THE ENEMY NEVER CAME

The Civil War in the Pacific Northwest

THE ENEMY NEVER CAME

The Civil War in the Pacific Northwest

Scott McArthur

CAXTON PRESS
Caldwell, Idaho
2012

ISBN 978-087004-512-7

Library of Congress Cataloging-in-Publication Data

McArthur, Scott.
  The enemy never came : the Civil War in the Pacific Northwest / Scott McArthur.
     p. cm.
  Includes bibliographical references and index.
  ISBN 978-0-87004-512-7
  1. Northwest, Pacific--History--19th century. 2. United States--History--Civil War, 1861-1865. I. Title. II. Title: Civil War in the Pacific Northwest.

  F852.M127 2012
  973.7--dc23

                        2012020052

Lithographed and bound in the United States of America

CAXTON PRESS
Caldwell, Idaho
182722

TABLE OF CONTENTS

ILLUSTRATIONS

ACKNOWLEDGEMENTS

I did most of my research for this book before much of the material was available on the Internet. Anyone who writes of history soon learns that his best friend is a librarian.

I thank the librarians and staff of Oregon Historical Society, the Idaho Historical Society, the Washington State Historical Society, the University of Washington, the University of Oregon, Western Oregon University, Oregon State University, the Polk County Historical Society, the Marion County Historical Society, the Clallam County Historical Society, the Salem Public Library, the Oregon State Library, the Oregon State Archives, the Oregon Military Museum, the Washington Military Museum, the National Archives both at Washington, D.C., and at its regional facility at Seattle, the Southern Oregon Historical Society, the University of Texas at Arlington, the Sacramento City Library and the Multnomah County Library.

Many thanks also to the research staff at the Library of the Benedictine Monastary at Mt. Angel, Oregon, which has a most complete library of Civil War material, and my good friends at the Monmouth Public Library who declare my research gave new meaning to the term "Interlibrary Loan."

Special thanks are due to my editor, Adair Law, who helped me make sense of what I learned, and to Colonel Warren Aney, historian of the Oregon National Guard.

— Scott McArthur, Monmouth, Oregon

PREFACE

Mention the American Civil War to the average American. If he remembers his high school history class at all, he will think of Abraham Lincoln, Gettysburg, Appomattox and maybe the battles for control of the Mississippi River.

But the Civil War in the Pacific Northwest? Why, he will protest, nothing happened out there.

To a great extent, that popular belief was true. There is no record of any actual Confederate military activity or presence in the Oregon Country—that then-remote corner of the country that today is Oregon, Washington, Idaho and part of Montana.

But people in the Pacific Northwest worried that the war might spill over into their sparsely settled frontier area. Add to that worry the continuing conflict with the Native Americans who did not willingly accept the destiny decreed for them by the invading whites.

The Civil War came to a Pacific Northwest sadly unprepared to cope with it.

Washington Territory was still reeling from the effects of a long and devastating series of Indian wars between 1855 and 1858. As a state, Oregon was barely two years old and was already torn by political controversy. Its newly-minted state government was firmly in the hands of so-called "Peace" Democrats who did not want war and did what they could to keep its citizens out of it.

The Pacific Northwest's ambivalence about the war grew from several factors. The area was a long way from the scene of actual North-South battles. Many felt that the struggle between the Confederate states and the Union was the problem of the East, not the West. The northwest economy expanded during the war and while part of the expansion was war-induced, a great deal of it came from the extraordinarily-rich gold deposits found east of the Cascade Mountains. Political dissent loses its allure to a society that is busy making money.[1]

Oregon and Washington Territory were at the very end of the communication pipeline. At the start of the war, with eastern telegraph connections only to Sacramento and San Francisco, it took days for a message or news from the East to get to the Pacific Northwest. The telegraph did not link that region to the rest of the nation until 1864 and roads were poor, the mails slow. This created a communications vacuum that bred rumor and fostered tales of non-existent threats.

Many northwest pioneers were from the so-called Border States. They came west to get away from internecine warfare and conflict. Others who emigrated from the South tacitly or expressly favored the seceding states. Still others just didn't like government, or at least a federal government that took powers they felt belonged exclusively to the states. This group was incensed at the thought of being forced into military service and even more offended by the clumsily designed Draft Act that allowed the well-to-do to buy their way out of service.

There were many political factions. At the start of the war, Republicans were a minority and Democrats were split badly. Some favored slavery. Some favored it in the Pacific Northwest. Others wanted it elsewhere but not in the region. Political conservatives believed in small government and states' rights. They felt the Southern states should be free to go their own way.[2] Others wanted to join the South, or to mold the Pacific Coast into a separate Pacific Republic free from the influences of the East.

Perhaps the best illustration of the maybe-we-will-maybe-we-won't stance is the statement of the Polk County Democratic Convention before the election of 1862:

> We are in favor of prosecuting the war for the purpose of suppressing rebellion, maintaining the Constitution and executing the laws; but we are opposed to any war for the abolition of slavery, or for any other purpose but for the maintenance of the Constitution and Union.[3]

It bespeaks the good sense of its people—and the artful handling of things by the military and political leaders in the Pacific Northwest and the Army's Department of the Pacific—that internal controversy seldom escalated above the level of harsh words and an occasional fistfight.

T. W. Davenport, a Silverton pioneer and father of Homer Davenport, famous Oregon artist, wrote many years after the war:

There was enough division in Oregon to have brought on
a destructive frenzy similar to that in Missouri, and would
have done so but for the long distance separating it from the
insurgent States, and the policy of the government in not
diminishing our home guard by recruiting here.[4]

Most of the regular army troops in the Pacific Northwest were
withdrawn at the start of the war. Locally recruited units from Oregon
and Washington Territory, as well as volunteers from California, took
over peace-keeping duties. Although poorly trained and inadequately
equipped, they did the job they were given. Department and division
commanders uniformly praised the volunteers for their ability to learn
and to adapt, for their bravery in infrequent combat against the Indians,
and for their steadfastness and endurance.

Newly-discovered gold deposits delivered huge amounts of gold
to help finance the war from Oregon, Washington Territory, and the
much-later Idaho Territory.

The Pacific Northwest emerged from the war politically and
economically stronger. Frightened away from the South because of
the war and the chaos that followed, investors looked to the West.
With its natural resources, the Pacific Northwest benefited greatly
from a huge infusion of capital.

The minority Republicans became a majority during the war. The
nascent government in Oregon and Washington Territory became
focused, although post-war scandals in Oregon's government brought
a revitalized Democratic Party back into control.

One of the true challenges in telling the story of this farthest-flung
corner of the Union is the lack of information. There is no single
complete account of what occurred in the Pacific Northwest during the
Civil War period.[5] The closest complete analysis was done by Glenn
Thomas Edwards, Jr. His master's thesis and doctoral dissertation
at the University of Oregon chronicled the military activities of the
District of Oregon (most of Oregon, Washington Territory and what
later became Idaho Territory, minus the Rogue Valley and southernmost
coastal area of Oregon which were linked with northern California in
the District of Humboldt) and the Pacific coast during the war.[6]

What is known today of that period comes from newspaper accounts
of varied political stripe, sparse official military and civil records that

survive from that time, and the confusing and often-contradictory memories of old men trying to recall what they did and what they saw when they were young.

Frances Fuller Victor, a principal historian of the period, bitterly complained of her difficulty in finding actual documentation of events in Oregon during the Civil War. In a footnote to an article in the *Oregon Historical Quarterly* she wrote:

> [I]t is almost, if not quite impossible, to find the printed reports of officers connected with these (Oregon Cavalry) expeditions, and other historical matter of date forty or forty-five years past. The state library does not contain them, the city and private libraries have been searched in vain, and the conclusion follows that the people have not, and the state officers have not, properly comprehended the value of such "documents," which should, if any still exist, be preserved by binding and placing where they can be found by students of history.[7]

Victor could have blamed the army.

In February 1866 an unnamed officer in the Commissary of Musters at Fort Vancouver complained to his superiors of the newly- formed Department of the Columbia:

> The records of the 1st Regiment of Infantry Oregon Volunteers...are still in this Office, which undoubtedly is not the proper place for them... It is indispensably requisite that a full and proper history of the Regiment should be made and kept by some officer, but as these books &c are here for the above length of time without any person appearing to inquire about them, or note the various incidental changes, I presume that the history of the Regiment is or will be very incomplete, and confused if some person don't take charge of and post them up.[8]

Notes

1   Van Winkle, Roger A., *A Crisis in Obscurity; A Study of Pro-Southern Activities in Oregon 1854-1865* (master's thesis, Western Washington State College, 1968), iv.

2   LaLande, Jeff, "'Dixie' of the Pacific Northwest: Southern Oregon's Civil War," *(Oregon Historical Quarterly, hereafter OHQ)*, 100(1999): 37.

3   Woodward, W.C., "Political Parties in Oregon," *OHQ*, 13(1912):30-31.

4   Davenport, T.W., "Slavery Question in Oregon", *OHQ*, 9(1908): 367.

5   Athearn, Robert G., "West of Appomattox, Civil War Beyond the Great River," *Montana, The Magazine of Western History*, 12 (Spring 1962): 2-11.

6   Edwards, Glenn Thomas, Jr., *The Department of the Pacific in the Civil War Years,* (PhD diss., University of Oregon, 1963); "Oregon Regiments in the Civil War; Duty on the Indian Frontier," (master's thesis, University of Oregon, 1960).

7   Victor, Frances Fuller, "The First Oregon Cavalry," *OHQ* 3(1902):163.

8   U.S. Army, Department of the Columbia, Letters Sent, n.p., National Archives Branch, Seattle, Wash.

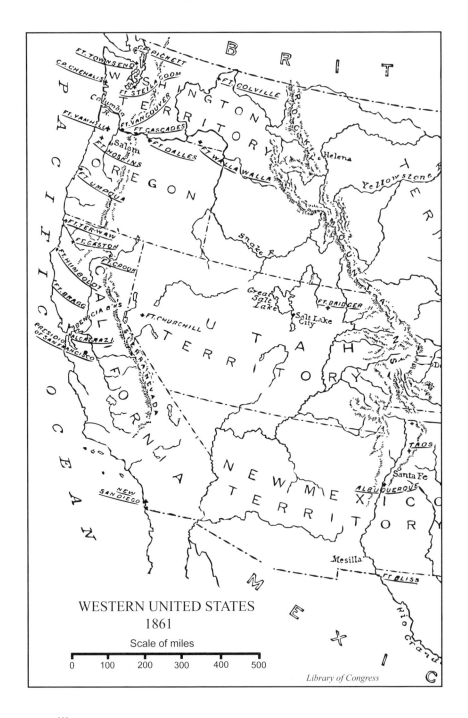

WESTERN UNITED STATES
1861

Scale of miles

0   100   200   300   400   500

Library of Congress

Chapter 1

PAST IS PRELUDE

At one time Spain, Russia, the United States, and Great Britain each claimed or looked possessively at the Oregon Country. The first permanent settlement came when American John Jacob Astor established his trading post at Astoria in 1811. Astor then sold it to the British North West Company in 1825. The Hudson's Bay Company (HBC) established a chain of fur trading posts and brought a dominant British presence to the Oregon Country. The HBC operated with a large network of trappers and traders. It attempted to populate the Oregon Country with farmers and settlers from eastern Canada. This effort failed, however, especially north of the Columbia River.

It was through the Convention of 1818 that both Great Britain and the United States, weary from the War of 1812, agreed that they would jointly occupy the Oregon territory for a period of ten years.[1] The convention was renewed in 1827 and by its terms the joint occupancy was to continue until both parties agreed otherwise. Recognizing that part, if not all, of the disputed territory would go to the United States, the HBC concentrated its fur-gathering efforts in what is now eastern Oregon and Idaho. Following the 1831-32 season, returns declined so markedly that the company abandoned its expeditions into the Snake River Country. According to historian Arthur L. Throckmorton, the area had become a virtual "fur desert."[2]

Two factors brought about American dominance of the Oregon Territory. Beaver hats fell out of favor in style-conscious Europe and the market for beaver fur collapsed. At the same time, there was the "great migration" of 1843, spurred by emigrant societies from other parts of the United States.[3] Britain and the HBC soon were overwhelmingly outnumbered by American settlers.[4]

American missionaries were accompanied by a flood of men and women anxious for free land. Now this young society needed laws. Things came to a head in 1841 when Ewing Young, arguably the richest American in the territory, died. It appeared that he died without heirs. To probate his estate, a primitive and totally extra-legal form of "provisional" government was formed. What originally was intended to be only a probate court eventually expanded into a full government with a code of laws, a court system, ten county governments, a prison, a single-house legislature, a governor, and a postal system.[5] This unique provisional government, which called itself Oregon Territory, had no basis in law. It worked, if imperfectly, because it had to.

In 1846, the United States and Great Britain finally agreed that Oregon Territory should be a part of the United States. But with the exception of a lone deputy Indian agent and erratic mail service, the Oregon Territory was without the benefits that came with being a part of the United States. During his 1845-49 term, President James K. Polk repeatedly demanded that Congress make Oregon a territory. By then, between 10,000 and 15,000 American citizens were living in what essentially was a lawless society.

At the time, slavery was the main issue in Congress, which delayed action on the Oregon bill.[6] Oregon was north of the so-called Compromise Lines of the Northwest Ordinance (1787), Mason-Dixon Line (1763) and Missouri Compromise (1820) that divided the free and slave territory.[7] In 1845, the legislature of the Oregon Provisional Government adopted as law the prohibition against slavery that was a part of the 1787 Northwest Ordinance. Pro-slavery leaders in Congress objected.

In 1846, Southern senators defeated a bill to make Oregon a territory.[8]

It took a tragedy to get the attention of Congress. On November 29, 1847 at the Whitman Mission near what is now Walla Walla, Washington, Cayuse Indians blamed the missionaries for an epidemic of measles that was ravaging the area. They killed Dr. Marcus and Narcissa Whitman, eleven other men, and two children. In response to pleas for help following the Whitman massacre, Congress created the Oregon Territory on August 14, 1848. After a long overland trip, Territorial Governor Joseph Lane was sworn in on March 3, 1849 at Oregon City and Oregon finally had a legitimate government.

TERRITORIAL DAYS

Now that it was a territory, contrary Oregon chafed under the administration of officials, most of them political appointees from the East. Although now a part of the United States, it was the most physically remote part of the United States. Oregon was so far removed from the political and population centers of the country that the frontier newspapers and Oregonians in their correspondence referred to "back East" as "the States."

Rancor soon rose. President Polk's Democratic appointee Joseph Lane declared the territorial government operational one day before Whig President Zachary Taylor took office.[9] Taylor sent his own replacement political appointees to fill Oregon Territory offices.

John Pollard Gaines became the new territorial governor. He brought federal funds with him to help the territorial government get started. The Democrat-controlled legislature decided to spread the wealth. It voted to build a capitol building at Oregon City, a university at Corvallis, and a prison at Portland.[10]

The settlers north of the Columbia River didn't like the fact that the territorial capitol was so far from them, nor that the bulk of the territory's money was spent in the Willamette Valley. They petitioned Congress for territorial status, and Washington Territory became a separate unit of the United States in 1853.

Conflicts between Gaines' Whig administration and Oregon's Democrat legislature brought demands as early as 1851 for statehood.

Congress's Kansas-Nebraska Bill of 1854 proposed giving each territory the right to vote slave or free. It stimulated intense debate in Oregon. In December 1854 Rep. Delazon Smith, a Democrat, introduced a series of bills in the territorial legislature that gave the Kansas-Nebraska measure Oregon's support. They passed.[11]

Stephen Douglas of Illinois introduced an Oregon statehood bill in Congress in 1854. However, Oregon's Whigs-turning-Republicans opposed statehood. They knew that Democrats would fill all state offices.

The slavery debate in Oregon was not based on its moral points. Many Oregonians did not abhor slavery as such. They simply wanted to avoid the trouble that other states had experienced because of the Negro, whatever his status.[12] They also feared that a Negro presence would undercut the value of white labor.

On July 28, 1857 the *Oregon Statesman* published a lengthy letter from George H. Williams, former chief justice of the Territorial Supreme Court. He was deemed by many as the most respected of Oregon political figures. In the letter, he claimed slavery would not work in Oregon:

> Slaves in Oregon, if they do anything at all, must necessarily be "jacks of all work." They will go everywhere and do everything. They will be free enough to see and learn all the vices of society and slaves enough to practice them without pride or self respect. I do not see how white men who expect to labor in Oregon can consent to have negro slaves brought here to labor with them....[13]

Oregon finally became a state February 14, 1859, even though it wasn't supposed to be one. Statehood arrived because Joe Lane lied and his fellow Democrats were nervous about the coming 1860 presidential election.

Under then-existing congressional policy, a territory could become a state when it had a population equal to the requirement for a seat in the House of Representatives. At that time, the number was 60,000.[14] House Republicans tried to delay statehood until a census showed Oregon had the required number of inhabitants. They failed. Joseph Lane, by then the Oregon Territory's non-voting delegate in the House of Representatives, piously declared he had no doubt Oregon had a population of not only 60,000 but more than 93,000.[15] Since he already had been elected one of Oregon's U.S. Senators to take office upon statehood, Lane was especially interested in statehood.[16] The upcoming 1860 presidential election also made urgent Oregon's admission to the Union. Democrats knew that the new Republican Party was rapidly gaining strength in the East. They figured that Oregon, at that time dominated by the Democrats, would deliver its three electoral votes for the Democrat nominee for president.[17]

The 1860 census showed Oregon with a population of 52,465, less than the number required to qualify Oregon Territory for statehood and far less than the 93,000 Joseph Lane had warranted two years earlier.[18]

DEMOGRAPHICS

At the start of the Civil War there were few white adults in the Pacific Northwest who had been born there. Almost all were transplants. Many were two-time transplants. These folks were born in the South or the East, moved to the Midwest or Border States and eventually to the Pacific Northwest. They brought with them the views and prejudices of their former home states.

Many of Oregon's early settlers were from the South.[19] But while their roots were in the South, they weren't automatic secessionists. Many vehemently declared that they left the South because of moral and economic objections to the slavery that existed there.[20]

Because many ex-Southerners viewed slavery with such disquiet, it led to a politically fatal split of the Democratic Party in the Oregon Country. Some felt that President James Buchanan had attempted to force slavery on Kansas and, with the aid of Senator Joseph Lane, was trying to promote it for the developing frontier states.

To a great extent, the Buchanan-Lane faction of the Democratic Party controlled the governments of both Oregon and Washington Territory.

THE PACIFIC NORTHWEST'S PECULIAR HISTORY OF SLAVERY

Along with all of the other factors that made the Civil War a complicating and unique experience for the Pacific Northwest was its own peculiar history of slavery. Prior to the coming of the white man, slavery was an established and economically significant custom among the native people.[21] The use of slave labor was important to the indigenous economy of the Pacific Northwest.[22]

The Canadian fur trader and agent for the North West Company, Alexander Ross, noted that the tribes that concentrated around the Columbia and Willamette Rivers and the Puget Sound country of Washington were primarily tradesmen, trading extensively in both furs and slaves.[23] Captain William Clark, who was in Oregon 1805-1806, commented on the custom of slavery among the coastal tribes as did the Hudson Bay Company's Sir George Simpson, who visited the Oregon Country in 1824 and 1825.[24] Earlier scholars even suggested that Oregon got its name from Indian slavery. An article in the *Washington Quarterly* posited that the name "Oregon" is derived from the Indian words "o-wah" (Chippewa name for "river") and "Wukan), the word for "slave." Thus: "Owah-Wakan"—river of the slaves.[25]

The life of an Indian slave was a difficult one. Generally, a slave was an item of property. He (or she) was worked, sold, traded, and often cast out to starve when no longer able to produce.[26] Some Indian slaves were adopted into their captors' tribes and accepted as equals.[27]

Coastal Indian slaves were identified by their naturally shaped foreheads. Free coastal Indians had a flattened forehead. The flattening was done during the first nine months of life. Infants were carried on cradle boards and after they were swaddled and lashed to the cradle board, a press made out of wood was attached to the still-soft skull of the newborn. A flattened forehead was the result and it was considered a thing of beauty. It identified them as a member of the privileged class.[28]

This cultural practice reportedly led to the death of some of the children born of early trappers and native women. The trapper fathers didn't want the heads of their children flattened and native mothers didn't want to raise a child with the appearance of a slave. Some mothers killed the infant children.[29]

Slave trade among the tribes was common up through the 1840s. An 1843 writer noted that a group of Klamath Indians brought slaves from the south to sell to other Indians at Oregon City.[30]

A slave market was convened periodically by the Indians on the banks of the Willamette River at what now is the foot of Eleventh Street in Oregon City. The *Oregon Journal* of January 8, 1920, recounted:

> Here, in the '40's and early '50s the Klamaths brought Indian slaves for sale, usually children captured in their frequent forays against the Shasta and Rogue Indians. The Klamaths traded these Indian slaves for blankets or other Hudson's Bay wares owned by the Willamette Valley Indians. Scores of these slaves were purchased from their Indian owners by the white residents of Oregon City. In most cases they were liberated. Occasionally they were adopted and educated.[31]

Former Oregon Governor Oswald West wrote that Indian slaves were gathered from their French Canadian owners and placed in the new government Indian reservations.[32] William Slacum, master of the *Loriot*, a ship sent by President Andrew Jackson to explore the Columbia River, reported to Congress that he found slavery endemic in the Oregon Country.

Slacum said that HBC employees not only married Indian women, but owned Indian slaves. He contended that the ownership of Indian slaves was encouraged by the HBC. He said, "Each man of the trapping parties has from two to three slaves, who assist the hunt and take care of the horses and camp, they thereby save the Company the expense of employing at least double the number of men that would otherwise be required on these excursions."[33] Alexander Ross mentioned his use of an Indian slave in his journal, but made no mention of ownership.

Dr. John McLoughlin, the HBC's chief factor at Fort Vancouver, reacted sharply to Slacum's contention. He said the HBC did not allow its employees to own slaves and did what it could to discourage slavery among the tribes.[34]

Elsie Frances Dennis reports a number of references to Indian slaves owned by both French and American settlers prior to the establishment of the Indian reservations in 1855-56.[35] She also recounts two instances when American and Japanese shipwreck victims were enslaved by Indian tribes in Washington and British Columbia.[36]

In 1843, a missionary at Oregon City reported that a slave sold for three horses or less. Slacum said a slave would bring eight to sixteen blankets and women were worth more than men.[37]

As disease decimated the native population and public sentiment among the new settlers turned against it, slavery of Indians faded. However, slavery among some Indians continued into the Civil War. In January 1864, the commanding officer of Fort Klamath, Oregon, wrote that he had taken a Pitt River Indian woman, held as a slave by a member of the Spokane tribe and abused by the owner's Indian wife, and had given her to a Klamath Indian who would treat her better.[38]

Royal Bensell, a diarist stationed at the Siletz blockhouse, wrote in his diary March 9, 1864 that Indians on the Siletz Reservation sold their women as slaves for a price of $5 to $50. He said some of the soldiers stationed at the Siletz blockhouse were purchasers.[39] The Superintendent of Indian Affairs for Oregon reported in 1871 that Indian girls between twelve and sixteen were sold or rented for cash payments.[40]

Negro slavery in the Pacific Northwest

In its early days, the Oregon Territory had few Negroes. Many of the leaders of the provisional government were from Border States and had witnessed the free vs. slave dispute. They worked to avoid the race problem by trying to exclude the race entirely.

The provisional government's legislative committee June 26, 1844 outlawed Negroes from Oregon Territory. The initial act required the owners of all Negro slaves to remove them from the territory within three years. Free Negroes were required to leave the territory within two years (for men) and three years (for women).

If they didn't leave voluntarily, the county constable was to administer twenty to thirty-nine lashes on the offender's bare back, a course of action to be repeated every six months until they left.[41] This Draconian law was soon amended to eliminate the lash. Instead, the offending Negro was to be sold into bondage to the highest bidder, who was charged with transporting the offender outside the boundaries of the Territory within six months.

Oregon was not the only jurisdiction to legislate the exclusion of Negroes. Similar laws were adopted in Illinois (1813), Indiana, and Iowa (1851).

Author Franz M. Schneider recounts the law's attempted use on two Negro merchants. Jacob Vanderpool was a West Indian sailor who had a cafe and boarding house in Salem.[42] Judge Thomas Nelson ordered him out of the territory in 1851. Abner Hunt Francis was a merchant in Portland. He and his wife were ordered out of the territory by the court in 1851, but remained until 1861.[43]

A petition was introduced in the state legislature in 1854 to permit Morris Thomas, a merchant of Portland, and his wife to remain in Oregon. Thomas was ordered to leave but the court's order was never enforced because it was discovered that the exclusion act had been unintentionally repealed.[44] The Oregon Constitution later required the legislature to enact exclusion legislation but it never happened.

The exclusion law caused at least two free Negro immigrants to settle north of the Columbia River, where, by apparent unwritten agreement, the so-called Anti-Black Act was not enforced. George Washington Bush, a free Negro from Pennsylvania, came to Oregon in 1844. Bush, whose wife was white, appraised Oregonians' attitude toward Negroes, and homesteaded near what is now Tumwater, where he became the first American settler north of the Columbia River.[45] Another Negro, George Washington (no relation to George Washington Bush), came to Oregon in 1850 and later moved north to found Centralia, Washington.

Notwithstanding the anti-Black Act, there were slaves who came to Oregon with their owners. The best known were Robin and Polly Holmes, who with their children came to Oregon as slaves of Nathaniel Ford, a Missourian who settled in Dixie (now Rickreall). Ford set the adults free but held on to the children. Robin Holmes found a friendly lawyer and filed suit in the Territorial Court at Dallas seeking custody of his three children.[46] After nearly a year, newly-arrived Territorial Supreme Court Justice George H. Williams, the fourth judge to be involved in the case, ruled that there was no slavery in Oregon. He ordered the children restored to their parents.

Oregon adhered to its no-Negro stand in the Constitutional Convention of 1857. Article I, Section 35 prohibited free Negroes and mulattos who were not residents of Oregon at the time of its admission from coming into the state.[47]

In the election of November 1857 adopting the Constitution, Oregon voters were specifically asked whether they wanted slavery in Oregon and whether they wanted to admit free Negroes into the state. Slavery was defeated by a vote of 7,727 to 2,645. The measure to exclude free Negroes passed 8,460 to 1,081.[48]

In an October 7, 1900 *Oregonian* editorial, editor Harvey Scott contended that all of Oregon knew that this provision of the constitution was unenforceable. He noted that Oregon felt so far removed from the rest of the United States that it believed no Negroes were going to come anyway.

Right or not, census figures show few Negroes in Oregon until well into the 1900s. The 1850 census showed fifty Negroes, and the 1860 census showed 128. It was unclear who was a Negro and who was not. Some Hawaiians and Indians were identified as Negro. Moses "Black" Harris, a pioneer trapper who guided at least one wagon train, is identified by author Martha Anderson as a pioneer Negro.[49] However Jesse Applegate in his memoirs described Harris, "...tho a white man, his face was the color of his (buckskin) coat."[50]

Oregon's constitutional prohibition against Negroes, made unenforceable by the ratification of the Thirteenth Amendment to the

U.S. Constitution in 1865, finally was repealed in the general election of 1926.

Chapter 1 notes

1   As early as 1820 Rep. John Floyd introduced a bill in Congress to annex Oregon to the United States. It was voted down. Hagemann, Todd, *Lincoln and Oregon* (master's thesis, Eastern Illinois University, 1988), 4.

2   Throckmorton, Arthur L., *Oregon Argonauts, Merchant Adventurers on the Western Frontier* (Portland, Or: Oregon Historical Society [hereafter OHS], 1961), 6-7.

3   Britain's attempt to colonize the Oregon Country with immigrants from its Canadian holdings fizzled.

4   The area north of the Columbia River remained a political no man's land. Frederick Merk, an authority on early Pacific Northwest immigration, claimed there were but eight Americans north of the Columbia River in 1845. Scott, Leslie M., "The Oregon Boundary Treaty of 1846," OHQ 29(1928):13, 15-16.

5   Bancroft, Hubert Howe, *History of the Pacific States,* (San Francisco: The History Company, 1886), 29:292-307.

6   Lockley, Fred, "Some Documentary Records of Slavery in Oregon," *Oregon Historical Quarterly* [hereafter *OHQ*] 17(1916):107-15.

7   Van Winkle, *A Crisis in Obscurity, A Study of Pro-Southern Activities in Oregon, 1854-1865*, iii.

8   Bancroft, *History of Pacific States*, 29:613.

9   Platt, Robert Trent, "Oregon and Its Share in the Civil War," OHQ 4(1903):91.

10 Bancroft, *History of Pacific States*, 30:146.

11 Hageman, *Lincoln and Oregon,* (master's thesis, Eastern Illinois University, 1988) 11-12.

12 Ibid., 8.

13 Williams, George H., "The Free State Letter," *Oregon Statesman*, July 28, 1857, 1, 2, reprinted in Ellison, Joseph. "Designs for a Pacific Republic, 1845-1862." *OHQ* 9(1908): 254-73.

14 *Weekly Oregonian*, March 19, 1859, 1. Shippee, Lester Burrell, "The Federal Relations of Oregon," *OHQ*, 20(1919):383, 389.

15 *Weekly Oregonian,* March 19, 1859. [p.1 also as in above note]?

16 In September, 1857 Oregon's constitutional convention adopted a state constitution and voters elected a full slate of state and federal officers--including Lane as one of the two U.S. senators--to take office when and if Congress made Oregon a state. Hageman, Todd, *Lincoln and Todd*, 13-14.)

17 In fact, it didn't. The Democrats split between Stephen A. Douglas and John C. Breckenridge. Abraham Lincoln won a plurality of the Oregon vote and the three votes in the electoral college by a margin of 270 votes.

18 Shippee, "The Federal Relations of Oregon," 383, 389.

19 George Himes, historian and founding secretary of the Oregon Historical Society, said that of 7,444 pioneers who came to Oregon before 1859, 50 percent were born in the Northern states, 33 percent in the Southern states and 11 per cent in twenty-one foreign countries. Hill, Daniel G., Jr., *The Negro Question in Oregon, A Survey* (master's thesis, University of Oregon, 1932), 9.

20 Johansen, Dorothy, *Empire of the Columbia*, (New York: Harper & Row, 1967), 260.

21 Merk, Frederick (Ed.), *Fur Trade and Empires, George Simpson's Journal*, (Harvard University Press, 1968), 352-56.

22 Oregon Federal Writers' Project, *Oregon Oddities*, 1940, 1-5.

23 Ross, Alexander, *Adventures of the First Settlers on the Oregon or Columbia River* (London: Elder and Co., 1849), 87, 92, 97, 99-100.

24 Merk,, *Fur Trade and Empires,* 352.

25 Meyer, J.A., "River of the Slaves or River of the West", *Washington Historical Quarterly*, 13(1922):4

26 Ross, *Adventures of the First Settlers,* 97.

27 Oregon Federal Writers' Project, *Oregon Oddities*, 1.

28 Ross, *Adventures of the First Settlers,* 99.

29 Merk, *Fur Trade and Empires*, 101.

30 Oregon Federal Writers Project, *Oregon Oddities*, 2.

31 *Oregon Journal*, Jan. 8, 1920, 10.

32 West, Oswald, "First White Settlers on French Prairie," *OHQ*, 41(1940):209.
33 Slacum, William A., "Memorial," *Senate Document No. 24, 25th Congress, 2nd session,* 10, cited in Dennis, Elsie Frances, "Indian Slavery in Pacific Northwest," *OHQ,* 31(1930):193.
34 Merk, *Fur Trade and Empires,* 354-55.
35 Dennis, "Indian Slavery in Pacific Northwest," 76-81, 181-82, 186-95.
36 Ibid., 76, 186.
37 Merk, *Fur Trade and Empires,* 355.
38 U.S. Army, Correspondence Files, First Oregon Cavalry, Fort Klamath, Oregon, National Archives, Washington, D.C.
39 Barth, Gunter, *All Quiet on the Yamhill,* (Eugene, Or.: University of Oregon Books, 1959), 131.
40 Report on Indian Affairs, Oregon Superintendency, 1871, 319, cited in Barth, Gunter, *All Quiet on the Yamhill,* 129.
41 Hageman, *Lincoln and Oregon,* 8.
42 *Oregon Statesman,* adv., June 6-September 16, 1851.
43 Schneider, Franz M., "The 'Black Laws' of Oregon" (master's thesis, University of Santa Clara, 1970), 17.
44 Ibid., 20.
45 Lockley, *Fur Trade and Empires,* 111-12.
46 The suit was *Territory ex rel Robin Holmes v. Nathaniel Ford,* Polk County District Court, Oregon State Archives, Salem, Or. Pauline Burch, a great-granddaughter of Nathaniel Ford, wrote that the suit was a friendly one to test the status of slavery in Oregon Territory and to determine Ford's obligation to his former servant. Burch, Pauline, mss. 107, Oregon State Library. But a letter from Ford to a friend in Missouri, James A. Shirley, asked that Shirley arrange to have a levy made upon the slaves to satisfy one of Ford's judgments so that Robin Holmes, his wife and the children might be returned to Missouri under the Fugitive Slave Act, and there sold. *Missouri Historical Review* January, 1931, cited in *OHQ* 32(1931):83-84.
47 Oregon Constitution, Art. 1, Sec. 35.
48 Curry, George L., Governor, Proclamation Declaring the Results of the Election [1857] for and Against Constitution, Deady, *The Organic and Other General Laws of Oregon Together With the National Constitution and Other Public Acts and Statutes of the United States, 1845-1984,* supra, 129.
49 Anderson, Martha, *Black Pioneers of the Northwest, 1800-1918, (n.p.,* 1980), 54.
50 Applegate, Jesse, "First Settlement of Polk County," *Polk County Observer,* March 13, 1903.

Chapter 2

POLITICS BEFORE THE WAR

Most of the pre-Civil War settlers of the Pacific Northwest were farmers. Even the doctors and lawyers who came west in the earliest years were farmers first. Those in the Oregon Country held the pragmatic, conservative views of the farmer.

But it was a politically fragmented society. Long after the Whigs had imploded in the East and scattered their adherents to the newly formed Republican Party, in remote Oregon Territory the Whig Party continued until 1858.[1] In the Pacific Northwest, the Republicans, a minority until the elections of 1862, weren't sure who they were.

Even though he had never set foot on Oregon soil, Abraham Lincoln had peculiar ties to Oregon. There are those who claim that without the support of Oregon, Lincoln might not have been elected president.

A one-term Whig congressman, Lincoln was appointed Secretary of Oregon Territory by President Zachary Taylor on August 9, 1849. Unfortunately, Taylor never asked Lincoln if he wanted the job.[2] And even had Lincoln wanted it, his fractious wife Mary did not. When the unsolicited commission as territorial secretary arrived at Lincoln's home in Springfield, Illinois, he sent it back to Secretary of State John Clayton, with this letter:

> Your letter of the 10th Inst., notifying me of my appointment as Secretary of the Territory of Oregon, and accompanied by a Commission, has been duly received. I respectfully decline the office.
>
> I shall be greatly obliged if the place be offered to Simeon Francis, of this place. He will accept it, is capable, and would be faithful to the discharge of its duties. . . .
>
> Your Obt. Servt. A. Lincoln.[3]

OREGON'S CONSTITUTIONAL CONVENTION

Oregon Territory, which thought that it was free of slavery, learned in 1854 that, perhaps, it was not. Delazon Smith, speaker of the Oregon Territory House of Representatives, contended that the 1854 passage by Congress of the Kansas-Nebraska Act, repealed that portion of the Oregon Territory Organic Act that prohibited slavery.[4] This fanned anew the free vs. slave argument that continued until statehood and set the ground for arguments that would split the state during the early part of the Civil War.

This led to a heated discussion in the 1855 Oregon Territorial Legislature and passage of a resolution supporting the principles of the Kansas-Nebraska Act that allowed Kansas and Nebraska Territory to vote free or slave.

The violence that followed in "bleeding Kansas" hastened the move in Oregon for statehood. Oregonians wanted the slavery issue in Oregon settled before people started killing each other.

Statehood was put to the vote in Oregon in June 1856. The measure failed by 249 votes.[5] The 1856 legislature resubmitted the issue and in June 1857, by a vote of 7,617 to 1,679, voters approved a call for a Constitutional Convention to draft a state constitution for Oregon. They also elected an overwhelmingly pro-South Democrat slate of delegates to that convention.[6]

Editorialists, writers of letters to the editor, and street-corner orators argued the slavery issue. Public debate became so robust that one California editor commented: "Oregonians have two occupations, agriculture and politics."[7]

The Constitutional Convention met August 17, 1857 in the county courthouse at Salem. Matthew Deady, a pro-slavery advocate and justice of the Territorial Supreme Court, was elected chairman.[8]

The Democratic majority, which figured that slavery would handily win if submitted to a popular vote, carefully left the issue of slavery out of the new constitution.

Oregon's proposed constitution specifically provided that no Negro or mulatto should be allowed to vote. The convention adjourned September 18, 1857. The election was held November 9, 1857. The voters were given three issues:

1. Adoption of the Constitution making Oregon a state: Passed 7,195 to 3,215.
2. Allowing slavery: Failed 7,727 to 2,645.
3. Prohibiting the admission of free Negroes into Oregon: Passed 8,640 to 1,081.[9]

Why did Oregon, which generally favored the South and slavery, vote it down? Because Oregon voters felt that the resulting tumult from slavery would be more costly than any benefits that might come from it.

By February 1858, the Democrats had split into pro-slavery and anti-slavery camps. And even though it was still not a state—Congress had yet to pass the Admission Act—Oregon elected its state officers in June 1858 with pro-slavery Democrats sweeping the ballot. The governor, secretary of state, and all Supreme Court justices were pro-slavery. The majority of the legislature was pro-slavery. Even the bulk of the local prosecuting attorneys were pro-slavery Democrats.

The state legislature met and elected Joseph Lane and Delazon Smith to truncated terms as Oregon's two U.S. Senators. This was all contingent on Congress finally voting to make Oregon a state.

The recently-elected senator from Oregon, Joseph Lane, suggested that Oregon not wait for Congress, but just go ahead and act like it was a state.[10] Cooler heads prevailed. Territorial officers continued as such. The Territorial Legislature met in December 1858. Among other things, it listened to an opening address by Territorial Governor George Curry that contained a lengthy discussion of slavery.

SENTIMENT FOR A PACIFIC REPUBLIC

One of the threats that spooked Unionists at the start of the Civil War—more philosophical than real—was that of the Pacific Republic. Its adherents proposed that Oregon, Washington, California, and other Pacific Slope territories withdraw from the Union as had the states of the Confederacy. They would form their own Pacific Republic.[11] The new Pacific Republic then would form an alliance with the Confederacy but remain a separate nation.[12]

The idea of an independent Pacific Republic was not a new one. Thomas Jefferson predicted that the Pacific Coast would become settled and split off as a separate nation.[13] The concept came up repeatedly after that.

Initially the argument for such a divide was the physical challenge of managing the remote Pacific Coast as a part of the United States. Later, as gold began to pour out of the California mines, Pacific Republic advocates argued that it would be cheaper for the Pacific Coast to go it alone rather than send federal tax revenues east and hope to see some of it returned.

Some wanted division for the sake of a smaller, more easily managed government. In 1853, Alonzo A. Skinner ran as a Whig for Oregon Territorial Delegate to Congress, promising to help make southern Oregon a separate territory. There were also proposals to divide California into two or three separate states.[14]

In every case, the real impetus for the Pacific Republic came from California because it had more at stake. It had the noisy political leadership and the producing gold mines. The Pacific Northwest was considered sort of a tag-along.

When Lieutenant Charles Wilkes surveyed the Pacific Coast in the early 1840s, he predicted that California, then a part of Mexico, would join with the Oregon Country as a separate nation. However, the first actual move for the Pacific Republic occurred in Sonoma, California in 1846 when a group of Americans forced the surrender of the Mexican garrison there and flew the Bear Flag of the California Republic.

In the mid-1850s, the Pacific Republic concept was reborn in California. Citizens claimed they paid more taxes to the federal government than they received services in return.[15] This time, leaders of Oregon's Democratic Party also backed a Pacific Republic.

Editors wrote on both sides of the issue. Alonzo Leland, editor of the Portland *Standard*, wrote:

> The vast chain of the Rocky Mountains presents an unmistakable boundary, and we have reason to believe that these boundaries, laid down by an over-ruling Providence, ought to be more strictly regarded....Let us think before we act. The growing disparity of habits between us and the Atlantic States, and the pecuniary advantages or disadvantages of a separation from the states are not the only questions which ought to be considered.[16]

The opposition Whigs, then in the process of morphing into the Free Soil Party (and soon to find itself the newly minted Republican party), blew up.

The *Oregonian* of July 28, 1855, thundered:

> Four years ago we repeatedly told the people of Oregon that the leaders of the self-styled Democratic Party designed at no distant day to throw off their allegiance to the United States government....The facts are upon record that these men have been constantly laying their plans for a revolutionary movement.

The clearest exposition of what a Pacific Republic might mean came when the *Oregon Statesman* in September 1855 reprinted a letter to a San Francisco newspaper outlining the claimed plans of the leaders of the Pacific Republic movement:

> A new Republic is to be formed, consisting first of ten states, three to be formed within the present limits of the State of California, three in Oregon Territory, two in Washington Territory and two from western portions of Utah and New Mexico....The great Pacific Railroad is to be abandoned, and every obstacle thrown in the way of its construction, which the argument at the hustings is to be made to the people that the government at Washington has refused the road to the people of the Pacific. The question of slavery is to be adjured and disclaimed until the plan is so far executed that there can be no retraction, after which the southern four or five states will adopt slavery.[17]

The 1856 election of President James Buchanan dampened again the fires of separatism, but as the threat of dissolution of the Union intensified, the movement revived.

In 1860, the *Oregon Statesman,* without attribution, claimed a conspiracy among the congressional representatives of California, Oregon, and Washington Territory to push for dissolution of the Union and division of the United States into three separate nations: the slave states, the free states and territories in the East and Midwest, with the Pacific Slope as the third.[18]

A leading proponent of the Pacific Republic was California Senator William Gwin. Gwin, a classicist as well as a politician, believed that the Pacific Republic should be patterned after the Venetian Republic. He favored hereditary titles for a white aristocracy and slavery for the Negroes and Sandwich Island natives who would be imported to do the heavy lifting. This vision caused political opponents and wags to give Gwin the nickname of "Duke."

James W. Nesmith and Edward D. Baker, elected by the legislature as Oregon's new senators, opposed the Pacific Republic.

In February 1861 two resolutions were introduced in the California Legislature: one supported the Union and the other proposed withdrawing from it. While both resolutions were debated, the arguments centered not on the ethics of slave state or free, but on which would cost the least. Debate ended when news reached California of the bombardment of Fort Sumter and the start of the war. What remained of the California Pacific Republic movement died after the substantial Republican victories in the September 1861 California elections.

The Washington Territorial Legislature condemned the designs for a Pacific Republic.[19] The Oregon Legislature followed suit, but not until after a strong pro-Union legislature was elected in 1862.[20]

Bear Flags were raised intermittently in California during the early part of the war. Generals Edwin V. Sumner and Irvin McDowell both expressed the belief that the Pacific Republic plots were more serious than the public believed.

THE ELECTION OF 1860, DEMOCRATS

Oregon entered the 1860 elections in a state of political turmoil. Voters had the choice of four major candidates for president: Lincoln the Republican, Douglas the Northern Democrat, Breckenridge the Southern Democrat and ex-Senator John Bell of Tennessee, whose Constitutional Union Party was an outgrowth of the Southern Whigs. The Constitutional Union solution to the slavery issue was to ignore it. To the others, the national future of slavery was the main issue.

The Democratic National Convention convened at Charleston, South Carolina. A pro-South presiding officer was elected and a pro-South credentials committee chosen. Then acute wrangling forced the convention to adjourn and reconvene in Baltimore. In Baltimore the Northern wing of the party took control. Southern Democrats and those favoring states' rights walked out. Oregon's delegates joined them.

In a meeting across town, the pro-South contingent adopted the platform rejected by the Douglas-dominated regular convention and nominated John C. Breckenridge, a senator from Tennessee, as its presidential nominee. Oregon's Senator Joseph Lane, who had been mentioned as a possible nominee for president, was nominated as vice president.

Oregon's six Democratic delegates, with three votes between them, were A. P. Dennison, Isaac Stevens, Lansing Stout, John K. Lamerick, R. B. Metcalf, and Justus Steinberger. Only Stout, Oregon's U.S. Representative, and Lamerick, a militia general in the Indian wars, were from Oregon. Stevens was Washington Territory's delegate to Congress. Steinberger, who later commanded the Washington Territory Volunteers in the war, lived near Tacoma. Dennison, elected vice chairman at the first Charleston convention, was a former Oregon Indian agent. R. B. Metcalf was another former Oregonian.[21] Lane coyly remained in Washington D.C., hoping for his party's call.

In Oregon, the Democrats had a lock on things political, but couldn't agree among themselves. The first glaring evidence of this was the futile three-week special session of the legislature that tried to elect a successor to Delazon Smith as U.S. senator.

The pro-South Delazon Smith had been elected to a bob-tailed term that ended March 3, 1859. Oregon did not become a state until February 14, 1859, which left Smith with the dubious distinction of serving the shortest term of any Oregon U.S. senator.

Upon statehood, the legislature elected Oregon's U.S. senators. Its U.S. representative was elected in a statewide election.

The Oregon Legislature met May 16, 1859 to choose a senator for a full six years. The Democrats had a thundering majority. The Southern element wanted to re-elect Smith, but the Douglas wing refused. After three weeks of wrangling, the legislature adjourned, passing no legislation and electing no senator. Joseph Lane remained as Oregon's sole senator, and for two years Oregon's second desk in the Senate chamber sat empty.[22]

In 1859, Lansing Stout, a rabid pro-slavery Democrat, was elected Oregon's sole U.S. Representative, defeating Republican David

Logan. Moderate Democrats defected from their party and voted for Logan. Out of 11,276 votes cast, Stout won by a margin of sixteen votes. His term expired in March 1861.[23] The Democrat-controlled legislature set the congressional election for June 1860, the same date as state and local elections.

There were no primary elections in those days. Candidates, including those who wished to be U.S. Representative, were nominated by party conventions. The Democratic state convention, which met without delegates from several pro-Douglas counties, nominated the pro-South George K. Shiel.

The Democratic State Central Committee met, chose pro-South presidential electors and expelled Douglas Democrats from the Central Committee.

Democrats controlled the September 1860 legislature. Yet, Edward Dickinson Baker, a Republican who had moved from California specifically to be a candidate for Senate, and James Nesmith, a Douglas Democrat, were elected as Oregon's two senators.

T. W. Davenport of Silverton later wrote that he helped engineer the election of a Republican and a Douglas Democrat to the Senate. Davenport said that he made the deal with C. P. Crandall, a leader of the Douglas wing of the Democratic Party.

The Republicans lacked the votes to put many, if any, of their party into the legislature. But the Democrats were badly fractured. On a hand-shake agreement, the Marion County Republican convention nominated no Republican candidates for the legislature. County Republicans—and those from other areas of the state—agreed to vote for Northern wing Democrats, whose spokesman was Salem Editor Asahel Bush. In exchange, the Douglas Democrats (Bushites) agreed to give one U.S. Senate seat to Baker.

Davenport later reported this post-election conversation with Richard "Uncle Dickey" Miller, leader of the Lane county Democrats:

Miller: Did you sell out to the Bushites?
Davenport: Surely we did not.
Miller: Well, what did you do?
Davenport: We bought in.[24]

However, the alliance between the Republicans and Douglas Democrats was no assurance Baker would be elected. The pro-South, or so-called Lecompton Democrats, held a significant block of votes. Author Elijah R. Kennedy told how pro-South members of the Oregon House of Representatives attempted to stop Baker's election:

> When the Lecomptonites learned that they were to have no voice in the election of Senators they determined to prevent, if possible, any election whatever by depriving one branch of the Legislature of a quorum; so many assemblymen withdrew. They went five miles outside town and were hidden in a capacious barn, where, it was promised, they should be secreted and fed "until the Baker danger should be passed." But the sergeant at-arms discovered their hiding place and took in enough of them to make a quorum. Thus, while a number of seceders remained in "Uncle Nick" Schram's barn, still hoping they might thwart the purpose of the majority, their unwilling comrades were locked in their legislative chambers and the Republicans and Douglas Democrats elected Colonel Baker and James W. Nesmith to the Senate.[25]

Democrats hoped that the fragmented national ticket would leave no presidential candidate with a majority of electoral votes. This would throw the election into the House of Representatives where the Southern states were organized and might prevail. Some thought that Joseph Lane might even thus become president. But that didn't happen.[26]

Lincoln won the electoral vote nationally. He won Oregon's three electoral votes, but by a tiny plurality.

Oregon voters followed their geographical origins in the election. Northern counties, with a majority of voters from New England, voted Republican. The middle counties of the Willamette Valley, with voters from the Border States, voted for Douglas. The rural counties of southern and eastern Oregon, with their strong population of voters from the South, chose Breckenridge and Lane.

THE ELECTION OF 1860, REPUBLICANS

Edward Dickinson Baker was a lawyer, an intimate friend of Lincoln's from Springfield, and namesake of his second son. Baker had been in Los Angeles and failed in an effort to be elected by the California legislature as U.S. senator. In December 1859, he moved to

Oregon at the behest of Republicans headed by David Logan. Oregon Republicans, successors to the extinct Whigs, had made a feeble beginning in the 1856 election. The Democrats, headed by Joseph Lane and John Whiteaker, still controlled Oregon politics. Oregon Republicans needed a powerful and persuasive leader. They figured Baker was their man.

After nearly three weeks of political wrangling, the Oregon Legislature in 1860 elected Republican Baker and Democrat James W. Nesmith as Oregon's U.S. senators.

Baker took his seat in the Senate. By all logic, Baker should have been a member of the cabinet. But Lincoln needed support in the Senate from the Pacific states. At the outbreak of the war, Baker turned down commissions offered to him by Lincoln as both brigadier general and major general. Instead, he accepted a commission as a colonel of volunteers, which allowed him to remain a member of the Senate. He was later killed in the Battle of Balls Bluff, October 21, 1861.

In the presidential election of 1860, Baker stumped Oregon for Lincoln. The 1860 GOP platform happily supported long-standing Oregon demands for a transcontinental railroad and an effective homestead law. This, plus the split between the Douglas Democrats and the pro-slavery Democrats of Lane and Whiteaker, gave Lincoln a squeaker victory in the election.[27]

Once elected, President Lincoln swiftly removed Buchanan's Oregon appointees, many of whom were actual or suspected secessionists. Filling the federal patronage positions with men both faithful and competent was a challenge but Lincoln had the help of well-placed and politically reliable advisors.

In addition to Baker, Lincoln had four old friends from Springfield, Illinois in Oregon. Simeon Francis (who was mentioned in Lincoln's letter declining the earlier job in Oregon) had moved to Oregon in 1859. Francis, former editor of the *Sangamon* (Illinois) *Journal* and Springfield's *Illinois State Journal*, was editor of the Portland *Oregonian.* Other friends were William L. Adams, editor of Portland's *Oregon Argus*, David Logan, and Dr. Anson G. Henry. All were leaders in the Oregon Republican party.[28]

Most of Lincoln's Oregon political appointees, and some for Washington Territory, were recommended by Baker. They included twenty-three men in positions ranging from superintendent of Indian affairs to surveyor for the Port of Portland.

Lincoln's principal Oregon political backers also got federal jobs. Simeon Francis was appointed Army Paymaster.

Doctor Anson G. Henry was appointed Superintendent of Indian Affairs for Washington Territory. Thomas J. Dryer was appointed Commissioner to Hawaii. He was replaced in 1863 by James McBride.

David Logan, who did not get along with Edward Baker, pointedly was not appointed to office.

William H. Wallace, another personal friend of Lincoln, was appointed governor of Washington Territory, but never came west to take up the job. Henry McGill, territorial secretary, was acting governor during the difficult early months of the war.

Lincoln's policies greatly benefited Oregon and the Pacific Northwest. He signed a new Homestead Act and the act financing the Pacific railroad as promised by the 1860 Republican Party platform. He approved an act providing federal financial support for the extension of telegraph service to the West Coast.

However, Lincoln's support of the Pacific Northwest was not all benevolence and politics on his part. The Pacific Northwest was responsible for over 40 percent of the total U.S. production of gold during the period 1861-1867, which helped greatly to finance the war.[29]

Chapter 2 notes

1 Weekly *Oregonian*, April 10, 1858.

2 President Taylor had trouble filling Oregon territorial posts. His first appointee as governor, Joseph G. Marshall of Indiana, also declined appointment. Kintzing Prichette, territorial secretary appointed by President James K. Polk, continued in office until September 18, 1849 when ex-General Edward Hamilton arrived to take over the secretary's job. Lincoln apparently also was considered for the governor's job, although this time he was asked first. In September 1849 Lincoln wrote John Addison, a Taylor confidant, that he didn't want the governor's job, either. Scott, Harvey, *The History of the Oregon Country,* (Cambridge, Mass., Riverside Press, 1924) 5:47.

3 Basler, Roy, (Ed.), *The Collected Works of Abraham Lincoln,* (New Brunswick, N.J., Rutgers University Press, 1953-55), 2:61.

4 *Oregon Statesman,* June 6, 1856.

5 Van Winkle, *A Crisis in Obscurity,* 2.

6 Johannsen, Robert W., "Spectators of Disunion, The Pacific Northwest and the Civil War," *Pacific Northwest Quarterly,* 54(June, 1953,): 107-08.

7 *Oregon Statesman*, April 14, 1857.

8 *Oregon Statesman*, June 28, 1857.

9 Van Winkle, *A Crisis in Obscurity,* 18-19.

10 Ibid., 23.

11 Kelly, Sister M. Margaret Jean, *The Career of Joseph Lane, Frontier Politician* (PhD diss., Catholic University of America, 1942), 187.

12 A resolution was introduced in the Confederate Congress October 2, 1862 to recognize the political neutrality of Oregon and California and urge the formation of a Pacific Republic which would become an independent nation allied with the Confederate States of America. Woodward, W.C., "Political Parties in Oregon," *OHQ,* 13(1912):21-22.

13 Hageman, *"Lincoln and Oregon,"* 24.

14 Wang, Peter Haywood, "The Mythical Confederate Plot in Southern California," *San Bernardino County Museum Association Quarterly*, 16:4(1969):14.

15 Ibid.

16 *Standard,* Portland, Oregon, July, 1855, quoted in Hull, Dorothy, *"*The Movement in Oregon for the Establishment of a Pacific Coast Republic," *OHQ*, 17(1916):182-83.

17 *Oregon Statesman*, July, 17, 1860, quoted in Ibid., 196.

18 *Oregon Statesman*, July 3, 1860.

19 Hansen, David Kimball, *Public Response to the Civil War in Washington Territory and Oregon 1861-1865,* (master's thesis, University of Washington, 1971), 13.

20 Ellison, Joseph, "Designs for a Pacific Republic, 1845-1862," 342.

21 Woodward, W.C., "Political Parties in Oregon," *OHQ*, 13(1912):311-13, Van Winkle, *A Crisis in Obscurity,* 32-34.

22 Van Winkle, *A Crisis in Obscurity,* 27.

23 Ibid., 26.

24 Davenport, T.W., "Slavery Question in Oregon," *OHQ*, 9(1908): 347-51.

25 Kennedy, Elijah R., *The Contest for California: How Colonel E.D. Baker saved the Pacific States for the Union,* (Boston, New York, Houghton Mifflin Co., 1912), 142-43.

26 Van Winkle, *A Crisis in Obscurity,* 41-42.

27 Hageman, *Lincoln and Oregon*, 20-23.

28 Ibid., 41-44.

29 Thomison, Joel D., "Old U.S. Mint at The Dalles is Monument to Argonaut Era," *OHQ*, 41(1940): 72-73.

Chapter 3

WAR COMES TO THE PACIFIC NORTHWEST

At 4 a.m. on April 29, 1861, the side-wheel steamer *Cortez* nosed up to a Portland wharf on the Willamette River. Oregonians learned that the country was at war and that it had been for nineteen days.

San Francisco newspapers told the story of the shelling and eventual capture on April 13, 1861 of the Union holdout at Fort Sumter in the harbor of Charleston, South Carolina. The story had been telegraphed from the East to St. Louis, where it was published April 14. It was then carried by Pony Express to Fort Churchill, Nevada, the end of the western telegraph line. It was republished in San Francisco on April 24, 1861, and then carried to Portland by ship.[1] The ocean trip from San Francisco took sixty hours, the speediest trip of record. (Overland to Portland from Sacramento by the weekly mail stage took seven days.) From Portland, the news was sent by ocean steamer around Cape Flattery to Olympia and Washington Territory.

Since January 1861 the struggling four-page newspapers of Oregon and Washington Territory had reprinted news from the eastern press telling of seceding Southern states' seizure of forts and arsenals in the South. So the Pacific Northwest was not surprised by the news of the outbreak of the war. The Portland *Oregonian* had started daily publication on February 4, 1861 and reported fully what news was available. Editorialists argued whether the rest of the nation should let the Southern states go, compromise by assuring the institution of slavery, or fight to force them to stay.

Oregon initially greeted the news of the fall of Fort Sumter with concern and muted displays of support for the Union. Word spread throughout the Portland streets, which at that time were essentially great mud holes because of the heavy rain that doused the Willamette

Valley in April 1861.[2] Flags flew from businesses and homes in Portland and Salem. Salem's *Oregon Statesman* warned that anyone interfering with the display of flags would pay for it.[3]

The *Oregonian* published the news of the fall of Fort Sumter on April 30, 1861. The *Oregon Statesman*, whose next regular edition was not scheduled until May 6, published an extra edition.

Along with the news of Fort Sumter, the *Cortez* also brought as a passenger Joseph Lane: ex-Governor, ex-war hero, ex-Territorial Delegate, ex-U.S. senator, failed candidate for vice president and now a thoroughly discredited Oregon politician. Lane had smugly declared on the floor of the Senate after Lincoln's election victory: "(W)hen war is made upon that gallant South for withdrawing from a Union which refused them their rights....The Republican party will have war enough at home."[4]

Lane, who was accompanied back to Oregon by his son Lafayette and two nieces, became a pariah. A drayman refused to carry his baggage from the wharf to the hotel. Friends who had proposed to welcome his return by firing cannon gave up the idea after being forcefully told that if they did, the cannon would be dumped in the Willamette River and maybe they would follow it.

One bystander solemnly claimed that two or three of the crates of Lane's personal belongings stacked on the wharf contained Sharps rifles intended to help arm a Pacific Coast insurrection. This claim was repeated in Unionist newspapers and in Hubert Howe Bancroft's *History of Oregon*.[5] But there is no proof of this allegation and Lane family correspondence indicates that any firearms brought back to Oregon likely were only two hunting rifles for Lane and his son.

Lane and his party stayed in Portland three days. Most of his friends avoided him. The women of the Southern Methodist Church invited him to a May Day dinner. His old friend and fellow Southern sympathizer Matthew Deady (now Oregon's federal judge) had Lane to supper. Deady later commented that no one else in Portland had made such an offer.

On May 2, 1861, Joseph Lane hired a team and wagon and the party headed south for his farm in Douglas County. They followed the old Territorial Road west of the Willamette River, and stopped the first night at the Eagle Hotel in Dallas. News of Lane's presence spread through the town. Unionists in the area wanted to be sure that Lane knew what they thought of him, so they ran the American flag up the flagpole and fired the town cannon thirty-four times—once for each state in the fractured Union. On leaving the hotel the next day, Lane noted that he had been hanged in effigy. The dangling dummy bore a hand-scrawled sign: "Jo Lane the Traitor."

Lane's son Nathaniel lived in Corvallis and here the temper was different. The former senator was honored at a public reception at the courthouse and this time there was welcoming cannon fire. Lane made a brief speech. Influenced perhaps by his very recent experiences, Lane forcefully rejected the idea of a Pacific Republic, urged peace, and told his listeners not to get excited about the happenings back east. Lane's speech was reported by the *Oregonian*, which labeled those who attended his address "a little squad of cackling secessionists and escaped negro stealers."[6]

Nearing Winchester, Lane climbed out of the wagon and caught the hammer of his pistol, which fired a ball through his chest and shoulder. It was a painful but not fatal wound that kept him housebound for several months.[7]

Prior to the news of the fall of Fort Sumter, sentiment in both Oregon and Washington Territory generally favored the withdrawal of the Southern states. Some favored slavery. Many felt the rights of the individual states were superior to those of the federal government.

The legislatures of both Oregon and Washington Territory were firmly Democratic. Washington's territorial governors had always been Democrats. Oregon's governor was a Democrat. Both Oregon and Washington were poor. In addition, Washington Territory was exhausted by its efforts in the Indian wars of the 1850s and the crushing debt incurred by the territory from those campaigns had not been repaid by the federal government.[8]

News of the secession of the Southern states initially was viewed with indifference in the Pacific Northwest. But with the start of actual war, opinions changed. As news of the early battles of the war and President Lincoln's call for volunteers struggled its way to the Pacific Northwest, patriotism rose in the breasts of its citizens. The formerly vocal supporters of Southern independence became remarkably silent.[9]

Letter writers to newspapers in both Oregon and Washington Territory championed the preservation of the Union. Some who wanted action headed east. Oregon Buchanan administration political appointees from the South also headed out and many of them joined the South.

Young Harvey Scott, future editor of the *Oregonian* and at the time a student at Pacific University, wrote the War Department in Washington, D.C. He would be happy to enlist, he wrote, if the government would pay his passage to the East. No answer came.[10] Scott stayed in Oregon, a civilian.

Speechmaking was a popular indoor entertainment in the 1860s and a Union mass meeting was held in early May in Portland's Willamette Theater. The program was a series of patriotic speeches calculated to stir the emotions of the crowd.

A string of Union clubs was organized throughout the state. The first was organized at Aurora on May 17 and Dr. William Keil, founder of the utopian Aurora Colony, was a speaker. Resolutions were passed pledging support of the government "against all foes from without or traitors within."[11] The Washington Legislature on February 28, 1861 adopted a resolution urging the preservation of the Union, decrying "all prospects of a Pacific Confederacy" and reaffirming its loyalty to the federal government.[12] On May 10, 1861, Acting Governor Henry McGill issued a call for enrollment of a territorial militia "to meet any requisition from the President of the United States or the governor of the Territory to aid in maintaining the laws and integrity of the Union."[13]

Oregon, whose legislature had adjourned, did nothing.[14] Governor John Whiteaker could have called the legislature back into special session but he chose not to. Instead Whiteaker, who apparently didn't spend any more time at the office than he had to, penned his "Address to the People of Oregon" on May 28, 1861, from his farm home at Pleasant Hill in Lane County. This missive initially was published in two Democratic newspapers. Whiteaker did not advocate resistance to the Union cause. But he didn't support it much, either.

He opined that the war was a matter of concern only to the East. Oregon, he said, should not involve itself in someone else's struggle, being too far removed from the scene of battle to get involved. Whiteaker derided the war as President Lincoln's doing and declared that Oregon would provide no troops for Lincoln's "fratricidal war." Besides, Oregonians had come from all corners of the Union. For

Oregon to side with one part against the other would "subject ourselves to the calamities which afflict them."

Whiteaker claimed that the purpose of the war was to end slavery and warned, "Have a care that in freeing the Negro you do not enslave the white man."[15]

President Lincoln called upon the states for 75,000 volunteers. Refusals came from the governors of Kentucky, North Carolina, Tennessee, Virginia, Maryland, Arkansas, Missouri, and Delaware, all of them Southern or Border states.[16] Oregon was the only state solidly in the North to refuse a request for troops.

Whiteaker's letter brought intense criticism. The pro-Union *Oregon Argus* flatly labeled Whiteaker "the biggest ass in Oregon."[17]

Through spring and summer 1861, public gatherings and flag-raisings were reported in the state's newspapers, especially in southern Oregon where many favored the South's right to secede. Unionists in Yoncalla, Phoenix, Kerbyvile, Table Rock, Applegate Valley, Ashland, Winchester, and Jacksonville held rallies, made speeches and raised the flag.[18]

The news that came was late and inaccurate. Philip Sheridan, who became a leading Union combat general, came to Oregon as a second lieutenant. His company headed to California when the war started and he was left in command at Fort Yamhill until replacements arrived.

It was September 1, 1861, more than four months after the start of the war, before Sheridan was able to turn over his post to Captain Philip A. Owen of the Ninth Infantry and head to Benecia Barracks, California and on to his place in history.

In his memoirs, Sheridan wrote:

> It was very difficult to obtain direct intelligence of the progress of the war. Most of the time we were in the depths of ignorance as to the true condition of affairs, and this tended to increase our anxiety. Then, too, the accounts of the conflicts that had taken place were greatly exaggerated by the Eastern papers and lost nothing in transition.
>
> We received our mail at Yamhill only once a week, and then had to bring it from Portland, Oregon, by express. On the day of the week that our courier, or messenger, was expected back from Portland, I would go out early in the morning to a

commanding point above the post, from which I could see a long distance down the road as it ran through the valley of the Yamhill, and there I would watch with anxiety for his coming, longing for good news....I earnestly wished to be at the seat of war, and feared that it might end before I could get East.[19]

As has been mentioned earlier, Oregon's principal tie to the East and to the Lincoln Administration was Senator Edward Baker. That tie was severed when Baker was killed at the Battle of Balls Bluff, Virginia, October 21, 1861.[20]

Baker's death shattered the hopes of the new recruits of the First Oregon Volunteer Cavalry Regiment, who had hoped that Baker would arrange their transfer to the battlefields of the East.[21]

It also opened the way for Oregon's anti-war Governor, John Whiteaker to appoint Baker's successor. Whiteaker appointed an avowed secessionist, Benjamin Stark, to fill Baker's Senate seat. Stark's appointment brought protests from Oregon's Unionists. They petitioned to bar his acceptance by the rest of the Senate, who had to vote to allow him to take his seat.[22]

The Salem *Statesman* branded Stark "a Secessionist of the rankest dye and the craziest professions." After some delay and debate, Stark was seated in February 1862. He served until September 1862 and exercised little influence in the Senate.

Chapter 3 notes

1 Payne, William Kenneth, *How Oregonians Learned About the Civil War* (master's thesis, University of Oregon, 1963), 81-85. *Oregon Statesman,* May 6, 1861.
2 Swing, William, "Civil War Falls Upon Nation; Rains Invade Portland Sector," *Oregonian*, April 9, 1961, 24.
3 Maxwell, Ben, "Free Negroes Unwanted in State as First News Came in 1861," Salem *Capital Journal,* Jan. 2, 1961, 1.
4 *Congressional Globe*, 2d Session, 36th Congress, Part 1, 43, cited in Kennedy, Elijah R., *The Contest for California: How Colonel Baker Saved the Pacific States for the Union* (Boston, New York, Houghton Mifflin Co., 1912) 136-43.
5 Bancroft, Hubert Howe, *History of Oregon* (San Francisco, The History Company, 1888) 2:455.
6 *Daily Oregonian,* May 9, 1861.
7 Hendrickson, James E., *Joe Lane of Oregon, Machine Politics and the Sectional Crisis*, (New Haven, Conn., Yale University Press, 1967) 250-52.
8 Snowden, Clinton A., *History of Washington* (New York: The Century History Co., 1909), 103-04.
9 Van Winkle, *"A Crisis in Obscurity,"* 46-52.
10 Klooster, Karl, "Portland's Part in the Civil War," *Oregonian*, Nov. 21, 1990. This Week Magazine.
11 Woodward, "Political Parties in Oregon," 322-34.
12 Hansen, *Public Response to the Civil War,* 11, 13.
13 Snowden, *History of Washington*, 104.
14 Carey, Charles H., *General History of Oregon Through Early Statehood*, (Portland, Or., Binfords & Mort, 1971), 626-27.
15 *Oregon Sentinel*, June 15, 1861, quoted in Carey, Charles H., *History of Oregon,* Author's Edition, (Portland, Or., The Pioneer Historical Publishing Co., 1922), 661.
16 Roberts, Allen E., *House Undivided, The Story of Freemasonry and the Civil War* (Richmond, Va., Macoy Publishing and Masonic Supply Co., Inc., 1990), 29.
17 Hageman, *Lincoln and Oregon*, 69.
18 LaLande, "'Dixie' of the Pacific Northwest," 44-46.
19 Sheridan, Philip H., *Indian Fighting in the Fifties in Oregon and Washington Territories* (Fairfield, Wash., Ye Galleon Press Reprint, 1987), 83-85.
20 Baker was not the first Oregonian to die in battle during the war. That unfortunate distinction fell to Capt. James W. Lingenfelter, of Jacksonville. Lingenfelter was a law student who enlisted in Baker's regiment of California (later redesignated Pennsylvania) volunteers. Lingenfelter died October 8, 1861 at Fortress Monroe, Va. (LaLande, Jeff, "Dixie of the Pacific Northwest: Southern Oregon's Civil War",OHQ (1999),47-8, Bates, Samuel P., *History of the Pennsylvania Volunteers, 1861-1865,* B. Singerly, (State Printer, Harrisburg, Pa., 1869-1871).
21 Platt, "Oregon in the Civil War," 95-98.
22 Hageman, *Lincoln and Oregon*, 44-45.

Chapter 4

THE WITHDRAWAL OF FEDERAL TROOPS

A t the start of the war the United States Army was in a terrible
fix. It faced a full-scale war with a federal army consisting of
14,663 men present for duty—1,700 less than its authorized
strength of 16,367.[1] As one of its first acts, the War Department
started pulling regular army troops back from the Far West to meet the
challenge of war in the East.[2]

On January 1, 1861, the regular army presence in Oregon and
Washington Territory consisted of twenty-seven companies. Of these,
sixteen were infantry, seven were artillery and four were mounted
dragoons.

Two Fort Vancouver artillery companies were sent to Fort Point,
California, February 28, 1861.[3]

Army posts at Fort Cascades, Fort Townsend, and Camp Chehalis—
all in Washington Territory—and Fort Umpqua at the south end of the
Siletz Indian Reservation in Oregon were ordered closed. The entire
military presence in the Pacific Northwest soon shrank to 700 men
and nineteen officers. There were 111 men at Fort Vancouver, 116 at
Fort Colville, 127 at Fort Walla Walla, forty-one at Fort Cascades,
forty-three at Fort Hoskins, fifty-four at Fort Dalles, and 110 divided
between Fort Steilacoom and Camp Pickett in the San Juans.[4]

The closure of the smaller scattered posts caused concern. A detail
was returned temporarily to Camp Chehalis after Indians in the area
were reported restive.

In Washington, D.C. there was labored debate over whether the
regular army units should be integrated into the huge new army of
volunteers or kept as separate units. Eventually, the regulars were kept
as separate units and the largely volunteer army formed around this
nucleus.

Before long, the regular army presence in the Pacific Northwest consisted of two lonely infantry companies and one of artillery, later shrinking to two infantry companies. One company of regulars remained at the politically sensitive post in the San Juan Islands throughout the war. The other was held at Fort Vancouver. Later in the war, one company of regular army infantry was sent from Fort Vancouver to build and staff the new coast artillery batteries at Cape Disappointment on the mouth of the Columbia River. A small ordnance detachment was kept throughout the war at the Fort Vancouver arsenal.

Until volunteers could be found to take their places, the last of the regular army line units couldn't be moved out of the Pacific Northwest. To man the Indian forts of Oregon and Washington Territory, units of the Second and Fourth California Volunteer Infantry Regiments were shipped in.[5]

On November 1, 1861, Captain Frederick T. Dent, a firm Unionist and Ulysses S. Grant's brother-in-law, marched his company of forty regulars of the Ninth U.S. Infantry Regiment out the gate of Fort Hoskins in what is now Benton County to Fort Vancouver and onto a ship headed for California. A hastily recruited company of the Second California Volunteer Infantry led by Captain J. C. Schmidt replaced them.[6]

The Californians, fresh from their steamship journey up the coast to a foreign environment, found they were short-handed and barraged with wild and unproven rural Oregon gossip. On November 25, 1861, Lieutenant T. B. Campbell, the post adjutant, wrote to headquarters at Fort Vancouver that guns had been given to the area Indians:

> Mr. Patton, a packer in the Indian Agency employ, came in and avers that when Mr. Newcomb (an Agency employee) was going away he distributed to the Indians guns and revolvers and ammunition, and he told them to fight for Jeff. Davis and the Southern Confederacy.

Campbell also heard continuous reports of:

> ...the disaffection prevailing around us. Yesterday Mr. Wisner substantiated to us as follows: Mr. Jerry Evans, of this valley, told him that Captain Dent gave him a box of ammunition containing 1,000 of rifle musket cartridges; that

he knew the said Evans to be a rank secessionists, and that Captain Dent must have known so also when he gave him those cartridges.

Campbell breathlessly repeated second- and third-hand claims that area secessionists, armed with weapons reportedly distributed by Captain Dent and Governor Whiteaker, were prepared to set the fort afire and shoot its tiny garrison. Campbell also requested the issue of fifty revolvers to buttress the firepower of the troops, who were armed with muzzle-loading muskets.[7]

The U.S. Army command had long been dominated by Southerners. As the clouds of war grew near, many of the army's best officers resigned and headed to the Confederacy. Nationally, four of the army's five commanders of mounted regiments resigned.[8]

Union Army leaders who served in the Pacific Northwest before the war included Ulysses S. Grant (stationed at Fort Vancouver), George McClellan (surveyed a wagon route over the Cascades), David Allen Russell (commanded Fort Yamhill), Philip Sheridan (served at Fort Hoskins and Fort Yamhill), and Joseph Hooker, who had left the army and was living in Salem at the start of the war.[9]

Washington agonized not over the adequacy of army troops on the Far West frontier, but over who was to command them. Two positions were at issue: command of the Department of the Pacific, which was all the troops west of the Rockies; and the subordinate command, a lesser degree command of its northernmost component the District of Oregon, which consisted of most of what now is Oregon, Washington, Idaho, western Montana, and a sliver of Wyoming.

THE DISTRICT OF OREGON

Benjamin F. Alvord, a tall, paunchy, and balding career Army officer, finally became the Civil War commander of all the army in the Pacific Northwest.

His appointment came almost by default. Colonel George Wright had taken over command from Brigadier General William S. Harney. Wright was transferred to command the District of Southern California in August 1861. In rapid succession, the job rotated through Colonel Benjamin F Beall[10] and Lieutenant Colonel Albemarle Cady,[11] two ranking regular army officers, and Colonel Justus Steinberger, ranking officer of the Washington Territory Volunteer Infantry, who had just recruited four companies of Californians to serve with the Washington Volunteers.[12]

When appointed July 7, 1862, Alvord was one of the few regular army officers left in the Pacific Northwest. Alvord had served with distinction in the Florida Indian War and was brevetted captain and major in the Mexican War where he was cited for "gallant and meritorious conduct" in the battles of Palo Alto and Reseaca de la Palma.[13]

Alvord was, at best, an unconventional army officer. Much of his first twenty years of service was as a member of the West Point mathematics faculty.[14]

Alvord served September 1852 to July 1853 as commander of Fort Dalles, Oregon. While there he authored a monograph, "The Tangencies of Circles and Intersections of Spheres" which was published by the Smithsonian Institution in 1856. He then was put in charge of surveying a road from the Umpqua River Valley to the Rogue River Valley of southern Oregon.[15]

In June 1854 Alvord was appointed major and paymaster of the then-Department of Oregon. For the next seven years he held pay call at the scattered military installations in the Pacific Northwest.

THE DEPARTMENT OF THE PACIFIC

At the outbreak of the war, the commander of all army troops on the Pacific Coast was Brevet Brigadier General Albert Sidney Johnston. A Texan, Johnston arrived in San Francisco to take over his command on January 15, 1861, and served a little more than three months. They were crucial months. Johnston was a 58-year-old West Point graduate who, after fighting in the Mexican War, had left the service. He served as adjutant general and secretary of state of Texas, and then returned to military service, commanding army units during the Mormon conflict in Utah from 1857 to 1860.

His loyalty was suspect because he was a Southerner, and because he was appointed to command the consolidated departments of Oregon and California during the waning months of the Buchanan administration.

Earlier, Johnston had turned down the command of troops in Texas because he knew that Texas might secede and he did not want to be called upon to take up arms against his adopted state.[16] Johnston did his job on the Pacific Coast well. He did much to preserve and protect federal installations as the nation lurched toward war. He transferred 10,000 stand of arms from the vulnerable Benecia Arsenal to more secure storage at Fort Alcatraz.[17] He recruited to fill vacancies in his regular army units and consolidated commands on the Indian frontier in northern California.

Climbing off a steamer at San Francisco on April 24, 1861, Brigadier General Edwin V. Sumner learned of the bombardment of Fort Sumter. The next day he presented himself at Johnston's office, displayed his orders and told Johnston he was fired.[18] Sumner took over command of the Department of the Pacific.[19] A tall white-bearded veteran of the Mexican War, Sumner came unannounced on a secret trip. No orders of his transfer had been published, he traveled in civilian clothes,[20] and his name was not on the ship's manifest. He was rowed to the steamer that was to carry him to Panama as it lay hove to in New York Harbor. The purpose: to outwit reporters who might report his departure.

Fearing that Johnston might side with those who would form a Pacific Republic, Sumner was sent by President Lincoln. There are two versions of how Lincoln came to suspect Johnston.

Erasmus Keyes, an aide to General Winfield Scott, wrote in his memoirs that Lincoln got word from Secretary of State Seward and Scott that Oregon's new Senator James W. Nesmith had been informed that Johnston was allied with secessionists.[21] How Nesmith came to learn of this is uncertain as Nesmith had left San Francisco on his trip east to Washington before Johnston ever arrived in California. Glenn Thomas Edwards, Jr. wrote that Nesmith may have maligned Johnston hoping to get the command sent over to his old friend, Colonel George Wright, commander of the District of Oregon. Or, it may have been paranoia that Nesmith shared with much of the rest of Oregon.[22]

The second version was told by *Sacramento Bee* editor James McClatchy. In 1880, McClatchy recalled that he wrote to Oregon's Senator Baker that Johnston intended to side with the South. McClatchy based this report on the statement of Edmund Randolph, a native Virginian then seeking appointment by the California Legislature as Senator from California. Randolph, McClatchy said, had told him, "I know this man Johnston," and predicted that he would plot to make federal installations vulnerable to takeover by "home rebels."[23]

Though insulted by his summary dismissal, Johnston also was relieved. Knowing that he could not fight against Texas, Johnston had sent his resignation to Washington two weeks before.[24] He moved to Los Angeles where he waited several weeks, and then joined with other Southerners in a cross-country trek to Texas and service in the Confederate Army.

Although Johnston has been accused since of an alliance with the South, Sumner absolved him of any wrong-doing while serving as commander of the Department of the Pacific. In his first report to Washington on April 28, 1861, Sumner wrote: "The command was turned over to me in good order. General Johnston...was carrying out the orders of the government."[25]

Chapter 4 notes

1   Huebner, Michael, "The Regulars," *Civil War Times* 33, 3(June 2000): 26.

2   Platt, "Oregon in the Civil War", *OHQ* 4(1903):99.

3   United States, War Department, *War of the Rebellion: A Compilation of the Official Records of the Union and Confederate Armies* (Washington, D.C., Government Printing Office, 1880-1901) (hereafter W.O.R), Series 3, 1:24.

4   Shablitsky, Julie M., *Duty and Vice: The Daily Life of a Fort Hoskins Soldier* (master's thesis, Oregon State University, 1996) 25.

5   Hunt, Aurora, *The Army of the Pacific* (Glendale, Calif., Arthur H. Clark Co., 1951) 228.

6   Onstad, Preston, "The Fort on the Luckiamute," *OHQ*, 65(1964):183.

7   W.O.R., Series 1, Pt. 1, 739-40.

8   Officers who joined the Confederacy after service in Pacific Northwest before the War included George Pickett, who served in the San Juan Islands, and James Archer and Robert S. Garnet, who were stationed at Fort Simcoe. Pre-war civil officials also served as leaders in the Confederate Army. They included Adolphus B. Hanna, U.S. Marshal for Oregon under Buchanan, J. Patton Anderson, the first U.S. Marshal in Washington Territory, Washington Territorial Governor Richard Gholson and John K. Lamerick, a brigadier general in the Oregon militia during the Southern Oregon Indian wars.

9   Robert J. Hendricks, in his confusing book, claimed 182 officers of general and flag rank who previously had served in the Pacific Northwest served the Union in the Civil War. But he included service in California and with the Wilkes exploration expedition of 1838-42. Hendricks, Robert J., *The West Saved America and Democracy*, (Salem, Or., n.p., 1939).

10 Ibid., 584.

11 Ibid., 656.

12 Ibid., 1014.

13 Bowyer, Gary C., "Archaeological Symbols of Status and Authority, Fort Hoskins, Oregon," (master's thesis, Oregon State University, 1992) 20.

14 Edwards, "The Department of the Pacific," 136, 257, 280-82.

15 Clark, Robert Carlton, "Military History of Oregon, 1849-59," *OHQ*, 36(1935): 55.

16 Johnston, William P., *The Life of General Albert Sidney Johnston* (New York, DaCapo Press, 1997), 248.

17 W.O.R., Series 1, V. 50, Pt. 1, 446-48.

18 Just to let everyone know how he felt, Sumner several months later crafted a General Order: "No Federal Troops in the Department of the Pacific will ever surrender to Rebels." Headquarters, Department of the Pacific, General Orders No. 20, September 3, 1861, University of Oregon Archives.

19 Edwards, "The Department of the Pacific," 61-62.

20 Josephy, Alvin M. Jr., *The Civil War in the American West* (New York, Alfred A. Knopf, 1991), 234-35.

21 Keyes, Erasmus, *Fifty Years Observations of Men and Events* (New York, Scribner and Sons, 1884), 420.

22 Edwards, "The Department of the Pacific," 57.

23 McClatchy, James, *Sacramento Bee*, Sept. 21, 1880.

24 Hagemann, "Lincoln and Oregon," 35.

25 Todd Hageman blames much of Lincoln's mistrust of Johnston on wild tales of dissent told him by Oregon's Senator James Nesmith. Hageman, Todd, "Lincoln and Oregon," 34.

Chapter 5

THE MILITIA — GUARDING THE HOMEFRONT

The Civil War was really able to start because of the work of the volunteer, part-time militia of the eastern states. The armies of the Confederacy were built on the militia units of the seceding states. Well-drilled militia units, primarily of the northeastern states, bulked up the small regular U.S. Army and provided badly needed manpower for the Union in the first few battles of the war. Most eastern states had active part-time militias which were part of a heritage of proud service rendered by citizen soldiers during the Revolution, the War of 1812 and Mexican-American War.

There were militia units in part of the Pacific Coast. But the departmental commander, General George Wright, refused to augment the sparse federal presence by asking for the mobilization of local militias.[1] Wright feared that armed, poorly trained troops roaming the West during times of internal dissent would lead to the abuses experienced in Kansas and Missouri before the war.[2]

THE OREGON MILITIA

Although Article X of the Oregon Constitution called for a militia, Oregon had no organized militia at the start of the Civil War. Article X automatically made militia members of every able-bodied male citizen aged eighteen to forty-five. It directed the governor, as commander-in-chief, to appoint an adjutant general and general staff and allowed the election of line officers by the men they commanded.[3] But what the state of Oregon had was a militia on paper only.

With its origin at Champoeg in 1843, Oregon's provisional government adopted a militia law and appointed several officers. But the militia was never organized as such.

In 1844, the provisional government formed the twenty-five-member Oregon Rangers, which drilled but saw no service.[4] After the December 1847 Cayuse Indian attack on the Whitman Mission at Waiilatpu, the provisional legislature authorized the formation of a fifty-member rifle company to relieve the mission and protect the survivors. Later, a 300-member regiment of volunteers was formed and spent the winter at Waiilatpu. Temporarily organized militia units saw service in the battles against the Cayuse and Rogue River Indians.[5] The First Oregon Mounted Volunteers served in the Yakima-Walla Walla country and the Second Volunteer Regiment in the Rogue River-Umpqua country of southern Oregon. However, with the advent of statehood in 1859, Oregon's new legislature did not fund a militia. Territorial Adjutant General Eli M. Barnum gave up the job and soon moved to Washington, D.C.[6] Relying on the regular army troops stationed through Oregon and Washington Territory, Oregon figured it didn't need a militia.

Most of the equipment gathered to support the Oregon troops during the Indian Wars of 1855-56 was sold by then-Quartermaster General Joseph Drew and his commissary officers. In the final session of the Territorial Legislature in January 1859, arguing over what the territory owned and what had happened to it consumed a significant amount of time. Drew balked at providing information to the legislature and was accused of stealing documents related to the claims for expenses from the desk of clerk of the Territorial House of Representatives.[7]

Oregon did have a few rifles and cannon left over from the Indian wars. With no one left to supervise their safekeeping, and no money to pay for it anyway, the state promptly delegated responsibility. The governor shipped what arms and equipment remained for safe-keeping to the various county judges. These county officers were men of great responsibility. They served as chairmen of their respective county boards of commissioners. They also were magistrates and probate judges and now were charged with keeping track of the state's military arms.

John Whiteaker, governor of Oregon at the outbreak of the war, had already made it clear that he thought Oregon ought to stay out of the war. He did little to raise troops for federal service and did nothing to organize a militia.

When Governor Addison Gibbs and a pro-Union legislature were sworn in on September 10, 1862, action commenced to organize an effective militia for Oregon. A handful of regular army troops and a thinly-spread force of federalized volunteers from Oregon, Washington, and California were the only military left.

The legislature promptly passed a comprehensive militia act, and repealed the territorial militia laws of 1854 and 1856. They gave Governor Gibbs only $5,000 to finance the formation and maintenance of the militia so the state was forced to do the job on the cheap. The job of listing all males eligible for militia service was delegated to the county assessors since they had to travel their counties anyway. The assessors were commanded to turn their lists over to the county clerks, who were to forward them to the adjutant general.[8] The few exempted from militia service were ministers of the gospel, the three judges of the Oregon Supreme Court, county judges, members of the legislature, county clerks, sheriffs, the secretary of state, the state treasurer, and clerks in telegraph offices.[9] All registrants were subject to a call-up if their services were needed. County judges were directed to provide necessary drill facilities and were told not to spend more than $50 a month to rent them—at county expense, of course.

Further militia expenses were to be paid from a $2 annual head tax levied by each county against males who were liable for service but who did not sign up and drill with organized militia companies.[10] Those who joined and drilled with the militia companies were members of the organized militia. Those who did not join were members of the unorganized enrolled militia.

Joel Palmer, superintendent of Indian affairs and commissary general of the provisional government troops in the 1848 Indian war, was appointed major general and commanding officer.[11]

Governor Gibbs appointed Cyrus A. Reed as Oregon's new adjutant general to do the day-to-day work. Reed was a man of many talents. An accomplished landscape artist, he'd made good money in San Francisco in 1849 as a sign painter. He came to Portland in January 1850 and helped build the first steam sawmill in Oregon Territory. After teaching a three-month term of school at Portland, he then became a partner in the sawmill he helped build.[12] He moved to Salem in 1852 and was a partner in the Willamette Woolen Mills. Reed also served as a member of the legislature from 1862-1870.[13] As head of the militia (which was an exempted position) he was able to hold two lucrative public offices at once.

Reed had no support staff, no military experience, and a salary of $800 a year. Secretary of State Samuel E. May (who, although he was exempt from service would command a Marion County militia company), fitted up Reed with an office in a room of the Holman Building, previously used as the state library. Now with the rank of colonel, the landscape artist-turned military leader set about creating a citizen militia and raising the six companies of full-time volunteers that would constitute the First Oregon Volunteer Cavalry.

Reed had no records and complained that even the muster rolls for the troops who had served as volunteers in the Indian Wars were missing.[14]

In November 1862, he wrote in longhand (with indifferent spelling and punctuation) to the county judges of each county. In the letter, he asked each judge to list any arms belonging to the state and their condition. If the arms had been distributed, was it practical to call them in? He asked to be informed "if you know of any person or persons in your County who would take an interest in getting up and organizing volunteer Companies...if you do please give me their names and post office address." He noted that having an organized militia was desirable, "living as we do upon the frontier surrounded by a savage and warlike rase (sic) we must of necessity be to some extent a military people."

His letters turned up four six-pounder cannons and 205 muskets held by the county judges in Jackson, Benton, Polk, Douglas and Clackamas counties.[15] The cannon were sent to militia artillery units as they were formed. The muskets, deemed useless, were never called in and remained in the hands of the county judges as late as 1878.[16]

The rest of the equipment once owned by Oregon had disappeared, although its practical use would have been debatable.[17] Reed told Governor Gibbs in his September 1863 report that several hundred steel-barreled jaegers (he spelled it yaugers)—short-barreled rifles of the type used during the Mexican War—had been given away to citizens of Marion County and remained unaccounted for.

Reed wrote the adjutant general in Washington on February 18, 1863 requesting "books of instruction." He wrote the California adjutant general, querying: How do you do your job and where do you find weapons?[18]

Over the next three years, eighteen companies of militia—fourteen of infantry, one of cavalry and three of artillery—were organized. One company was at Ashland Mills in southern Oregon,[19] one at The Dalles and the rest in the Willamette Valley.[20]

The troops had to provide their own uniforms and were paid for drill only during the annual muster, held in conjunction with the State Agricultural Fair at Salem.[21] Finding weapons for the militia troops was a challenge, for without weapons they weren't much of a home guard. They were an unpaid, part-time army with nothing to shoot at and nothing to shoot with. This made recruitment slow and retention difficult.[22]

Governor Gibbs drew on the $5,000 the legislature appropriated for the organization of the militia and bought 360 cavalry sabers. They weren't much, but Gibbs claimed he got a good buy—$2.50 each plus shipping charges.[23]

In spring 1863, rumors of secessionist plots spread throughout Oregon. Gibbs wrote to General Alvord on May 7, 1863 to let him know that:"I think I shall call on you for arms in a few days. General Wright told Secretary (of State) May that I could get all I needed. Secretary May returned (from San Francisco) on the last steamer."

Three days later, Gibbs formally asked Alvord for arms.[24] Alvord directed Captain Theodore J. Eckerson, the storekeeper of the arsenal at Fort Vancouver, to ship to Gibbs 400 rifled muskets[25] and accessories and 16,000 rounds of ammunition.[26]

Alvord told General Wright, his immediate superior, what he was doing by letter.[27] The letter left Fort Vancouver May 7. It got to headquarters in San Francisco May 20. Wright immediately telegraphed Alvord:

"Arms cannot be supplied to Oregon militia."[28] But they had already been shipped.

Alvord had acted in part upon the representation of Secretary of State May[29] that Wright had assured approval of the issuance of the arms.[30] Wright wrote his superiors he said no such thing.[31]

After some dithering, Wright agreed that Oregon didn't have to give the weapons back, and by mid-June they had been issued to the then-operating companies of militia.[32]

It wasn't that the army didn't have the weapons handy. At the inventory dated November 1859, the Fort Vancouver arsenal reported an inventory of 3,763 muskets and 126 rifles.[33] Some of the estimated 45,000 stand of arms at the Benecia, California armory were sent back east at the start of the war. Part of the Vancouver arsenal's equipment was ordered shipped south to Benecia. But not all of it.

Under an 1808 law, each state and territory was entitled to an annual issue of military equipment. The distribution to states was based on the population at the last decennial census.[34] The issue was made up of muskets, or other equipment of comparable value. Arms were issued, however, only to the states and territories that reported an active, organized militia. With no organized militia and therefore making no report, Oregon had received none of the weapons due from the federal government for over two years. The 400 muskets issued from Vancouver were charged against weapons due in the future to Oregon.

Oregon's militia units drilled at home. Form was important to the groups, with each adopting rules and regulations for the conduct of their internal affairs. The Ashland Mountain Rangers, the militia group at Ashland Mills, filed three separate versions of its constitution with the adjutant general.

The highlight of the year was the annual muster at the state fair at Salem. An August 10, 1864, letter sent to Adjutant General Reed from Captain Ivan D. Applegate, commanding officer of the Rangers, emphasized the volunteer nature of Oregon's militia. He said his troops couldn't make it. "[O]ur company is made up entirely of farmers...and as much as they would like to come down it would be impossible for them to do so, and save their harvest."[35] The Ashland Rangers held their own drill at Camp Sublimity, in the Cascade Mountains along the major Indian trail into the Rogue Valley.

Prizes were given at the state fair to the militia companies who showed most proficiency in drill. But the display of arms was not uniformly welcomed. In September 1864 the militia drilled on the state fair grounds. J. Quinn Thornton, a Peace Democrat, led a rump meeting of the Agricultural Society, which owned the fair grounds. By a voice vote, the Society agreed to ask the militia to do its drilling somewhere else. The state ignored the vote. Reed claimed the vote was not among society members but among hangers-on. Shortly thereafter the fairgrounds was used as a muster site for the First Oregon Volunteer Infantry.

The Oregon militia was never called to service during the war. Yet, as noted in Secretary of War Redfield Proctor's 1889 report on Oregon war claims, it did act to champion the cause of the Union and to suppress any attempts at outright revolt by supporters of the Confederacy.

In 1865 the legislature repealed the $2 head tax on all eligible males who did not participate in the organized militia, and used the $23,300 remaining in the military fund to help build the penitentiary. In his February 1866 report to the governor, Reed complained that the repeal of the head tax removed the incentive for militia service and resulted in the disbanding of half of Oregon's militia companies. He urged that the state rent or erect a fireproof armory building to store the state-owned military equipment. His recommendations were ignored.

The Oregon Militia continued as an organization after the Civil War. Legislative efforts to require the counties to finance and construct armory facilities were struck down by the Oregon Supreme Court in 1887.[36]

Reed hung on as adjutant general until 1870. Most of the militia units disbanded. An exception was Multnomah County, where membership in the organized militia became a matter of social prestige. Reed's main job was to administer the redemption of bonus certificates given to those who enlisted in the Oregon Volunteer Infantry and Cavalry units.[37]

In October 1870, the legislature abolished the adjutant general's office and gave the Secretary of State responsibility for all records and equipment of the office.[38]

Reed went into the real estate business and returned to painting, doing a landscape panorama of the Northwest that was exhibited at the Philadelphia Centennial Exposition in 1876.[39]

THE WASHINGTON MILITIA

At the start of the Civil War, Washington's militia organization wasn't much better than Oregon's, but Washington had an adjutant general, a supply of arms, and the skeleton of an organization. It also had a territorial government willing to get things done.

There were three factors that helped the organization of the home guard Washington Territorial Militia. The first was that Isaac I. Stevens was Washington's first territorial governor. At the start of the war he was Washington Territory's non-voting delegate to Congress. A military man, Stevens was first man in his class at West Point in 1839, and resigned his commission as a brevet major in the U.S. Army to accept appointment as governor. As governor he set about to organize a strong militia, although it took him until 1855 to get the territorial legislature interested.

The second was that Washington Territory had suffered severe Indian uprisings that extended throughout the territory between October 1855 and July 1856. Without a militia in the territory during the spring of 1855, the tiny white population would have been annihilated.[40] During that war, the coordinated efforts of army regulars, militia, a navy sloop, and a handful of marines and civilian volunteers kept the Indians at bay. They erected sixty-one forts, stockades, and blockhouses at or near virtually every inhabited neighborhood in the territory.[41]

Third, while Oregon quibbled over what to do with its equipment and arms at the end of the Rogue River Indian War in 1856, the ordnance officer of the Washington Territory volunteers meticulously accounted for 2,434 muskets, rifles, and sabers received from the federal government.[42] In his final report, William V. Miller, commissary general of the volunteers, boasted to the governor that his troops ended up with more horses than they started with and that he had sold horses, mules, and wagons belonging to the militia at more than they originally had cost.[43] A record was kept of all military equipment, including forty-seven rifles issued to the various members of the territorial legislature.

Washington Territory continued to draw its share of the $200,000 worth of military equipment parceled out by the federal government annually to its states and territories. The 1858 allotment was two twelve-pound mountain howitzers, carriages and equipment, six packsaddles and harness, and twenty-six percussion rifles "and appendages" worth a total of $920.[44]

The federal turnover, for some reason, was not made in dollars, but in thirteenths of the value of a musket. In January 1861 the army chief of ordnance reported to the territory that it was entitled to the equivalent of 135 9/13 muskets. The territory could accept delivery in army equipment according to a Statement of the Cost of Small Arms, Field Artillery, Etc., at Their Equivalent in Muskets.[45]

Continued Indian troubles east of the Cascades kept the citizens of Washington on edge. There were pitched battles between regulars and Indian renegades in the Spokane area in 1858.

In January 1861 Lieutenant Colonel Silas Casey sent two companies of regulars from Fort Steilacoom to the Muckleshoot River area to put down an uprising of hostile Indians. President Lincoln called for federalizing 75,000 militia troops nationwide on April 15, 1861, but the call wasn't received in Olympia until May 10, 1861. Acting Governor Henry McGill issued a proclamation for all able-bodied men to organize into militia companies. On May 14, 1861, Adjutant General Frank Matthias at Seattle appointed enrollment agents in all Washington counties. Six companies shortly were organized.

A new panel of enrolling officers was appointed and a second call for militia members was issued on January 15, 1862. Militia enrollment lagged. A year later, on January 28, 1863, the territorial legislature adopted yet another militia act. This stated that all men aged eighteen to fifty not "disqualified by bodily infirmity" were liable for service. The act compelled the county assessors to compile a list of those eligible, as in Oregon, and made the county commissioners responsible for drawing and issuing arms provided by the territory to the militia groups when organized.[46]

In March 1863, vexed with a long series of Indian raids against immigrant trains and prospector parties, a 111-member company of volunteers naming itself the Boise Rangers organized and called itself to duty at Placerville. The company was headed by Jefferson Standifer, a towering six-footer and a leader in the mining community.

Standifer's group apparently attempted to organize itself under the Washington Territory Militia Act. It had the complement of officers (captain, three lieutenants, four sergeants and four corporals) provided by the Washington act. It reported its organization to Militia Brigadier General John W. Moore, a member of the Washington Territorial Council (Senate) who lived at Pierce City, Idaho.

Word of the call-up reached Washington Governor Pickering on May 18, 1863. Pickering responded to Moore that he couldn't approve the unit because Idaho had been a separate territory since the preceding

March 3.[47] Not that it mattered. By then the Rangers had formed, done its duty, and disbanded.

The newly-organized Idaho Territory was crippled by a defect in the federal act creating the territory that left Idaho without any laws until ten months after its formation.[48] This, and the healthy percentage of its voters who were refugees from the South, left Idaho with no militia act. Idaho contributed no volunteer units to the war.

The Idaho militia finally was organized in 1873.

Chapter 5 notes

1 Technically, state militia units could be called to duty only by act of the governor. Once activated by the state or territorial governor they could be federalized. In some states early in the war, newly formed federal volunteer units were made up largely by volunteers from militia forces.
2 Edwards, "The Department of the Pacific," 83.
3 Deady, M.P., *General Laws of Oregon, 1845-1864* (Portland, Or., State Printer, 1866), Art. X, Sec. 1-2, Oregon Constitution.
4 Field, Virgil F., *The Official History of the Washington National Guard,* (Tacoma, Wash., Washington Military Department, 1961), 1:23.
5 Clark, Robert Carlton, "Military History of Oregon," 15-18.
6 Oregon Adjutant General, "Report for the Year 1863", House of Representatives Journal, Oregon Legislature, 1864, Session, 111.
7 Oregon Legislature, *Journal of the House of Representatives*, (1859 session), 97-105.
8 Deady, Matthew P. and Lane, Lafayette, *The Organic and Other Laws of the State of Oregon, 184-7, Portland*, Or., E Semple, State Printer, 1874) Ch. 36.
9 Carey, *General History of Oregon,* (Portland, Or., Binfords & Mort, 1971), 632.
10 Oregon Legislature, *Journal of the House of Representatives*, (1864 Session), Governor's Report.
11 Carey, *General History of Oregon,* 644.
12 Scott, *History of the Oregon Country,* 3:106, 380.
13 Corning, Howard McKinley, *Dictionary of Oregon History* (Portland, Or., Binfords and Mort, 1956), 208.
14 Oregon Adjutant General, "Report for the Year 1863," House Journal, Oregon Legislature, 1864 Session.
15 Ibid.
16 Oregon Governor's Office, Executive Order of November 19, 1878, Oregon State Archives.
17 Oregon Adjutant General, Correspondence File, 1862-1863, Oregon State Archives.
18 Ibid.
19 Ashland was one of the few communities in Southern Oregon to openly support the war. Much of Oregon's Rogue River Valley was anti-war Democrat. LaLande, Jeff, "'Dixie' of the Pacific Northwest," 32.
20 Oregon Military Department, *Historical Annual,* (National Guard of the State of Oregon, 1939) 209.
21 The style of uniform was prescribed by Adjutant General Reed in this letter to a prospective recruiter: "All uniforms must be similar to that of the same arm of the service in the U.S. Army with a distinctive mark upon the hat or cap..." Oregon Adjutant General's office, Correspondence file, 1862-1863, Oregon State Archives. In practice, the style of uniform varied. One Multnomah County unit wore uniforms of gray.
22 Oregon Adjutant General, Correspondence File, 1862-1863, Oregon State Archives.
23 Oregon Legislature, "Journal of the House of Representatives", (1864 session), Governor's Report, 195.
24 W.O.R., Series 1, Vol. 50, Pt. 1, 429.
25 Until 1855 the U.S. Army equipped its troops with flintlock smooth bore muskets. Starting in 1855, the army's Springfield Armory began the production of a much more accurate muzzle-loaded rifle

musket that had a rifled barrel and fired a minie bullet. Rifle-muskets distributed to the Oregon militia were flintlocks that had been converted to percussion cap rifles.

26 W.O.R., Series 1, Vol. 50, Pt. 1, 450.

27 U.S. Army, District of Oregon, Correspondence File, 97; National Archives, Washington, D.C.

28 W.O.R., Series 1, Vol. 50, Pt. 2, 449.

29 May might have been somewhat elastic in the truth. After he left office, May was indicted in March 1872 by the Marion County grand jury and charged with multiple counts of malfeasance—primarily theft--while in office. He was tried but acquitted. *State v. Samuel E. May*, Marion County Circuit Court records, Oregon States Archives.

30 W.O.R., Series 1, Vol. 50, Pt. 1, 462.

31 Ibid., 483.

32 Oregon Adjutant General's office, Correspondence File, supra.

33 W.O.R., Series 3, Vol. 1, 1.

34 Field, *The Official History of the Washington National Guard,* 222.

35 Oregon Adjutant General, Correspondence File, supra.

36 Oregon Legislature, Act of October 20, 1870. *Vincent v. Umatilla County*, 14 Oregon Reports 375, 12 Pacific Reports 732 (1887).

37 Oregon Adjutant General, *Report for the Years 1865-6*, 115-16.

38 Oregon Legislature, Act of October 20, 1870.

39 Oregon militia units were called to service during the Modoc Indian war (1872), the Nez Perce outbreak (1877) and the Bannock Indian War (1878). The militia was reorganized as the Oregon National Guard in 1887. Units were activated to assist in civil unrest in Vale (1892), the lower Columbia River (1896) and at Roseburg (1896). Units served in the Spanish-American War, World Wars I and II and in Iraq and Afghanistan. (Oregon Military Department, *Historical Annual,* National Guard of the State of Oregon, 1939, supra).

40 Field, *The Official History of the Washington National Guard,* 35-39.

41 Ibid., 169-70.

42 Ibid., 167-68.

43 Ibid., 168-69.

44 Ibid., 175.

45 Ibid, 176.

46 Ibid., 211-15.

47 Ibid., 222.

48 *Territory v. Williams*, 1 Idaho Supreme Court Reports, 85,(1864); (anonymous author), "The Year Without Laws," *Idaho Yesterdays, the Journal of the Idaho Historical Society*, 25, No. 1(1981):13.

Chapter 6

RESPONSIBILITIES, RESISTANCE AND THE DRAFT

The start of the Civil War brought new responsibilities to the army in the Pacific Northwest. The army already was working hard to keep the peace. This often meant resolving disputes that arose between the incoming white settlers and miners and the Indians who didn't want them there. The army explored and mapped new territory, opened and improved wagon roads and trails, assisted the emigrants who traveled those roads, and helped speed new avenues of transportation and communication to the frontier. Because of those responsibilities, much of the army's pre-war manpower was located in the West.

At the start of the Civil War these soldiers, and the hastily recruited volunteers who took their places, were charged additionally with preventing the invasion of Confederate and foreign forces and insurrection by anti-Union elements at home.

RESISTERS

In the Pacific Northwest, first or second generation ex-Southerners formed the majority of the passive resistance to the Civil War. These men and women sympathized with their friends, kinsmen, and cultural cohorts in the seceding states.[1] In the rough-and-tumble frontier mining camps, there were others who just wanted to mine gold. They wanted the government, of whatever stripe, to leave them alone—except, of course, when it came to protecting them from the Indians.

Civil War resisters expressed their objections in a range of ways—often while under the influence of alcohol. Some did it verbally. Others raised the Confederate flag, objected to the display of the American flag, or talked with their fists. Sometimes bored soldiers tried to goad secessionists into a fight.[2] Few if any of the resisters went beyond huff-and-puff in their opposition.

On July 17, 1862 Congress took firm steps to dampen the fires of resistance from those who owned property, by authorizing the forfeiture of all tangible and intangible property of any men or women in the Northern states and territories who gave aid and comfort to the rebellion.[3] The U.S. Land Office restricted homestead grants to those "loyal to the United States."[4]

On the West Coast, pro-secessionist sympathies were strongest in California. Accounts of pro-South militancy there and among U.S. expatriates in British Canada were reported breathlessly by a Pacific Northwest press short on news and long on political expression.[5]

Civilian reports of threatened insurrection flooded military headquarters, especially in California. Although few if any of the civil reports proved true, almost uniformly they asked for troops. Editorialists claimed that local situations were often exaggerated because local schemers knew that there were profits to be made from military contracts and payrolls.[6]

In the District of Oregon, there were threats and reports of threats to the Union but the army took no direct action against secessionists. General Alvord figured that most of the resisters were more mining camp blowhards than a threat to security.

In southern Oregon, then a part of the District of Northern California, there were at least three arrests of civilian protesters. Two men tried to prevent the recapture of deserters from Fort Lincoln near Crescent City. The noisiest objection seemed based on the fact that the pursuing troops came from California. The third had offered a toast to Jefferson Davis' health in a tavern.

In 1863, there were no civilians taken into custody in the district of Oregon because of anti-government activities. It was only at the very end of the war, when Patrick H. Mulkey was jailed at Eugene for loudly lauding the assassination of Abraham Lincoln, that anyone was jailed.

THE DRAFT AND JULIUS KEELER

Early in the war, it was soon apparent that there were not enough volunteers and activated militia units to fight America's Civil War.

The draft started in 1862 in the East. It was resisted in many parts of the country. In all, only 46,000 men were drafted nationwide. The law permitted a man subject to the draft to hire another to take his place, if he had the money to do it. This brought another 118,000 substitutes (some of dubious military value) and was a contributing factor to the draft riots in some eastern cities.[7]

The draft was really never considered for the Pacific states and territories.[8] President Lincoln specifically excluded Oregon, Washington Territory, California, Nebraska, New Mexico, Utah, Colorado, Nevada, and Idaho from his draft proclamations throughout the war.[9] Some contend that this was because the manpower of the West was needed to produce gold to finance the Union's war efforts.[10] In fact, the actual war was fought with troops from the eastern and midwestern states. The Pacific Coast and the western frontier was left to fend for itself with men mostly recruited in the West.

Although no one was ever drafted in the Pacific Northwest, registration of all draft-age men was required. Along with appeals to patriotism and state, federal, and local bonuses, the threat of a military draft that did not exist was used to promote volunteer enlistment in Oregon units. Oregon's draft registration began in July 1863.

Julius M. Keeler, a cavalry veteran of the Army of the Potomac, was sent to Oregon to organize the registration for the draft. After arriving in the state that July, Keeler promptly announced that it was unlikely that any man would be drafted in Oregon. He then appointed enrolling agents in eighteen separate districts in Oregon and set about listing all draft age white men.

Many of the rugged frontiersmen of the Pacific Coast did not cheerfully accept being made potential draftees. The rumor mill worked overtime and resistance was feared throughout Oregon. The opposition most feared was from organized secessionists.

For Keeler, an Oregon pioneer, his assignment to duty in Oregon was a homecoming. He first came to Oregon in 1852, was the principal of the Tualatin Academy at Forest Grove from 1852 to 1856, and was its principal when it was renamed Pacific University.[11] As a Whig he was elected county school superintendent of Washington County, when Portland was included within its boundaries.[12]

Keeler set up the first graded public school in Portland and taught the first government Indian school at Forest Grove, before it became

Chemawa School at Salem. A take-charge sort of a person, he was a likely fellow for this new challenge. He had served as an officer of the Connecticut Volunteers and he had a good record. Most importantly, he knew Oregon and its people.

Accompanied by his second wife, their infant daughter and a son from his earlier marriage, Keeler came via Panama to Portland in July 1863.[13] He was sent to Salem, because it was the state capitol, where he rented an office on the second floor of J. D. Boon's two-year-old building.[14] The building was used primarily as a general store. Oregon's capitol building had burned in 1854, so Boon's building also served as the state treasury. Oregon's government business was conducted in various rented space scattered about Salem. Boon was the state treasurer, and conducted such business as the state treasury required in his own quarters.[15]

Born in 1829 in the county seat town of Malone, eleven miles south of the Canadian border in upstate New York, Keeler claimed the benefit of a classical education and was a sort of Renaissance man. In 1849 he and seventy-nine other men from the eastern states banded together to seek their fortune in the newly discovered California gold fields. Regular transport to California was difficult to find, so Keeler and his associates solved their transportation problems as did other adventurers. They formed a mutual benefit and joint stock company, bought a run-down old sailing ship, stocked it with a year-and-half of supplies, hired a captain and crew, and set sail for Cape Horn and California. Keeler was elected president of the group.

If ever a group needed leadership to get to California, it was this one. Desperate to get to California before the claims were all staked, Keeler and his associates looked for "anything that would float." Keeler later told one of Hubert Howe Bancroft's researchers that they got what they sought—an old New Orleans packet, the *Arkansas*. The ship leaked, ran out of water and was blown toward Africa and into the path of icebergs by adverse winds. It took twenty-five days days to beat their way around the Horn. Five months and three weeks after leaving New York City, the tattered *Arkansas* and its worn-out adventurers—minus two who died and were buried at sea—staggered into San Francisco harbor on December 18, 1849. The ship arrived on a stormy day, was blown onto the rocks of Alcatraz Island, and wrecked. The company had been wise enough to insure the ship, so they got some recompense from the underwriters.[16]

Keeler mined in California for two years before heading to Oregon in 1852. He returned to California in 1855, where he was superintendent of schools at Napa until shortly before the outbreak of the war.[17]

As part of his duties in 1863, Keeler divided Oregon into registration districts and hired deputies to superintend the registration. The southern Oregon deputy was Alonzo A. Skinner, then the county clerk of Lane County. Skinner formerly was the sole judge of the Provisional Government's Circuit Court and would later become an associate justice of the Oregon Supreme Court. Nathan Olney, former Indian Agent at The Dalles who was to command the company of cavalry volunteers mustered for four months of emergency duty in the Indian country of eastern Oregon in the summer of 1863, was employed as an enrolling agent.[18]

Rumor was a staple of every day life in Civil War Oregon. Tales of planned revolt, resistance to the draft, and overthrow of the government were epidemic. Keeler pursued them and reported them to his superior, Major Pinckney Lugenbeel. Lugenbeel had been ordered from command of Fort Boise in August 1863 to superintend Keeler's work and that of his counterpart for Washington Territory, Captain J. W. Porter, who conducted his efforts from Fort Vancouver.[19] Lugenbeel had his office at Portland.

Existing files show that on several occasions during the two-and-a-half years he served as provost marshal at Salem, Keeler perceived serious internal threats against the Union.[20] None of them resulted in arrest and some were pooh-poohed by his superiors.

Lugenbeel was succeeded in the supervisory position at Portland in November 1863 by Lieutenant Colonel Thomas C. English. In October 1864 Keeler wrote English of rumors that Southern sympathizers in the southern Willamette Valley were fully armed, well-trained and prepared to rise up in case of a draft, or in case of Lincoln's victory in the November election. He also said he had reports that seventy-five barrels of arms were secreted on a farm sixty miles from The Dalles.

English reported to General Alvord that "Captain Keeler's report is undoubtedly made in good faith....I cannot but believe that it is highly colored."[21] Independent investigation was made of the arms report at the Wasco County farm. None were found.

In November 1864 Keeler hired James A. Riley, a one-time California sheriff, as a spy to infiltrate "secret organizations in this District inimical to the Administration and Government."[22] Keeler later reported that his spy had learned of 300 stand of arms secreted by rebel sympathizers. No arrests were made. English told Keeler to discharge his spy.

Keeler got along well with Lugenbeel, but English found him a timid man. When Keeler asked what procedure he should follow in arresting those who publicly exulted in the death of President Lincoln, English waspishly replied by letter of April 22, 1865:

> [A]s you seem to desire positive directions from this Office for all your Official Acts, without in the least relying on yr. own judgment and discretion, you are hereby ordered to inquire into and fully investigate all such charges, and if you find that good reasons exist for believing the parties guilty of the offenses alleged, you will at once arrest and send them to Fort Vancouver W.T. informing me of your action, and transmitting to this office written charges against the offenders (in each case separate and distinct) together with the names and addresses of the witnesses....[23]

On November 4, 1863, Keeler's boss, Major Pinckney Lugenbeel, the assistant provost marshal for the army's Oregon District, wrote to his chief, Provost Marshal Colonel J. B. Fry in Washington, D.C. He reported that Oregon's enrollment was nearing completion. Washington Territory's enrollment hadn't started because the enrollment commissioner and surgeon hadn't been appointed. Nothing had been done in Idaho Territory, which he said was thickly populated with deserters from the U.S. Army and ex-Confederate soldiers.[24] Lugenbeel noted that in Oregon's Linn and Lane counties, there were reported threats of armed resistance to enrolling officers. Both Keeler and his deputy in Eugene City, County Clerk Alonzo A. Skinner, asked for federal troops to put down threatened resistance to the enrollment in Lane County.[25]

While others stewed over the rumors, Lugenbeel decided to leave his office at Portland and investigate for himself.[26] He came back November 13, 1863 and reported that no resistance was anticipated.

He said that objections to the draft appeared economic, not political. He wrote to Provost Marshal Fry:

> No armed organizations are making or have been made of persons hostile to the Administration or Government. Very many of the inhabitants are very ignorant and easily excited but I believe the Secessionists are very few in number and generally are very old and feeble.
>
> I regret however to inform you that there is a very general objection to any Draft being made except in case of a foreign war or to chastise hostile Indians.
>
> They say that the floating population has gone to the mines and laborers cannot be obtained at any price to cultivate the soil. In case a draft is made I would respectfully recommend that the draft be first ordered in the Commercial Counties....[27]

In December, the enrolling officer at Canyon City, who had collected 200 names for his draft registry, asked for military assistance and said he had been threatened "with bloodshed and loss of business and property."[28]

Headquarters for the Washington Territory provost marshal was established at Fort Vancouver. Enrolling officers were appointed for each county in the territory.

Walla Walla County, a rough and tumble part of the territory, was heavily populated by deserters from both North and South, and didn't favor the prospect of service in the army. As the enrolling agent sat in a saloon doing his work, he was doused with a bucket of water. On another occasion a string of firecrackers was set off under his chair. Eventually, seven men were arrested and convicted before a United States commissioner for interfering with the draft.[29]

Things were even stickier in Idaho Territory. Lugenbeel told Fry that a draft in Idaho would trigger an exodus north to Canada. He said a large number of Idaho men otherwise eligible for the draft were deserters from the U.S. and Confederate forces.[30]

Keeler's wartime activities in Oregon were not confined to enrollment and counterespionage duties. The files of the *Oregon Statesman* report Keeler helped organize and judge the militia review at the 1863 Oregon State Fair at Salem.[31] He raised funds for the Sanitary Aid Society at Salem and The Dalles. Notwithstanding his military office, he was a political activist and spoke to the Lincoln-Johnson political clubs at Salem and Eugene before the presidential election of 1864.

He also had time to care for himself. He explored and staked silver deposits known as the "Keeler Lode" in the Quartzville mining district of eastern Linn County in August 1864.[32] He was an incorporator of the Crescent Gold and Silver Mining Co.[33] In 1864 Keeler was listed as an incorporator of the Pacific Gold and Silver Mining Company at Salem. He also appears to have hired his son, P. J. Keeler, as clerk of his office about August 1864. There is reference in the Portland Provost Marshal General's correspondence file relating to an oath of allegiance, required of all civilian employees and contractors, signed by P. J. Keeler. Bancroft indicates that P. J. Keeler was born of the union of Keeler and his first wife, Sylvia. This would have made P. J. Keeler no more than eleven years of age in 1864.

However, nepotism was not unknown in the Civil War military. Major Lugenbeel had James P. Lugenbeel (relationship unknown) as an employee in his office.

After the war, Keeler went into partnership at Salem with N. O. Parrish in the book and stationery business. He continued his interest in mining and helped open the first wagon road to the Quartzville mining district. He remained prominent in community affairs.

In December 1866 he and his wife hosted a benefit at their home for the Rev. Obed Dickinson, the controversial pastor of the First Congregational Church.[34]

Keeler was appointed U.S. Marshal for Oregon in August 1866.[35] He later moved to New York City where he was in business as a commission merchant.[36] He returned to San Francisco in 1872 and got into the mining business again, this time in Inyo County, which includes Death Valley. He was superintendent of the Owens Lake Mill and Mining Co., erected a ten-stamp silver quartz mill and platted the town of Keeler, now a wide spot in the road on the dusty eastern edge of Owens Lake, whose waters were taken for the Los Angeles Aqueduct project.

Keeler represented Inyo and Mono counties in the 1884 California Legislature, and served as Deputy U.S. Collector of Internal Revenue for those counties. At the time of his interview by Bancroft's researcher in 1888 he was the president of the Inyo Marble Co., which for some years quarried deposits of marble in Inyo County.[37]

Keeler died at San Francisco January 30, 1890.[38]

Chapter 6 notes

1 Carey, *History of Oregon*, 3:663.

2 Platt, "Oregon in the Civil War," 97-104. Richter, Sara Jane, "Washington and Idaho Territories, The Civil War in the Western Territories," *Journal of the West*, 16,2(1977):34. Barth, *All Quiet on the Yamhill*, 106, 109.

3 Department of the Pacific, U.S. Army, General Orders No. 34, September 17, 1862, University of Oregon Library, Eugene, Oregon.

4 *Oregon Statesman*, March 3, 1862.

5 *Jacksonville (Or.) Sentinel*, January 11, 1862, quoted in Hageman, "Lincoln and Oregon," 47-48.

6 *San Francisco Alta*, August 6, 1864.

7 Wiley, Bell Irvin, *The Life of Billy Yank*, The Common Soldier of the Union, (Garden City, N.Y., Doubleday, 1971) 284.

8 W.O.R., Series 1, Vol. 50, Pt. 2, 1093.

9 W.O.R., Series 3, Vol. 4, 1269.

10 Hageman, "Lincoln and Oregon," 57.

11 Scott, *History of The Oregon Country*, 1: 318-319 and also Corning, *Dictionary of Oregon History*, 132.

12 *Oregon Statesman*, June 27, 1854.

13 *Oregon Statesman*, July 27, 1863.

14 Ibid.

15 The building still exists as Salem's oldest business building at 888 Liberty Street NE.

16 Bancroft, Hubert Howe, manuscripts, Inyo Marble Co. and Julius M. Keeler, Bancroft Library, University of California, Berkeley, Cal.

17 Scott, *History of the Oregon Country*, 2:276.

18 For a list of registrars and the results of the registration, see the exhibit to this chapter.

19 W.O.R., Series 3, Vol. 3, 687.

20 U.S. Army, District of Oregon, Office of the Acting Assistant Provost Marshal General, correspondence book (hereafter District of Oregon Provost Marshal correspondence book) National Archives Branch, Seattle, Wash., 81-82.

21 District of Oregon Provost Marshal correspondence book, 187-88.

22 Ibid., 85-86.

23 U.S. Army, District of Oregon, Office of the Provost Marshal General, Letter Book, Record Group 110, National Archives Branch, Seattle, Wash., 251-52.

24 District of Oregon, Provost Marshal correspondence book, 5.

25 W.O.R., Series 1, Vol. 50, Pt. 2, 669.

26 District of Oregon, Provost Marshal correspondence book, 6.

27 Ibid., 5.

28 W.O.R., Series 1, Vol. 50, Pt. 2, 699-700.

29 Snowden, *History of Washington*, 11.

30 District of Oregon, Provost Marshal correspondence book, 5.

31 Ibid., March 7, 1864.

32 Ibid., August 8, 1864.

33 Ibid., August 15, 1864.

34 *Oregon Statesman*, December 25, 1865.

35 Ibid., August 13, 1866.

36 Scott, *History of the Oregon Country*, 2:277.

37 Bancroft, manuscripts, Inyo Marble Co. and Julius M. Keeler.

38 Scott, *History of the Oregon Country*, 5:258.

Chapter 7

THE SUPPRESSION OF THE COPPERHEAD PRESS

The greatest assault on individual liberties during the Civil War in the Pacific Northwest was the suppression of the anti-government—or Copperhead—press. Six newspapers were closed down in Oregon. Each was an outspoken critic of the Lincoln administration and of the Union position in the war.[1] There were critics in the Washington Territory press, but none of its newspapers fell under the censor's control.[2] In California, there was censorship of several newspapers.[3]

The most complete study of this event is Kathleen O. Winkerwerder's unpublished master's thesis, "Treated as Enemies: The 1862 Suppressions of Oregon's Copperhead Press," (University of Oregon, 1985).

Congress in 1851 and 1852 gave newspapers free postage within their county of publication, and half-rate outside. The purpose: To spread the news of government and political thought.

During the summer of 1861, fearing that unbridled criticism of the war would foster open rebellion in the North, Postmaster General Montgomery Meigs closed the mails to the more vocal opponents of the North and its policies, effectively putting them out of business.[4] Nationwide, twelve newspapers were suppressed in 1861.

In 1862, the War Department took over suppression duties. On February 28, 1862, General Wright, saying he had seen Oregon newspapers "filled with abuse of the President and the Government of the United States," ordered Lieutenant Colonel Albemarle Cady, then commander of the District of Oregon, to send him copies of "traitorous sheets" so he could have them barred from the mails.[5]

Over a period of eight months in 1862, six Oregon newspapers were barred from the mails. Five of them ceased publication immediately.

The other died some months later. These newspapers all espoused the Copperhead or Peace Democrat political philosophy.

The offending newspapers and the dates of their suppression were:

Oregon Democrat, Albany, February 15, 1862
Southern Oregon Gazette, Jacksonville, March 11, 1862
Democratic Register, Eugene, October 3, 1862
Albany Inquirer, Albany, October 3, 1862
Evening Advertiser, Portland, October 3, 1862
Oregon Weekly Union, Corvallis, October 31, 1862

Most Oregon newspapers were founded for and supported by political parties and, at best, there was a hazy dividing line between editorial comment and news reports. News was viewed from the political standpoint of the editor. If you didn't like what the editor wrote, there were other newspapers to read.

Editors followed the "Oregon Style" of journalism, a vicious form of calumny in which those out of favor of the editor might find themselves called anything and accused of everything.[6] Today, such reports would bring immediate and repeated civil suits for libel. Then, the "Oregon Style" was viewed as fair comment, even if it was followed by the occasional fistfight or invitation to duel.

Over a period of nine months, every opposition newspaper in Oregon was barred from the mails. None advocated outright rebellion. Their sins—if they were sins—were outright, rabid criticism of the Lincoln administration and the war. Their complaints followed a consistent pattern:

1. President Lincoln was unfit by training or education for his office and served merely as a tool of the abolitionists.

2. The Republican-controlled federal government forced the rupture of the Union by its obdurate refusal to negotiate with the South and recognize its long history of slavery.

3. The Unionist (mainstream) press was but a tool of the federal government and its abolitionist masters.

4. The military leaders of the North were inept. The terrible Union military losses in the early years of the war resulted principally from the incompetence of Northern military leaders.

5. The South had superior political and military leaders and could never be defeated.

6. And, after it was begun, the suppression of the anti-administration press was the unconstitutional use of naked federal power to repress dissent and extinguish all political opposition.

Nowhere in the Pacific Northwest did the Copperhead Press advocate open resistance. Compared to the virulent anti-government speech and press of America's Vietnam and Iraq war periods, the criticism of the opposition press of Oregon during the Civil War was mild indeed, although more crudely expressed.

However, the 1860s is not today. We were then, as a nation, not only less tolerant of dissent but rigidly conformist, even in Oregon. Add to that the fear of some that Oregon might side with the Rebellion, or join the rumored Pacific Republic.

Oregon's questionable political heritage may well have induced a less-forgiving attitude toward dissent.

Here is a list of the newspapers that were suppressed, those who controlled them, and some of the things they said:

Oregon Democrat

The *Oregon Democrat*, of Albany, was founded by Delazon Smith, later a Breckenridge delegate to the 1860 Democratic National Convention. Smith died soon after the convention. The newspaper passed to W. B. Henley, who hired Patrick J. Malone as editor. Malone previously wrote for the two principal newspapers in the state, the *Oregonian* and the *Oregon Statesman*. Malone railed against the war, the Republican Party and its principal voice, the *Oregonian*, which he labeled "the Niggeronian." The Postmaster General barred the *Oregon Democrat* from the mail on February 15, 1862. The newspaper immediately ceased publication.[7]

ALBANY INQUIRER

Soon, the *Albany Inquirer* made its appearance as the successor to the *Oregon Democrat*, again with Patrick Malone as the editor. That paper was barred from the mails by order of General Wright, October 3, 1862.

The sole existing copy of the *Albany Inquirer* had commented upon the inauguration of Governor Addison C. Gibbs, the War Democrat-Unionist. The *Portland Times* reported that as Gibbs took his oath of office, he rolled his eyes heavenward as he repeated the phrase, "So help me God."

Malone, who did not attend the inauguration, commented on the *Portland Times* report. He wrote scathingly:

> The correspondent does not unfortunately give any of the particulars. He does not tell us whether any of the old women fainted, or whether any, or how many little children screamed. He should have given us the entire effects that immediately followed this startling phenomenon. We had, immediately following the inauguration, refreshing showers of rain, almost entirely unknown heretofore at that season. Did the lifting of the governor's eyes produce that result?... [W]e trust that the legislature...will pass a joint resolution requesting his Excellency, at stated intervals during the coming season, to lift his eyes to heaven, so that the gentle rains will be called down by that powerful electrical effect, our usual dry weather avoided, the pastures to be clothed with continual verdure and the earth be crowned with fatness.[8]

SOUTHERN OREGON GAZETTE

The *Southern Oregon Gazette* at Jacksonville started publication August 14, 1861 and was closed March 11, 1862.

James O'Meara published the paper. The *Gazette* was a successor to another failed Jacksonville paper, the *Oregon Democrat,* in which O'Meara also had a role. Earlier, O'Meara had been with the *Democratic Standard* in Portland.

O'Meara fulminated against the abolition of slavery, saying that it would:

[R]esult in the subjugation and vassalage of the whites of the south...and the cruel slaughter [of the Southern whites] by the infuriated slaves which shall be armed and incited on to destruction and carnage by the abolitionists.

O'Meara repeatedly criticized the conduct of the war, and railed against the Lincoln administration in ways that today appear childish, but were powerful criticism at the time.

DEMOCRATIC REGISTER

The *Democratic Register* of Eugene started in March 1862. It had as part-owner and writer Cincinnatus (Joaquin) Miller, who in later years won acclaim as a poet. Miller later became county judge of Grant County, Oregon, and led a company of volunteers who pursued Indian raiders during the Indian troubles in 1864.

Miller's partner was Anthony Nolter, another the Peace Democrat editors who had rotated among the dozen or so Democratic publications that bloomed and withered in early Oregon.

Nolter excoriated the *Oregon Statesman* of Salem and the *Oregonian* of Portland. He protested the suppression of anti-administration newspapers and predicted his own newspaper's demise. He roundly criticized the arming of black troops, the levying of a federal tax to finance the war and the good works of the U.S. Sanitary commission.

In the issue of August 23, 1862, he wrote:

Abraham Lincoln is today as much of a traitor as Jeff. Davis. Both have broken the laws of their country; both have drenched their country in human blood and both alike should be brought to answer for their crimes. The only difference...is one has come out boldly before the world and openly declared hostility to the Constitution...while the other has professed to be true to the Constitution and the laws of his country, while he...like a thief in the night, was quietly and surely...tearing down and placing under his feet the laws that bound him as a servant of the American people, and now he stands forth robed in the authority of a dictator, with the prisons filled with men who dared to raise a voice against him.[9]

The last issue of *Register* was September 27, 1862. The suppression notice was issued six days later.[10]

OREGON ADVERTISER

The *Oregon Advertiser*, a weekly, and the *Portland Evening Advertiser*, a daily, were founded by S. J. McCormick. McCormick was a delegate to the constitutional convention of 1857 and was mayor of Portland in 1859.

George L. Curry, three times territorial governor of Oregon, was co-editor.

At the start of the war, the *Advertiser* was pro-Union. As the war wore on, the newspaper's political outlook changed. Lincoln and his policies were criticized, and the war blamed upon the ambitions of Lincoln and the Republicans. Curry left the paper in February 1862.

It may be that General Wright's suppression order of October 3, 1862, came too late. The *Oregonian* reported that the *Advertiser* had suspended publication several days before the suppression order was received.[11]

OREGON WEEKLY UNION

The *Oregon Weekly Union* of Eugene was the only newspaper to publish after it was barred from the mails. But it died an economic death shortly after the order that barred it from the mails was lifted.

Publisher J. B. Slater opposed the war. He, like Governor Whiteaker, espoused a "hands-off" policy and thought Oregon should sit out the war.

In September 1861 Slater sold the newspaper, which the previous July was merged with the *Democratic Herald,* to Patrick Malone, who earlier had worked on the *Oregon Democrat* and the *Albany Inquirer.*

The *Union* was not included in the blanket suppression order of October 3, 1862. The *Oregonian* commented that the *Weekly Union* should have been suppressed also, and Malone fired back with pyrotechnic fury:

> Oregon Sniveldom is in a ferment! The Abolition warhowlers feel their inability and want of brains, to cope in argument with the appeals of Democrats to the Constitution; to law; to reason and common sense....The whole Kennel of Vampires who feed out of the official servile tub...are in full chorus yelping on the track of the only Democratic newspaper left in this State. What the imbecile minded asses cannot do by argument, they hope to accomplish by clamor. A

semi-idiot, upon whose face Nature stamped the vacant stare of the unfeeling and uncaring fanatic writing from the Niggeronian, thinks the reason that General Wright did not suppress the Union was that he did not see it!! We can inform the Nig that General Wright gets the *Union* mailed to him regularly....General Wright can see for himself that the Oregon Union is not disloyal, but neither is it servile.[12]

Malone did not confine his contempt to the *Oregonian*. He referred to the Unionist-dominated legislature as "a putty headed set of nincompoops" and claimed Lincoln's Emancipation Proclamation was a move intended to please the abolitionists.

The notice suppressing the *Oregon Weekly Union* was issued by the postmaster at San Francisco on orders of General Wright. It was printed in the *Union*'s issue of November 8, 1862.

Malone continued to publish and announced he would distribute the newspaper through his own "*Union* Pony Express," delivering by private courier to subscribers, including those in southern Oregon.

The *Union* limped along with mainly political news until the postmaster general rescinded all Oregon suspension orders December 25, 1862.

The return of access to the mails did not help the *Union*. Plagued with "financial embarrassments," the *Union* published its last issue March 28, 1863.[13]

Chapter 7 notes

1 Winkenwerder, Kathleen O., "*Treated as Enemies; The 1862 Suppression of Oregon's Copperhead Press,*" (master's thesis, University of Oregon, 1985), 29-30.

2 Ibid., 36-39.

3 In California, five Copperhead newspapers were suppressed. They were: *Stockton Democrat, San Jose Tribune, Tulare Post, Visalia Equal Rights Expositor* and the *Los Angeles Star.*

4 No appeal process was provided and apparently no publisher of a suppressed newspaper attempted appeal. Fowler, Dorothy Canfield, *Unmailable* (Athens, Ga., University of Georgia Press, 1977), 48.

5 W.O.R., Series 1, Vol. 50, Pt. 1, 897.

6 Lyman, Horace S., *History of Oregon; The Growth of an American State,* (New York, North Pacific Publishing Society, 1903), 4:289.

7 Winkenwerder, "*Treated as Enemies,*" 51-58.

8 *Albany Inquirer,* Sept. 17, 1862.

9 *Eugene Democratic Register,* Aug. 23, 1862.

10 Winkenwerder, "*Treated as Enemies,*" 71-79.

11 *Portland Oregonian,* Oct. 14, 1862.

12 *Weekly Union,* Oct. 25, 1862.

13 Winkenwerder, "*Treated as Enemies,*" 83-93.

The steamer *Brother Jonathan* sank off Crescent City, June 30, 1865. Brig. Gen. George B. Wright, en route to command troops in the Pacific Northwest was among the dead. His death resulted in the appointment of volunteer Army commanders who launched a series of winter campaigns that resulted in the final pacification of rebellious Indians.

Major General Isaac Stevens
Killed at the Second Battle of Bull Run.

Southern Oregon Historical Society No. 17062
Major William Rinehart
He led troops in Eastern Oregon Indian campaign. Later, he was Malheur Indian Agent.

Oregon Historical Society No. CN020568
Colonel George B. Currey
He assumed command of Northwest troops after the death of Brig. Gen. George Wright.

Southern Oregon Historical Society No. 17063
Lieutenant Colonel John Drake
He led the winter campaign in Eastern Oregon that ended the Indian raids.

Fort Walla Walla, Washington Territory, in 1862. Fort Walla Walla was a principal military installation east of the Cascade Mountains before and during the Civil War.

Oregon Historical Society No. 22072

FORT STEVENS BATTERIES. The interior of Fort Stevens was photographed shortly after the end of the war. Fort Stevens, one of three coast artillery installation at the mouth of the Columbia River, remained in service until the end of World War II. The only action the Columbia River forts ever saw was a random shelling by a Japanese submarine in the early months of World War II.

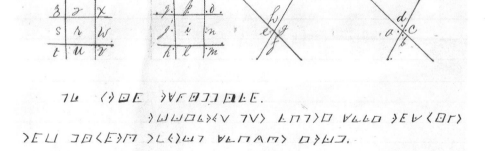

Oregon Historical Society Mss. 685, A. C. Gibbs Papers

THE SECRET CODE OF THE UNION LEAGUE. This code was used for correspondence by the Union League, formed in Oregon to counter the Knights of the Golden Circle Translated: "Approach the Outer Door and give any signal except double raps."

Oregon Historical Society No. 1671
Colonel R. F. Maury
Commander of Pacific Northwest troops.

Oregon Historical Society No. OrHi 11494
Paiute Chief Paulina

U.S. Army Military History Institute
Lt. Colonel Charles S. Drew
He established Ft. Klamath, Oregon.

Oregon Historical Society No. 53881
Brigadier General Benjamin Alvord
Long-time professor of mathematics
at West Point, Alvord commanded
troops in the Pacific Northwest 1862-
June 1865.

Oregon Historical Society No. CNN003832
Captain James Lingenfelter
Served with Baker's Pennsylvania Volunteers; was first Oregonian
killed in Civil War.

Author's Collection

Army troops lined up for pay call at Fort Lapwai, Idaho Territory.

Laws Railroad Museum, Bishop, California
Captain Julius M. Keeler
He organized the Oregon draft.

Oregon State Archives
John Whitetaker
Oregon anti-war governor who resisted the enlistment of Oregon volunteers at the start of the war.

Oregon State Archives
Addison C. Gibbs
Oregon's war-time governor.

U.S. Army Military History Institute
Colonel Justus C. Steinberger
Commander, 1st Washington Territory Volunteer Infantry Regiment.

73

San Juan Island National Historic Park

This is the parade ground at Camp San Juan Island, formerly Camp Pickett U.S. and British troops jointly occupied the San Juan Islands in Washington Territory throughout the Civil War. Eventually the Islands were declared part of the United States.

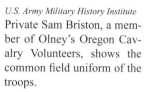

U.S. Army Military History Institute
Private Sam Briston, a member of Olney's Oregon Cavalry Volunteers, shows the common field uniform of the troops.

Southern Oregon Historical Society
Zany Ganung chopped down the flagpole at Jacksonville that displayed the rebel flag.

Columbia River Maritime Museum
The Revenue Cutter *Shubrick* was the import duty collector, mail boat, lighthouse tender and what passed for a Navy in the Pacific Northwest during the Civil War. It also was a prize of a planned but failed plot by Confederate sympathizers to capture and convert the ship to a privateer.

75

Southern Oregon Historical Society, No. 6319

Officers of the Applegate Rangers, a militia company at Ashland Mills, Oregon, pose in uniform and with their state-issued sabers. The sabers were their only arms for a while. The state couldn't afford muskets.

Oregon Historical Society No. 13415

Portland held a grand parade to celebrate the surrender of General Robert E. Lee at Appomatox, which signaled the end of the Civil War.

Chapter 8

THE KNIGHTS OF THE GOLDEN CIRCLE

Duuring the Civil War, the pro-South Knights of the Golden Circle organization was a misunderstood threat to the stability of the Pacific Northwest. It was misunderstood for several reasons. Communication within the Pacific Northwest was primitive at best. The organization of the Knights was steeped in mystery. Its members made it that way. They swore an oath of secrecy, pledging to resist the government of the United States. Members of the Knights identified each other in a ritual that was cumbersome, convoluted, and larded with symbolism.[1] Existing reports of its ritual vary wildly, but the claimed ritual resembles that of the Order of Freemasons, which was preeminent among the numerous secret men's lodges of the time.

The secrecy and ritual likely contributed to the Knights' inability to do little other than talk about rebellion. The Knights' mysticism alienated some. It was difficult to recruit members to an organization whose members kept their membership secret.

ORIGINS

The Knights of the Golden Circle was an outgrowth of a series of pre-war regional political associations. These organizations weren't formed for purposes of revolt. Their goal was to prevent the intrusion of the federal government into state affairs and to protect the South against domination by non-slave holding Northern states.

The first Knights of the Golden Circle was organized in Cincinnati in 1854. Its founder was George W. Bickley, a physician from Boone County, Indiana. It quickly spread to the South.

The group's initial goal was to occupy Mexico and then annex it to the United States as slave territory. Other countries around the Gulf of Mexico were to follow. The ultimate purpose was to add these to the

United States as slave-owning states, thereby neutralizing dominance of non-slave owning states in U.S. politics.

After the Southern states left the Union, the Knights of the Golden Circle extended its activities into the North. It was absorbed in 1863 into the Order of American Knights, a better-organized group, which in turn changed its name in 1864 to Order of the Sons of Liberty.

There were myriad organizations besides the Knights of the Golden Circle. Some were separate groups that shared membership and purposes with the Knights. Others were a part of the Knights organization. Some of these gloriously-titled organizations were: Corps de Belgique, Southern League, Paw Paw, Union Relief Society, Illini, Democrat Invincible Club, Democratic Reading Room, Knights of the Golden Square, McClellan Minute Guard, Knights of the Columbian Star, Union League, Mutual Protection Society, Circle of Honor, Loyal League, Knights of the Order of the Sons of Liberty, Peace Organization, and Star Organization.

Most of the groups had the same basic structure. There were three or more levels of membership, akin to the three degrees of Freemasonry. Members of the lower level knew little if anything of the workings of the upper echelons of the organization. Generally, the organization was a handful of leaders who were the only ones with a true command of the goals and activities of the order. Some reportedly admitted women as members.[2]

THE KNIGHTS' ACTIVITIES DURING THE WAR

Because of the group's secretive nature and the sensational reporting of the press of the day, it's difficult to define the extent of the Knights' activities during the war. Yet it's clear that the presence of the Knights and its various successors was most felt in the midwestern states of Missouri, Illinois, Indiana and Ohio.

The "Peace" Democrats or Copperheads spawned various secret societies that were constantly being dissolved and reformed, often with the same officers and members. The usual cause of dissolution was infiltration by government spies. This meant that the members of the new organization[3] then had to learn a fresh array of passwords, signs of recognition, and handshakes.[4]

Historians disagree about whether the Knights really posed a serious threat. Some scholars conclude that the Knights did a lot of talking, but took little action. At its lower levels, the Knights functioned as little more than a Democratic social club. Rodney Patton, a scholar of the Knights, contends that contemporary newspaper accounts and official reports were exaggerated by the anxiety that accompanied a terrible war.[5]

General Joseph Holt, the army's judge advocate general, reported to Secretary of War Edwin M. Stanton on October 8, 1864, what his spies had learned about the Knights of the Golden Circle. He described them as "A large army of well-armed men, constantly drilled and exercised as soldiers." He also opined that most of the organization's members had joined, "supposing it to be a Democratic political association."[6] Whether these unknowing lower-level initiates would actually come to arms against the Union was never really tested.

The Knights and its successors, financed in part by Confederate money from Canada, made three serious but ultimately unsuccessful efforts to free and arm Confederate prisoners from Union prison camps in Illinois and Indiana.[7]

THE KNIGHTS IN CALIFORNIA

The Knights of the Golden Circle and its successors were active in California during the war, and their presence caused concern in the Pacific Northwest. A self-appointed group of patriots wrote Secretary of War Edwin Stanton in 1861 to claim that there were 16,000 members of the Knights of the Golden Circle in California.[8] In 1864, The Sacramento Army provost marshal sent a spy into the Knights of the Columbia Star organization (a successor to the Golden Circle) who claimed that the two Knights organizations had a combined membership in California of 50,000.[9]

Author Robert Treat Platt claimed there was a planned but unexecuted plot by 800 Knights of the Golden Circle to capture the Benicia Arsenal and, once armed, to seize the Pacific Coast.[10]

Army records of the period have frequent reports of secessionist efforts in California. Whether these plots were a part of an organized conspiracy or acts of individual groups of dissidents is unclear. It's also unclear whether the plots were real. Many reports were accompanied by pleas from the local community who wanted a detachment of troops stationed locally, a decision that would have been of great benefit to the local economy.[11]

An editorialist in the *San Francisco Alta*, derided "the howler on our side who goes in for civil commotion, for he sees great pecuniary advantage in transportation contracts, in conduct of sutler's stores, in following the army and picking up whatever he may find lying around loose."[12]

However, the activities of the Knights of the Golden Circle and the Knights of the Columbian Star, disappeared toward the end of the war. No report of these organizations in California appears in the army's published records after 1864.

THE KNIGHTS IN OREGON

In Oregon, the Knights of the Golden Circle started organizing in 1861. By the end of the year, it was claimed there were ten lodges or "circles" in Oregon. The location of nine of them was listed: two in Portland, two in Salem, and one each in Albany, Scio, Dallas, Jacksonville, and Yamhill County.[13] Adjutant General Cyrus A. Reed kept an eye on the Knights, and later claimed that he had two spies in the organization.[14]

As 1861 ended, the Oregon Knights were split by internal wrangling. Most members wanted to leave the Union and join in a Pacific Republic. But they disagreed whether this should be accomplished by peaceful means or by open revolt.

In a most perplexing July 12, 1862 letter, Washington Territory Governor William Pickering wrote General Alvord to inquire whether army commissions should be given those suspected of membership in the Knights of the Golden Circle, whom he referred to addressed as "Barons, Lords, Earls, Dukes and Princes of Treason."

Alvord answered:

> I have no knowledge of the existence on this coast of the Knights of the Golden Circle. If there are any then they keep very secretive. As they are and necessarily must be a dead faction here, they will not be likely to show their heads...."[15]

As the war progressed, supporters of the North reasoned that if the secessionists had their secret organization, so too should the Unionists. The Union League was organized in the East and organization soon followed in Oregon. On December 14, 1863, the Grand Council of the Union League was organized at Portland. Its president was

Governor Addison C. Gibbs.[16] The financial records of the Grand Council show that constituent lodges were organized at: Dallas, Portland, Salem, Dayton, Lafayette, McMinnville, St. Helens, School House No. 2 (Multnomah County), Dalles City, South Portland, Ames Chapel (Washington County), Bethel, Corvallis, Amity, Eugene City, Forest Grove, Sandy Precinct, Hillsboro, Wilterville Forks, Auburn, Humboldt Basin, Canon (sic) City, Silverton, Catherine Creek and Union School House (Washington County).

Business and political leaders of Oregon were prominent in the affairs of the Union League. General Joel Palmer, Oregon's first Indian agent, organized the nineteen-member Union League lodge at Belle Passi, near Woodburn.[17]

The Union League started with a bang. Fearful that the Knights would intercept its mail, the Union League devised its own cipher. The most mundane correspondence was laboriously transcribed into a runic code before being posted. One sample of that cipher remains in the papers of Governor Gibbs at the Oregon Historical Society library.

Yet once organized, the Union League didn't have much to do.[18] The Knights, if they existed, were hard to find. Rent with internal squabbling, the Union League soon dissolved and as of its meeting on April 29, 1864, the Grand Chapter's minutes ceased.

Oregon's Knights of the Golden Circle went through several permutations. By the time of the 1864 state fair, they called themselves The Jones Family, and solicited and initiated members at the fair.[19]

There is a real question whether the Knights of the Golden Circle ever really had much of a membership in the Pacific Northwest. Because most of the existing reports of the Knights of the Golden Circle and its successors in Oregon are second-hand at best or are reminiscences told or written years after the end of the war, the evidence is conflicting.

Historian Charles H. Carey quoted former Adjutant General Reed as contending the Knights had 2,500 members in Oregon in 1863. In a 1912 article in the *Oregon Historical Quarterly,* W. C. Woodward quoted Reed as saying that he then had a complete list of the Knights membership that included nearly every Democratic editor and politician in Oregon.[20] The adjutant general's files for that period contain no reference to the Knights.

In 1903, Robert Treat Platt quoted an unnamed "historical authority" who said he had a file of cipher documents of the Knights. Its whereabouts now apparently is unknown.[21]

Well after the war, Reed said that the Knights planned to assassinate him, and that they made plans on several occasions to capture federal arms. A rumored threat to seize weapons bound from Portland to Eugene City after the November 1864 election did cause the mustering of an escort of militia from Corvallis.

It was reported that a group of secessionists headed by Patrick Henry Mulkey of Lane County had organized to travel to Fort Vancouver to blow up the federal arsenal there. Word reached the army's district headquarters at Fort Vancouver and Lieutenant Ivan Applegate and a squad of men from Company K, First Oregon Volunteer Infantry, located the men in a saloon at Eugene City and sent them home.[22] There's a question whether Mulkey and his friends were truly plotting or just talking drunk. In later years Mulkey would once again rise to the public's attention for drunken conduct. (See Chapter 17).

T. W. Davenport wrote at length in 1908 of a discussion recounted to him many years before by B. F. Harding, a prominent lawyer. Harding said in February 1863 that a client of his—a leader of an identified secessionist faction—told him that the factions proposed to gather groups from Lane, Benton, Linn, Douglas and Jackson counties near Scio to "go on the warpath." Whether or not this was a serious threat, Davenport said Harding claimed to have convinced his rebel friend of the futility of starting a war against a professional military while armed only with hunting rifles and no organized source of food or supplies.[23]

In 1910 D. H. Jones, a veteran of the First Oregon Volunteer Infantry, wrote that after enlisting in the Oregon Volunteers in 1864 he was called to Governor Gibbs' office and sent to search out and report on organized Knights units. Jones claimed he found five organized companies in Salem, totaling 200 men, one of which drilled a block from Adjutant General Reed's home. He said he found 230 more Knights at Crabtree in Linn County, fifty at Burnt Woods in Benton County, one company at Forest Grove, three others "west of the river", three companies at Portland and one at Lake Labish in Marion County. Each of these was openly drilling[24] and a couple of them, he said, were using Hardee's *Infantry Tactics* as their drill manual.[25]

In 1862, Oregonians panicked. At Hillsboro a deep, wide trench and high barrier was erected around the county courthouse.[26]

Students at Pacific University at Forest Grove, claimed as a prank to have infiltrated a local lodge of the Knights.[27]

One apparently authentic report is that of John O. Shelton, one of Reed's spies, who reported from Portland on February 10, 1865, and from Dallas on February 22, 1865. Shelton (not the John Shelton, M. D., who practiced medicine at Monmouth at the time) claimed that the Knights organization had not made its appearance in Oregon until fall 1864, when a man he identified only as "Woods" brought it north from California. Shelton reported attending a meeting of about forty men near Dallas, and said the Knights, which he said went in Oregon by the name The Old Guard, had 120 members at Independence.

Shelton indicated that the Oregon Knights group had as its goal "to put down the present Administration, to resist the draft as an attempt should be made to enforce it, and to improve the first favorable opportunity of erecting a 'Pacific Republic.'" The one meeting Shelton reported attending was consumed in reviewing changes in the elaborate ritual and signs of recognition adopted by the organization.

He identified only sixteen members, some of them only by their last names: Caton, Curl, John F. Miller, James D. Fay, James O'Meara, Holbrook from Idaho, and LaFayette Lane (Joseph Lane's son). Nine members were listed from Polk County. They were Judge Hayden (Benjamin Hayden of Eola was the County Judge of Polk County), Dempsey, Dr. Sites, Dr. T. V. B. Embree, John Jeffrey, Matthew Brown, Joe Sligell, George Russell, "Squire" Hole, and McDaniel.[28]

Whatever the extent of the organization in Oregon, except for the tensions at the time of the 1864 elections, the army took no action against the anti-government element, organized or otherwise. Through June 1863, not one arrest was made for disloyal acts.[29]

On March 17, 1865, after being informed of his removal as commanding general of the District of Oregon, General Alvord wrote to the army's Judge Advocate General, Joseph Holt, that "I have had ample evidence that the secret and treasonable plots described by you in your published report (on the Knights of the Golden Circle)... have extended to the State of Oregon and the Idaho and Washington Territories...." However, Alvord opined that the outbreaks in the Midwest would not be repeated in the Pacific Northwest because "The

leading men of the opposition party have discouraged any outbreak...
[and] as a large majority of the population is loyal, the malcontents
should have been easily put down."[30]

David Kimball Hansen wrote that the Knights organization
continued through the end of the war, but its political activities were
rendered ineffective by internal bickering and limited membership.[31]

Whatever its membership or name, the Knights of the Golden
Circle made noise and caused a great deal of concern to Oregon's pro-
Union government, but it accomplished little else.[32]

Chapter 8 notes

1 Patton, Rodney L., "Knights of the Golden Circle: Fact or Fiction," (master's thesis, Kansas State College of Pittsburg, 1964), 6.
2 Morrow, Curtis Hugh, "Politico-Military Secret Societies of the Northwest, 1860-1865," (PhD diss., Clark University, 1929), 4-7.
3 See the Appendix A for the rituals used in Oregon by the Knights of the Golden Circle in 1865.
4 W.O.R., Series 2, Vol. 7, 930-953, Holt, Joseph, Adjutant General, U.S. Army, Report. W.O.R., Series 1, Vol. 50, Pt. 2, 999.
5 Patton, "Knights of the Golden Circle," iii.
6 W.O.R., Series 2, Vol. 7, 930-953.
7 Morrow, "Politico-Military Secret Societies," 466.
8 W.O.R., Series 1, Vol. 50, Pt. 1, 589-591.
9 Edwards, "The Department of the Pacific," 227. Also Wang, "The Mythical Confederate Plot in Southern California," 5.
10 Platt, "Oregon in the Civil War," 106-7.
11 Edwards, "The Department of the Pacific," 225.
12 *San Francisco Alta*, August 6, 1864, quoted in Edwards, "The Department of the Pacific," 225.
13 Carey, Charles H., *General History of Oregon*, 633-34.
14 Pollard, Lancaster, "Golden Circle Knights Opposed Union Banner," *The Oregonian,* December 31, 1961, 19.
15 Field, *The Official History of the Washington National Guard,* 1:198-99.
16 "Constitution, Bylaws and Minutes of the Multnomah Council of the Union League of the State of Oregon, Dec. 28, 1863 – May 3, 1864," Mss. Multnomah County Library, Portland, Or.
17 Spaid, Stanley, "Life of General Joel Palmer," *OHQ* 55(1954):321.
18 Carey, *History of Oregon,* 666.
19 Williams, Catherine, "The Confederate Underground," *Sunday Oregonian, Northwest Rotogravure Magazine,* August 15, 1956.
20 Woodward, W.C., "Political Parties in Oregon," *OHQ,* 13(1912):22.
21 Platt, "Oregon in the Civil War," 106.
22 Shelley, James M., Mss. 391, OHS.
23 Davenport, T.W., "Slavery Question in Oregon, 365-67.
24 If the local Knights were attempting to master the drills set forth in Hardee's manual, they would have had a tough time of it. Brevet Lieutenant Colonel W.H. Hardee's *Rifle and Light Infantry Tactics* was a two-volume work published under direction of the War Department in 1855. It was the Bible of the American Infantry during the Civil War. It consisted of by-the-numbers drill procedures that covered everything from loading the musket (in four defined steps) to the formation of a square to defend against cavalry charges. At the start of the war, Hardee joined the Confederacy.
25 Jones, D.H., Mss. 898, OHS. Hardee, W.H., *Rifle and Light Infantry Tactics for the Exercise and Manoeuvres of Troops When Acting as Light Infantry or Riflemen* (Philadelphia, Lippincott, Grambo & Co., 1855).
26 Bancroft, Hubert Howe, *History of Oregon*, (San Francisco, The History Co., 1888), 2:489.
27 Robertson, James H., "Origin of Pacific University," *OHQ,* 6(1905): 136.
28 Shelton, John O., "Statements in Regard to Secret Political Organizations in Oregon," July 10, 1865, Mss. 468, OHS.
29 Edwards, "The Department of the Pacific," 198.
30 District of Oregon, U.S. Army, Letter Book, Benjamin F. Alvord to Joseph Holt, March 17, 1865, National Archives Branch, Seattle, Washington.
31 Hansen, "Public Response to the Civil War in Washington Territory and Oregon, 1861-65," 28-29.
32 Schablitsky, "Duty and Vice: The Daily Life of a Fort Hoskins Soldier," 26.

Chapter 9

INDIANS AND ARMIES

During the Civil War, for many in the Pacific Northwest the paramount concern was not the war itself but the native Indian. In the 1850s and 1860s various bands of natives threatened the lives and property of the emigrants who crossed their lands.

Any ideas white emigrants carried about the native population likely were shaped by the Indians of the Northeast or the Midwest, who were different from the native people of the Oregon Country.

The emigrants might have carried in their minds Jean Jacques Rousseau's idea of the noble savage or the famous couplet from the eighteenth century British poet/essayist Alexander Pope's *Essay on Man*:

Lo, the poor Indian! whose untutor'd mind
Sees God in clouds, or hears him in the wind;
His soul proud Science never taught to stray
Far as the solar walk or milky way.[1]

"Lo!" was a nickname for the native used by Oregon's editors and by individuals in their diaries and daily correspondence.[2] The English and the French enjoyed the notion of a theoretical Indian, and many Pacific Northwest editors likely would have preferred the theoretical to these seemingly foreign and unknown men they were dealing with. But noble or ignoble, "Lo, the poor Indian" was an object of derision and sometimes of fear.

As the first whites to visit the Pacific Northwest, fur traders had little conflict with the indigenous natives. They cooperated with and accommodated the native, perhaps because they had no intention of staying. The majority of the American settlers who followed did not understand the Indian and few of them had the desire to do so.

Many white settlers felt that the Indians could never be civilized and that they were squandering valuable land. As late as 1873 the *Washington Standard* in Olympia opined: "[Indians are] but in reality human weeds, vegetable men, occupying the earth in its primitive form, as it were in trust until a superior race supplants them."[3]

Anxious for more help from the army, Oregon's Territorial Legislature decided to document its pleas by compiling a list of the whites who died at the hands of the Indian. The list was presented on February 3, 1858 by its Military Affairs Committee to the Territorial Council (Senate).

Those reports listed 273 white deaths at the hands of Indians between 1834 and 1858, each identified by name, date, and location of death.[4]

Some years later, Frances Fuller Victor, the eminent historical writer who did Hubert Howe Bancroft's research and wrote extensively on Pacific Northwest history, was hired by the Oregon Legislature to write the story of Oregon's early Indian wars. She totaled 1,896 whites killed by Indians in what are now the states of Oregon, Washington, and Idaho between 1828 and 1878. The greatest number of deaths came from 1860 to 1862.[5]

EARLY CONTACT

Prior to their first contacts with whites, the natives of the Pacific Northwest led a relatively simple existence. Those on the coast and along the river valleys had abundant food. Those who lived inland were less fortunate. In the 1840s, the Belgian Catholic priest Father Pierre DeSmet said the Snake Indians were so named because the lack of game forced them to dig in the dirt for their sustenance. Camas and other roots provided a staple of their diet.[6]

Some limited contact with European ship-borne adventurers is reported in the late 1700s. When Lewis and Clark came to the Pacific Northwest in 1805, they found iron tools and other evidence of earlier Indian trade with the white man.

The Indian population was significant. Dr. John McLoughlin estimated that in 1824, when the Hudson's Bay Company sent him to Fort Vancouver, there were 100,000 Indians in the Pacific Northwest. He estimated 30,000 in the Columbia River Basin.[7] Admittedly this was an educated guess. But as the leader of the organization that had the greatest contact with natives throughout the region, it's the best guess available.

With the exception of the Nez Perce, the tribes generally were small, lacked powerful chiefs and were primarily hunters and gatherers. Early white travelers described them as dirty, underfed, and ill-clad. In the 1850s, Lieutenant Lorenzo Lorain, who had traveled throughout the Pacific Northwest, wrote to his wife that the natives he encountered were "miserable creatures when compared to the Indians of romance." Another described the Indians of Humboldt Bay, California, as "poor, harmless...miserable creatures...and the most loathsome looking human beings that I have ever seen."[8]

The Indians the earliest settlers encountered generally welcomed them and often were helpful to distressed travelers.[9] They were interested in trade. But the influx of white speculators, miners, and settlers meant more than trade goods. To the Indian of the Pacific Northwest, their arrival brought a swift and wrenching transition from a near-Stone Age existence to a complex technological society that was at best baffling. This influx was accompanied by strange diseases that came close to annihilating the Indians as a race and shattered their existing tribal society.

EPIDEMICS

Outsiders brought disease that decimated the Indians of the West Coast. Written and oral history shows, as does archaeological research, that there were five early wide-spread epidemics among Pacific Northwest Indians. They were:

1520   Smallpox that spread through much of the West Coast, likely from shipwrecked or visiting Asian sailors.[10]

1770s   Smallpox on the lower Columbia River, Lincoln County in Oregon, and north along the coast to the area of Sitka, Alaska.

1770s   Venereal disease, apparently from the Cook expedition.

1824-25 Smallpox over the Columbia plateau and southern Oregon coast.

But most terrifying was the malaria epidemic that started in 1830.[11]

Malaria first broke out among the whites and Indians at Fort Vancouver. It likely came aboard one of the four sailing vessels—three American and one British—that visited the Columbia River in 1829 and 1830. Malaria was endemic in Hawaii and other Pacific islands visited by trading vessels of the time. Over the next three years the disease spread throughout the Willamette Valley and the Lower Columbia, going upstream as far as The Dalles.

Mortality among the white population was low. The native population, however, had no natural defenses against this disease. When contracted, malaria was to them a sentence of death. The accepted native remedy—a sweat bath followed by a plunge into cold water—accelerated the end.

Dr. John McLoughlin estimated that 90 percent of the natives in the area visited by the disease perished. Three-fourths of the Indians in the vicinity of Fort Vancouver died in 1830. Others estimated the mortality rate as high as ninety-nine in 100. Nathaniel Wyeth, who led two expeditions to the Oregon Country in 1832 and 1834, wrote that tribes on Sauvie Island near Portland all died. When settlers first moved onto Sauvie Island in the late 1830s they found brush growing over old Indian villages that were littered with relics and unburied human bones.[12] The epidemic returned each summer through 1835. Likely carried by trappers and other travelers, the epidemic spread south to the Sacramento area, killing up to 75 percent of the native population there.

Researcher S.F. Cook declared that the epidemic "destroyed the Indians as effective social and biological units."[13]

The devastation of the native tribes in the Willamette and Lower Columbia areas left the survivors with no enthusiasm to oppose the invasion of their native lands by the whites. However, disease did not spread to the tribes in Puget Sound, southern Oregon, and east of the Cascades. It was there that the Indian wars occurred.

CAYUSE WAR, 1847-1850

In 1836, Marcus and Narcissa Whitman, sponsored by the American Board of Missions, a Presbyterian-Congregational-Dutch Reformed organization, settled a mission at Wailatpu, in the Walla Walla country. Whitman was a physician, who along with his wife, Narcissa, had been called to the church.

This was the land of the Cayuse Indians, who were strong warriors and relatively untouched by the earlier epidemics. The Indians first welcomed the Whitmans. Then they became increasingly concerned over the whites' interference with their traditional hunting and fishing. The white emigrants also brought a plague of measles with them which infested the Walla Walla country. White people got sick, but recovered. The Indians got sick and died.

With the Great Migration of 1843, the number of white immigrants in the Oregon Territory increased rapidly. Tensions between the natives and the white interlopers rose.

On November 29, 1847, leaders of the Cayuse tribe knocked on the kitchen door of the Whitman quarters at Wailatpu Mission. They invited themselves in, and murdered thirteen of the seventy-two whites who were there, including the Whitmans, and held hostage fifty-three women and children, many of whom were badly mistreated.[14][15]

By virtue of the 1846 treaty with Great Britain, Wailatpu and the Oregon Country had become a part of the United States. But Congress, deadlocked over the issue of slavery in the newly annexed country, left the Oregon Country as an unorganized territory. The federal government did appoint Dr. Elijah White as a deputy Indian agent. But it sent no military.

Oregon, the only part of the U.S. to organize its own provisional government, didn't wait for the federal government. It sent out a hastily organized militia to catch the murderers and to pacify the whole tribe.

In January 1848 the Indians battled fifty members of the militia at The Dalles. Eventually, the local troops drove them back to the Deschutes River. The war against the Cayuses continued intermittently. Federal troops joined the local militia in 1848. Finally, the Cayuse leaders surrendered five men at The Dalles who were identified as the principals of the Wailatpu murders. In the first significant trial of the new Oregon Territory courts, they were tried in Oregon City in 1850, and hanged.

A NEW CHALLENGE FOR THE ARMY

The army was charged with keeping the peace. But what had worked in the eastern states did not work in the West. In the East, the frontier was agricultural. Farmers sought new land and staked their claims in a steady movement to the West. Farmers generally were family men, and stayed at peace with the Indians who had occupied the land before them.

But the Far West wasn't settled in an orderly fashion. The tide of this different civilization did not advance with order. White settlements sprang up where the soil promised a good crop or where some far-ranging miner found signs of gold. The mining element was a fractious one.

The invading whites decimated herds of buffalo which had provided subsistence for the Indians of the Plains, and interfered with the free-range hunting and fishing practices of the Indians of the Pacific Northwest.

The army predicted the conflict that was to come. In his report of November 20, 1850, Quartermaster General Thomas S. Jesup[16], warned:

> The buffalo have been rapidly diminishing for many years past, and now afford the Indians a very scanty supply...Brave men in a savage state, with arms in their hands, never starve themselves, nor allow their women and children to starve, when subsistence can be won by prowess or skill.[17]

General Ethan Allen Hitchcock reported to the Secretary of War in 1852:

> The whites go upon Indian lands, provoke the Indians, bring on collisions, and then call for protection, and complain if it is not furnished, while the practical effect of the presence of the troops can be little else than to countenance and give security to them in their aggressions; the Indians meanwhile looking upon the military as their friends, and imploring their protection.[18]

Because the native population was so decimated by the 1830s malaria epidemic, there was little Indian trouble on the lower Columbia or Willamette. Three minor armed clashes were recorded in the Willamette Valley during the decade or so before the Civil War--at Oregon City, near Molalla, and south of Salem. Each involved Indians from eastern Oregon traveling through the area.

White settlers also had economic concerns. They worried that they could not get title to the lands they homesteaded until the existing native rights were extinguished. On July 20, 1849 Governor Joseph Lane and the Oregon Territorial Legislature asked Congress that the federal government buy up the rights of the Indians and remove them from the areas being settled.[19] In 1850, Congress extinguished the Indians rights to land in Oregon west of the Cascades. Anson Dart arrived in October 1850 as Superintendent of Indian Affairs. Territorial Governor John P. Gaines, Alonzo A. Skinner, and Beverly S. Allen were appointed a commission to treat with the western Oregon tribes for the relinquishment of their lands.[20]

RESERVATIONS

The federal government had a fixed Indian policy. Settlers were entitled to land under the Donation Land Act of 1850 and later legislation. Yet the United States acknowledged the Indian's title to the land and that title had to be extinguished. To accomplish this, Congress in 1854 authorized treaties with the various tribes of Oregon and Washington Territory.

Between 1854 and 1856, fifteen separate treaties were made with Pacific Northwest Indian tribes. Each had six basic elements:

1. The Indians gave up their claim to the land.

2. The government would pay the Indians annually certain amounts of goods and equipment.

3. The Indians would be given buildings, mills, men to teach them to use them and how to be farmers, and physicians.

4. The Indians acknowledged that the federal government had jurisdiction over them.

5. Fishing rights were reserved to the Indians.

6. Most critically, the Indians must move onto the reservations within one year.[21]

Reservations for the dislocated Indians were established where the government thought the pressures from white settlers would be minimal. The huge Siletz-Alsea Reservation on the Oregon coast was established in 1855 because no whites had settled the coastal valleys.[22] By 1860, this reservation held an estimated 3,000 treaty and non-treaty

Indians. That year there were an estimated 7,000 Indians in Oregon and 17,000 in Washington Territory.[23]

The reservation idea did not work for a variety of reasons. Some tribes were sent to share the same reservations with traditional enemies. Congress was slow in ratifying the treaties. The promised buildings and supplies were slow in coming, when they came at all. The government's Indian support efforts often were tarnished by graft and incompetence.

Worse, from the government's point of view, was that some of the land set aside for reservations was found to have desirable natural treasures. Gold was discovered in the Rogue River Valley Indian lands of southern Oregon. White miners with little concern for treaty law invaded.

Resistance to the whites soon spread through the inhabited portions of Oregon and Washington Territory.

ROGUE RIVER WARS

Southern Oregon was settled late. But the California gold rush that started in 1849 increased the traffic of white men through the Rogue River basin.

Governor Joseph Lane negotiated a treaty with the southern Oregon tribes in 1850. But then gold was discovered on the Rogue. The resulting flood of miners onto lands set aside by that treaty to the Indians led to the Rogue River War of 1853.[24]

A second treaty at Table Rock in 1853, ratified by Congress a year later, attempted again to set aside a part of the Rogue River area for the Indians. But pressures of the continued white intrusion set the Indians off again. The second installment of the Rogue Indians Wars broke out in early October 1855 and was accompanied by almost simultaneous uprisings throughout southern Oregon, northern California and eastern Washington Territory.[25]

The Oregon Militia and regular army units from the Willamette Valley managed to quell the uprising.

THE YAKIMA WARS

On September 13, 1855, Indians murdered the eastern Washington Indian Agent Andrew J. Bolon. Major Granville Haller set out with a detail of green troops from Fort Dalles into the Yakima Valley in pursuit.

Haller met up with an unexpected and superior force of Indians. He fought a pitched battle then retreated under fire to Fort Dalles, suffering casualties of five dead and fifteen wounded.

Oregon Territorial Governor George L. Curry recruited eight companies of militia and sent them to help quell the Indians.

The Yakima Indian War spread throughout Washington Territory including the Puget Sound region. During the Battle of Seattle on January 26, 1856, a coordinated Indian attack upon the waterfront community was repelled by sailors, marines, and cannon fire from the U.S.S. *Decatur* and a hastily assembled group of local volunteers.[26] In January 1856 there was also an attempt by a mixed band of Yakima, Klickitat, and Cascades Indians to wipe out settlers along the Columbia and to capture two steamboats moored at opposite ends of the Chenoweth portage at the rapids of the Columbia.[27]

In April 1856 Colonels George Wright and Edward J. Steptoe raided the Yakima Valley and broke the rebellion. Indians were returned to reservations. Fort Simcoe, halfway between The Dalles and Yakima, was established.

CAUSE OF THE WARS

In the Oregon Country there was much concern about the Indian, but little concern for his welfare. Politicians and editors railed against the Indian. The *Oregonian* was most vituperative, claiming that the Pacific Northwest Indians were to a man unfriendly to the whites, demanding: "These inhuman butchers and bloody fiends must be met and conquered, vanquished—yes, EXTERMINATED; or we can never hope for, or expect peace, prosperity or safety."[28]

Some of the Indian uprisings were fomented by non-tribal members, half-breeds, provocateurs from other tribes or white men who had their own reasons for fanning rebellion.

Major General John E. Wool, commander of the Department of the Pacific at the time of the Indian wars, criticized the brutal treatment of the Indians by the whites. He charged publicly that the Indian wars were prolonged in part to crush the Indians more completely, and also to squeeze extra money out of the federal government for the payment of militia expenses in fighting the Indians.

Wool claimed that the governors of Oregon and Washington territories intended "to plunder the treasury of the United States under the pretense of enriching the people of the Territories, and to promote their own ambitious schemes and that of pecuniary speculators."

The people of the Oregon Territory didn't like Wool any more than Wool liked them. In February 1856, the Territorial Legislature had asked for Wool's recall, claiming that he had refused to give federal equipment to the volunteers and attempted to discourage merchants from equipping the territorial troops privately.[29]

One of the complaints against Wool was that his criticism would delay the payment by the federal government of Oregonians' claims for their costs in the Indian wars.

They were right. Attempts to get federal funds to reimburse the cost of the Indian wars were foiled in the 1856 Congress. Finally a special commission, chaired by Lafayette Grover of Salem, later governor of Oregon, and two army captains, Rufus Ingalls and A. J. Smith, tallied up the amount they felt due the territories of Oregon and Washington. This, they said, was $6,001,497.36. The Third Auditor of the Treasury was asked to review. He determined the amount due at $2,400,000. He fixed many costs at what the army paid in the East for similar supplies and services, ignoring the inflation of the Oregon frontier.

Congress appropriated this amount. The militia members and those who supplied them were eventually paid, but with greenbacks, which traded at a significant discount to gold.[30]

UTTER-VAN ORNUM MASSACRE

In the fall of 1860 with the presidential election looming and the Union slowly disintegrating, the Pacific Northwest was shocked with news of murder and kidnapping.

On September 13, 1860 a wagon train of forty-four immigrants was waylaid by a band of about 100 Indians near Castle Creek, on the Snake River in what is now southwest Idaho, about 320 miles east of Fort Walla Walla. Some said the Indians were Bannocks. Others claimed that the group was drawn from several tribes.

The whites were outnumbered and outgunned. Initially they gave much of their food as tribute to the Indians, who then drove off the cattle and horses and killed eleven of the immigrant party.

The survivors then began a desperate flight on foot. Several were picked off by the Indians as they struggled on. Four of their number—discharged soldiers who had joined the train en route—deserted the settlers, whose women and children could not keep the pace. Two of the survivors stumbled into the Umatilla Indian Agency to tell their tale of horror.

Reduced by starvation, and after resorting to cannibalism, eleven survivors were rescued October 25, 1860 by an element of the Ninth Infantry from Fort Walla Walla under Captain Frederick T. Dent.[31] This event also is referred to as the Salmon Falls Massacre, the Van Ornum Massacre, the Utter Train Massacre, the Myers Massacre (after members of the party) and the Sinker Creek Tragedy.[32]

The killings occurred two weeks after their escort of army troops (figuring that the wagon train was well past the point of Indian danger) had turned and headed back to its temporary station at then-abandoned Fort Hall.[33]

The loss brought howls of outrage from the Oregon Legislature, then in session. Although its members were at the same time ignoring the organization of their own state militia, they promptly adopted two memorials to Congress. These memorials demanded the establishment of military posts at Fort Boise and elsewhere along the immigrant trail. While they were at it, they also asked for new military roads and a land office at The Dalles.[34]

The Utter-Van Ornum Massacre inspired one of the classic tales of the Wild West.

Alexis Van Ornum (sometimes spelled Van Orman) was a member of the train. He, his wife, son Marcus, and four other members of the family were found slain and mutilated near the present town of Huntington, Oregon. Four of the family—three girls and a boy Reuban, aged about ten—were taken captive by the Indians.

The girls died of starvation and abuse while in Indian custody. Reuban Van Ornum was recovered nearly two years later by Major Edward McGarry and a detail of the Second California Volunteers from Fort Douglas at Salt Lake City.

Reuban's recovery was due to the single-minded pursuit of his uncle, Zachias Van Ornum, a six-foot tall, black-haired gold miner from Oregon. Everyone else had written off the possibility of additional survivors from the massacre. But, believing that they had survived, Zachias spent two years in pursuit of Reuban and his sisters.

Some time after the massacre, Zachias learned from an unnamed relative that a white boy about Reuban's age had been seen with a band of Indians. The relative claimed he had tried to buy the boy from the Indians, but that they asked an exorbitant price. In September 1862, Zachias sought the aid of Lieutenant Colonel Justus Steinberger, commander at Fort Walla Walla, who sent Zachias and a companion to join the three companies of Oregon Volunteer Cavalry under Lieutenant Colonel R. F. Maury then on a tour to protect the emigrant wagon trains through what now is southern Idaho.

Zachias Van Ornum signed on with Maury's expedition as a civilian interpreter. He stayed with the column until it reached the Bruneau Valley. Then he left and went to Salt Lake City. There he got the promise of help from Colonel P. E. Connor, commander of federal troops in Utah Territory. Van Ornum met McGarry's company of the Second California Volunteer Infantry in the Cache Valley of Utah on November 22, 1862 and went to the Bear River area on the boundary between Utah Territory and what now is Idaho.

There McGarry's unit fought with Bear Hunter, an Indian chief and his group.[35] Bear Hunter and three of his men were captured by McGarry and his men and held hostage until Reuban was returned to camp. The boy's face had been painted in an attempt to mask his race. But his light hair and blue eyes gave him away.

A reporter from a California newspaper reported that Reuban, by then acclimated to his Indian life, did not return voluntarily, but kicked and fought as the soldiers washed the paint from his face.

Zachias Van Ornum later applied for a federal pension for his service in recovering the boy and for his service during the January 1863 Bear River campaign near what now is Preston, Idaho. In his pension application (now in the Oregon Historical Society files), Van Ornum said that after recovering the boy he stayed in the territory for a time, acting as a scout for Connor's troops.

What eventually happened to Reuban Van Ornum is not reported. Author Hubert Howe Bancroft said Reuban may have grown up to be the person "known as 'Mountain Jack', who killed a number of Indians in revenge for their mistreating and killing of his sister Eliza."[36]

MEDOREM CRAWFORD AND THE EMIGRANT PROTECTIVE CORPS

The Castle Creek slayings startled the Pacific Northwest and finally goaded Congress into expanding military protection to emigrant wagon trains on the Oregon Trail.

For several years, travelers on the trail had been subject to flying attacks by bands of Indians, especially in the desolate area between old Fort Hall and Fort Walla Walla.

Led by Oregon's lame duck Senator Joseph Lane, in the spring of 1861 Congress appropriated $50,000 to finance additional protection for the emigrants. The army previously had attempted to control the Indian marauders by showing the flag. Expeditions of cavalry were sent from both the east and west ends of the trail. But they were ordered to stick to the main trails and escort wagon trains where it seemed appropriate. They were told not to pursue the Indians into the wilds.

One of the hallmarks of national political and military thought during the Civil War was to spend no more than was absolutely necessary. Lane suggested that the army do it on the cheap and Secretary of War Simon Cameron agreed. It was too expensive to make up an escort of regular army soldiers or even three-year volunteer enlistees. The army would have to pay to send them west and then pay to bring them east and feed them until it was time to head west again.

Cameron crafted an Emigrant Protective Corps consisting of a handful of officers and civilian supervisors. The ranks were filled by temporary soldiers enlisted to serve only during the trip, and to be discharged at the end of the trip.

Lane's successor in the Senate, Edward D. Baker, wanted Medorem Crawford, an Oregon politician and 1842 pioneer then in the East, to head the escort. Crawford had served as a member of the Oregon Provisional Government Legislature from Clackamas County. He had come west with Elijah White's party in 1842 over the same trail he was to patrol. Most importantly, as a member of the first state House of Representatives from Yamhill County, he had championed and helped to elect the two winners—Senators Baker and James W. Nesmith. It was pay-back time.

Cameron, however, figured that the law required a regular army officer to handle the funds for such a project. He had just the man for the job, Captain Henry E. Maynadier, late of the Tenth Infantry Regiment, a competent army officer with frontier experience. Maynadier was from Virginia. He didn't want to fight against the South. Nor did he want to resign his commission and fight for the South. Figuring that the marauding Indians of the frontier were an ideal foe for Maynadier,

Cameron gave him the job.[37] Crawford, given a commission as a captain of volunteers, was Maynadier's assistant. Crawford did the bulk of the work during the initial expedition in 1861. He took total command of the expeditions in 1862 and 1863.

Each expedition fielded fifty-five to eighty men, including a clerk, four assistants, a hired civilian doctor, and a wagon master. Since patronage was an accepted practice at the time, who better to help out than a trusted member of the family? For the 1861 expedition, Crawford hired his brother, LeRoy Crawford, as his chief clerk. In 1862 Crawford promoted LeRoy Crawford to his chief assistant, and hired their father, Samuel G. Crawford, as clerk.

In spring 1864, Crawford resigned his commission. With the help of Senators Nesmith and Benjamin F. Harding and Representative John R. McBride, Crawford got his brother LeRoy appointed as commander of the 1864 expedition.

Volunteers were easily found. The government paid the cost of their transportation to the starting point at Omaha. They received $13 a month and their keep during the trip west. At the end of the trip they were discharged. Best of all, in return for their service they got a free trip to the gold country of the Pacific Northwest.

One of Crawford's short-term soldiers during the 1862 expedition was Joseph Dolph, a young lawyer who later served, 1883-1897, as U.S. Senator from Oregon.

Each man was equipped with a Colt revolver and a Wesson breech-loading rifle. The officers rode horses and the men rode mules. Horses were in short supply. Mules cost less. The mules that were provided were unbroken and breaking them was the soldiers' problem. One of Crawford's volunteers, William P. Berger, later of Portland, said "It took us over two weeks before we could get those mules saddled and moving forward instead of up and down."[38] Mule-drawn wagons were filled with equipment and supplies. Beef cattle—rations on the hoof— were herded along with the expedition.

During the latter part of May each year, the expedition left Omaha. Most of the emigrants had left earlier, but Crawford's troops caught up with them and their slower ox teams.

The army acted as both guard and road service. Medorem Crawford wrote in his report at the end of the 1862 trip: "We cured their sick, fed the destitute, hauled their baggage and families, mended their wagons, repaired the roads and in some instances drove their teams."

In 1861 and 1862, the expedition ended at Fort Walla Walla, where Crawford sold the remaining supplies, horses, and mules and discharged his men. The 1862 expedition covered 1,620 miles in 104 days.

In 1863 and 1864 the army group's journey ended at the newly established Fort Boise. In 1862, 1863, and 1864 a separate but similar Corps of Volunteers was outfitted under separate command to escort travelers from Fort Abercrombie near present-day Fargo, North Dakota, to the Montana gold fields.

The Emigrant Protective Corps served its purpose. The availability of an escort led to better-organized wagon trains that were more adequately outfitted and stayed to an assigned trail.

In 1862 only about fifteen travelers were killed on the trail. All had traveled well in advance of the column.[39]

No deaths were reported in 1863. Much credit for this was due to Colonel P. E. Connor's California Volunteers from Salt Lake City. They made a sweep through the Fort Hall area earlier in the summer after wiping out a large band of Indian marauders at Bear Valley on Utah's northern border.

Also that year Lieutenant Colonel Reuben F. Maury and three companies of the First Oregon Volunteer Cavalry went from Fort Walla to meet Crawford's expedition at Salmon Falls, Idaho.

After 1864, the army began construction of new forts across the empty Indian lands of the West. The end of hostilities with the South freed up additional regular troops to guard the emigrant routes.

Crawford was rewarded for his service. He was appointed collector of customs at Portland from 1864 to 1869, and was appraiser of customs between 1871 and 1875. He also obtained an appointment to West Point Military Academy for his son, Medorem Crawford, Jr.[40]

Chapter 9 notes

1 Bartlett, John, *Familiar Quotations*, Tenth Edition, (New York, Halcyon House, 1919), 315.
2 Hilleary, William, *A Webfoot Volunteer: The Diary of William M. Hilleary, 1864-1866.* (Corvallis, Or., Oregon State University Press, 1965) 167.
3 *Washington Standard*, Olympia, Washington Territory, Oct. 28, 1871.
4 Oregon Legislature, "Report of the Committee on Military Affairs, Territorial Council, 1858-59 Sessions."
5 Victor, Frances Fuller, *The Early Indian Wars in Oregon (Salem, Or., State Printer, 1894), 499-500.*
6 Scott, *History of the Oregon Country,* 2:324.

7   West, "First White Settlers on French Prairie," 209.
8   Edwards, "The Department of the Pacific," 209.
9   Tobie, Harvey Elmer, *No Man Like Joe*, (Portland, Or., Binfords and Mort, 1949), 148 and John Mintog "Reminiscences," *OHQ*, 2(1901):213-14.
10 The first documented European sailors to cruise the Oregon Coast did so in the early 1540s.
11 Boyd, Robert, *The Coming of the Spirit of Pestilence*, (Seattle, Wash., University of Washington Press, 1999) 18-22.
12 Seaman, N.G., "The Amateur Archaeologist's 50 Years in Oregon," *OHQ*, 52(1951): 148.
13 Cook, S.F., "The Epidemic of 1830-1833 in California and Oregon," *University of California Publications in American Archeology and Ethnology*, 43(1955):303-26.
14 Sager, Elizabeth, and Wilson, Mrs. E.M., *The Last Day at Waiilatpu*, (Walla Walla, Wash., Whitman College, 1897.)
15 Part of the reason for the murder of the Whitmans may have been the traditional Indian practice of killing the medicine man whose cures did not work. Measles came to the area. Whitman, a physician, treated all who were afflicted. The whites who had an inbred immunity to this and other European-based disease, survived. The natives did not.
16 General Jesup's first name was Thomas, but all of his published correspondence was signed "Th. S. Jesup." A veteran of the War of 1812, he served as the Army's Quartermaster General from May 1818 to June 1860.
17 Jesup, Th. S., "Report of the Quartermaster General," Nov. 20, 1850, quoted in Cross, Osborn, *March of the Regiment of Mounted Riflemen to Oregon in 1849*, (Fairfield, Wash., Ye Galleon Press, 1967) App. 1-4.
18 Edwards, "The Department of the Pacific," 14-15.
19 Schablitsky, "Duty and Vice," 11.
20 Field, *Official History of the Washington National Guard*, 1:28.
21 Ekland, Roy E., "The 'Indian Problem,' Pacific Northwest," *OHQ*, 70(1969):114.
22 Schablitsky, "Duty and Vice," 11.
23 *Weekly Oregonian*, December 15, 1860.
24 Clark, "Military History of Oregon," 26-31.
25 Hendricks, Robert, *Innnnnnng Haaaaaaaa!, The War to End the White Race*, (Salem, Oregon, n.p., 1937), 18.
26 Phelps, Thomas Stowell, *Reminiscences of Seattle, Washington Territory and the U.S. Sloop of War Decatur During the Indian Wars of 1855-56*, (Fairfield, Wa., Ye Galleon Press, 1971) 24-33.
27 Winther, Oscar Osburn, *The Great Northwest* (New York, Alfred A. Knopf, 1952), 175.
28 *Weekly Oregonian*, Oct. 20, 1855, 2.
29 Clark, "Military History of Oregon," 44.
30 The Oregon Legislature in 1903 and 1905 approved additional state money to pay the surviving officers and enlisted men of the Oregon militia what had been promised them. In 1913 the seven aged survivors of the war from Polk County finally were paid for their lost horses or mules.
31 Dent, Captain F.T., Report of November 8, 1860, "Indian Depredations in Oregon," Executive Document No. 29, U.S. House of Representatives, 36th Congress, 2nd Session, 85-90.
32 Historians have not always been objective in chronicling killings between the whites and the Indians. When Indians did the killing, it was labeled a massacre by newspapers and government reports. But the word massacre was not used when Indians were wiped out by the whites.
33 Carey, *A General History of Oregon*, 625-26, 661.
34 Oregon Legislature, Session Laws of Oregon, First Regular Session, Begun September 10, 1860, Memorials, 11-15, Governor's Message, 42-44.
35 W.O.R., Series 1, Vol. 50, Pt. 1, 167-68, 181-87.
36 Hart, Newell, "Rescue of a Frontier Boy," *Utah Historical Quarterly*, (Fall, 1963):51-54. Cannon, Miles, *Idaho Sunday Statesman*, July 17, 28, August 21, 1924.
37 W.O.R., Series 1, Vol. 50, Pt. 1, 460-61.
38 Berger, William P., quoted in Lockley, Fred, "Impressions and Observations of the Journal Man," *Oregon Journal*, Portland, Or., March 24, 1934.
39 W.O.R., Series 1, Vol. 50, Pt. 1, 153-55.
40 Crawford, Medorem, *Journal of Medorem Crawford*, (Fairfield, Wash., Ye Galleon Press, 1967) Foreword. Also Fendall, Lon W., "Medorem Crawford and the Protective Corps," *OHQ*, 72(1971): 54-77.

Chapter 10

INDIAN EXPEDITIONS 1860-63

The end of the Indian Wars of the 1850s did not mean that the army's job in the Pacific Northwest was over. There still were two serious challenges. The first was that no one was keeping the so-called Treaty Indians on their designated reservations and keeping the white trespassers off. The other challenge was keeping the non-treaty Indians—who ranged the unsettled areas east of the Cascade Mountains—from raiding the emigrant wagon trains and the miners and settlers who streamed into the country.

The army faced a significant challenge in protecting the settlers. The great range of the unsettled West and the hit-and-run tactics of its native warriors were not well met by a military trained and equipped to fight the Napoleonic wars. Congress failed to provide enough men, equipment, or supplies to do the job, which left the army struggling to catch up.

The major Indian troubles were in the vast expanse east of the Cascades. The bulk of the difficulty came from the so-called Snake Indians. These Indians were a loose amalgam of small, independent bands. Some called themselves Paiutes. They were joined by Shoshones and Bannocks and a relatively small number of Klamath and Modoc Indians.

These wanderers lived a nomadic life, feeding themselves upon roots, seeds, game and fish, supplemented by what they could steal. Their earlier victims were other Indians. The comparatively wealthy whites soon became prey.

Emigrant wagon trains were their initial targets. But when the military began patrolling the Oregon Trail and escorting the wagon trains, the Indian marauders shifted their attention to miners and the homesteaders who moved onto previously ignored farm and ranch lands.

Drifting throughout the territory, the Snakes practiced a hit-and-run form of warfare. They attacked, assembled their booty and retreated, many to remote valleys where they wintered until springtime, and the season to renew their wanderings.

Frances Fuller Victor noted that they knew where to find water and grass and could sleep peacefully while the army wore itself out looking for trails that the Indians were careful not to leave.

The Snake Indians were consummate guerrilla warriors and ruthless victors who took no prisoners. Because they expected like treatment from the army, those Indians who couldn't escape usually fought to the death.

The first military escort of emigrant trains came in 1859 after the country around Walla Walla was opened to settlement. Captain Henry D. Wallen provided an escort through the area east of the Cascades. Wallen's dragoons, infantry, and engineers kept the Indians away from the wagon trains. There were no reported Indian attacks that season.

1860

In 1860, General William Harney sent out two expeditions. Major Enoch Steen went east from the Crooked River country of Oregon and had several brushes with Indians but experienced no fatalities. A smaller force under Captain A. J. Smith, a veteran of the earlier Indian wars, was attacked near the Owyhee River. That same season, non-treaty Indians attacked the Umatilla Indian Reservation.[1]

The bloodiest experience of the season was the Utter-Van Ornum Massacre. The Oregon Legislature was in session when news of the massacre reached Salem. A memorial to Congress wisely predicted that a campaign against the Snakes would be useless unless pursued year-round.

1861

As the nation lurched toward Civil War in the early months of 1861, things were difficult in the Indian areas of the Pacific Northwest. Emboldened by the withdrawal of regular army troops, the Indians also were aggravated by the federal government's failure to make payments provided by treaty.[2] They began to push back at the "civilization" that was encompassing them.

104

Oregon Governor John Whiteaker demanded a greater federal military presence. Colonel George Wright, commander of the army's District of Oregon, replied on January 3, 1861, saying the army was doing its best.[3] Wright sent Nez Perce Indian scouts to the Snake Indian country to search for signs of the Van Ornum children, kidnapped during the Castle Creek massacre.

Three days later the effects of the threatened war in the East were felt as the first two companies of artillery were ordered south from Fort Vancouver to San Francisco.[4] In mid-January troops were sent from both Fort Walla Walla and Fort Dalles to apprehend Indians who had robbed settlers and stolen livestock along the Umatilla River and Willow Creek areas of eastern Oregon.[5] In Washington Territory a settler at the mouth of Skykomish River on Puget Sound was murdered.

Troops from Fort Walla Walla and Fort Dalles captured the Indians responsible for the theft of cattle and robberies in eastern Oregon. A detachment of dragoons from Fort Walla Walla captured and summarily executed two Indians. The detail from Fort Dalles captured two more who were turned over to civil authorities for trial.

Gold seekers on the Columbia River near the U.S.-Canada border got into a pitched battle with nine Indians. Two white men were killed and four others wounded. Four Indians were killed and one wounded.

In August, Joseph Bailey, recently elected to the Oregon Legislature, and two other men were killed by Modoc and Pit Indians while driving a herd of 800 cattle to the Nevada mines.[6]

Meantime, Lieutenant John Mullan was sent from Fort Walla Walla with three officers, a surgeon, and one hundred men on a planned sixteen-month expedition to map and construct a wagon road from Fort Benton, Montana to Fort Walla Walla. The intent was to open a new wagon road to the Pacific Northwest for military travel.[7] The project soon was halted due to the war. But some of Mullan's data was used by later railroad expeditions. In 1865 Mullan, then a civilian, published and sold his *Miner's and Traveler's Guide to Oregon, Washington, Montana, Wyoming and Colorado*, which incorporated material from the army explorations.[8]

By mid-year, Colonel Wright made a requisition on Oregon Governor Whiteaker for one company of volunteer cavalry because of Indian depredations in The Dalles area. Whiteaker, who did not like the war, failed to raise troops and the recruitment of volunteers in Oregon was taken over by the army.

At the start of the year, General Joseph Johnston, commander of the Department of the Pacific, was reluctant to send troops into either northern California or the territory east of the Cascades.[9] He preferred to concentrate troops in the San Francisco area to meet the anticipated dissolution of the Union. But he did understand Indian warfare. He ordered the troops who were in the field to stay no longer than three days in any one camp site. By keeping Indians on the move he intended to save white settlers and travelers from Indians who would be kept too busy to raid them.[10]

Military affairs in the Pacific Northwest were not managed in a uniform manner. Colonel Wright was transferred from Fort Vancouver in August 1861 to take command of the District of Southern California.

In rapid succession after Wright's transfer, command of the District of Oregon rotated through two regular army officers, Colonel Benjamin Beall and Lieutenant Colonel Albemarle Cady, and through Colonel Justus Steinberger, ranking officer of the Washington Territory Volunteer Infantry.[11] But until mid-1862, things were pretty much run long-distance from San Francisco.

1862

Pacific Northwest Indians became even more aggressive as 1862 opened. In the fall of 1861 George Wright, now a brigadier general and commander of the Department of the Pacific, shipped newly recruited California Volunteers to Oregon and Washington Territory posts to replace the regulars withdrawn to California and eastern posts. On October 28, 1861, 350 volunteers arrived and were sent to man Fort Yamhill in Oregon and Fort Steilacoom in Washington Territory. On November 20, five more companies arrived. They were sent to Forts Colville and Walla Walla in Washington and Fort Dalles in Oregon.

By January 1862, the total military presence in Oregon and Washington Territory was forty-eight officers and 686 men. The army had only five companies of foot-bound California Volunteer Infantry, one company at Fort Dalles and two companies each at Fort Colville and Fort Walla Walla, to cover the vast area east of the Cascades where the serious Indian problems existed. There was no mounted unit in the District of Oregon.

The new First Oregon Volunteer Cavalry, all six companies of it, was raised in spring 1862.

A detail raised at The Dalles under Captain George B. Currey was the first Oregon unit to see action. When he was ordered from Fort Dalles to seek out a party of Simcoe Indians, Currey had only twelve men ready for duty. The Indians were from the same tribe that had robbed and rustled from settlers on the Umatilla River the year before. This time a party of prospectors had been murdered on the John Day River.

Currey and his men left The Dalles in March 1862. Currey displayed the initiative which he carried with him throughout the war and later culminated in his effective defeat of the renegade Indian tribes during the winter of 1865-66. Currey and his men raided a number of Indian villages and took several aged Indians hostage to secure the good behavior of their tribes. The murderers they sought escaped. The detail returned to Fort Dalles well-experienced in forced marches and sleeping on the ground.[12]

On July 7, 1862, Major Benjamin Alvord was brevetted Brigadier General of Volunteers and appointed commander of the Military District of Oregon. As one of the few regular army officers left in the Pacific Northwest, that may have been one of his qualifications for the post.

Although the army couldn't cover its assigned territory, no great uprising occurred in 1862. But Charles H. Carey wrote that on several occasions, residents of mining camps east of the Cascades outfitted detachments of vigilantes at their own expense to pursue and punish bands of Indians who killed and robbed miners.[13]

In its earlier treaty, the Nez Perce tribe had been assured of extensive reservation grounds in northeastern Washington Territory, including what is now northern Idaho. Figuring it was well out of the way of the white man, the white negotiators believed it would be a good way to keep the Indians and the emigrants apart. Then gold was discovered and shortly 15,000 miners, very interested in gold and unconcerned with Indian treaty rights, swarmed onto the reservation.

Indian Agent J. W. Anderson complained to General Alvord that the reservation was "infected with a great number of lawless white men, who sell whisky to the Indian, steal their horses and debauch their women."

Congress failed to provide much of what was promised to the Nez Perce by the treaty. The usually peaceful Nez Perce muttered of war.

On July 18, 1862 General Alvord sent Major Jacob Rinearson and Company F of the Oregon Cavalry to a camp near Lewiston. Rinearson was instructed to "use every exertion to preserve order and quiet between whites and Indians." He was especially asked to prevent the sale of spirits or wine to the Indians.[14]

Rinearson arrived on site and quickly realized the futility of his assignment. Keeping the peace was impossible. Renegade whites stole the Indian horses. The Indians stole them back. Whiskey was peddled openly. Soldiers caught the whiskey peddlers and poured out their wares. The peddlers went to Lewiston, got a new load, and headed back to the Indian country.

There was suspicion that secessionist miners' actions in goading the Indians were grounded in political as well as economic interests. Lawyer, one of the Nez Perce chiefs, certainly thought so. He cursed Jefferson Davis and told Robert Newell,[15] a white man on the reservation, that he hoped Davis might be captured, fitted with a ball and chain, and forced to saw wood "for two or three years at some military post." William V. Rinehart, then a lieutenant in Rinearson's company, wrote that he and his troops spent the summer futilely "pursuing renegade Whites and Indians alternately."

Alvord was worried about an outbreak. He traveled by steamboat and horseback to the reservation. In October, he gathered Nez Perce leaders and delivered a windy and promise-filled address. He admitted that his troops were not doing what the government promised—keeping the white man off the reservation. He promised to do better, then ordered more troops east of the Cascades, told Rinearson to try harder, and issued a supply of light weapons to the more responsible of the local white citizens just in case.[16]

This was also the first year that Captain Medorem Crawford's military escort accompanied emigrant wagon trains along the Oregon Trail. Lieutenant Colonel Maury and a detachment of Oregon Cavalry were sent from Fort Walla Walla to meet Crawford's train near Salmon Falls, Idaho.

Maury credited the presence of his command with keeping Indian activity along the western end of the trail at a minimum. He said

Indians freely visited the emigrant trains but avoided most contact with his troops.

A second expedition was sent from Fort Walla Walla in August. William H. Barnhart, Indian Agent at the Umatilla Reservation, asked military help in corralling a band of "refractory" Indians who left the reservation. Through harassment and threat of violence they had driven away settlers from the Grand Ronde Valley. The leader of this band was Tenounis, a sub-chief who wanted to keep the Grande Ronde Valley for his own. He and his followers called themselves the Dreamers or the Soul-Sleepers. Tenounis, a true terrorist before the term was ever coined, and his band surrounded isolated farm cabins and warned the inhabitants that if they were not out of the country by nightfall, the following day they would be killed.

Currey tracked down Tenounis and tried to convince him and his men to return to the reservation. Currey and a sergeant were in the subchief's lodge with Tenounis and his chief deputy, Wainicut-hi-hi. Currey's men were lined up outside. Members of Tenuonis' band and others who apparently followed the soldiers to see the action were clustered outside.

After at least two hours of discussion, Currey reported Tenounis and Wainicut-hi-hi drew weapons from their hiding place beneath the blankets. Currey drew his revolver, and fatally shot both men. At that point Indians outside drew on the soldiers, who were armed with obsolete muzzle-loading short rifles. Two more Indians and a horse were killed. No soldiers were injured.[17]

The Indians scattered. Currey headed back to the reservation. The slaying brought temporary quiet to the area.[18]

1863

Medorem Crawford's escort company and roving cavalry from Fort Walla Walla drove the renegade Snake Indians away from their usual prey of emigrant wagon trains along the western end of the Oregon Trail. The natives then turned to miners and ranchers.[19]

Again, the Indians were restive because the whites did not honor their treaty promises. In addition, because some tribes had split, there were many Indians who had not been party to the treaties. There were also other bands of Indians who had no real tribal affiliations.

Sometimes the Indians were assisted by white renegades. In the dead of winter 1862-63, government pack mules were driven from pasture at the north end of the military reservation at Fort Walla Walla. Company E of the First Oregon Volunteer Cavalry was sent in pursuit with Captain George B. Currey in command. Currey and his company followed, swam through the slush ice of the Snake and Columbia Rivers, and came upon the thieves. The leader, a white man identified only as Stubbs, was killed. His Indian helpers were captured. The captives and the mules were returned to Fort Walla Walla, where the mules went back to pasture and the Indians were turned over to the civil authorities.[20]

Some—including Captain Currey—thought that they were north of the British America-U.S. border when the thieves were apprehended, which would have meant that Currey and his men had no jurisdiction. But Currey wanted results. He said he didn't know exactly where he was and really did not care.

On January 10, responding to pointed complaints that Oregon had raised far too few troops, Governor Addison C. Gibbs called for the recruitment of six additional companies of cavalry to bring Oregon's truncated First Volunteer Cavalry Regiment up to strength. Only one company was raised.[21]

General Alvord had pestered his superiors for all matter of men and equipment since his appointment as commanding general in July 1862. He particularly lobbied for authority to establish permanent installations in the Indian country and on the Oregon Trail between Fort Hall and Fort Walla Walla. On January 14, 1863, Alvord was ordered to establish a post near the old Hudson's Bay Company Fort Boise. He sent Major Pinckney Lugenbeel to scout the area. On July 4, 1863 Lugenbeel established Fort Boise, some forty miles east of the old Hudson's Bay Company site.[22] A factor in determining the location was a site for a sawmill located on a creek ten miles from the post. The mill would provide lumber, otherwise unavailable in the unpopulated area, for construction of the buildings at the fort. Lugenbeel and his men erected temporary quarters for three companies of infantry and two of cavalry.[23]

Fort Boise was originally conceived as a summer operation. Alvord noted in his report to Adjutant General Lorenzo Thomas in Washington, D.C., "During this winter for want of forage the cavalry, with the exception of twenty-five men, will withdraw to Fort Walla Walla."[24]

General George Wright also ordered the establishment of a new post at Klamath Lake and directed that the Oregon Volunteer Cavalry company at Camp Baker (near Phoenix in southern Oregon) be transferred there. This meant the withdrawal of all troops from Oregon's Rogue River Valley, an area heavy with Southern settlers feared to be secessionists. Oregon's Governor Gibbs protested and asked that troops be retained at Camp Baker. In April, Wright directed the post commander, Lieutenant Colonel C. S. Drew, to leave a detail at Camp Baker for the time being.[25]

Fort Klamath was built by Company C of the First Oregon Volunteer Cavalry and a crew of civilians. Some buildings were of logs. Most were of lumber cut in a primitive sawmill built on nearby Fort Creek.[26]

On January 29, 1863, Colonel P. Edward Connor, four companies of California Volunteer Cavalry, and one company of infantry fought with a large band of Indians at Bear River, on the boundary between Utah and Washington Territory (now Idaho), killing 224 Indians. Twenty-one army men were killed and fifty-three were wounded.[27] It was the largest Indian battle of the Civil War period in the Pacific Northwest. Connor was promoted to brigadier general.

In March word spread throughout Oregon's Benton County that the army was considering abandoning Fort Hoskins. Forts Hoskins, Umpqua to the south, and Yamhill to the north originally were established to keep the Indians on and the whites off the Siletz Reservation on the central Oregon Coast. Fort Umpqua was abandoned shortly after the start of the Civil War. Army strategists questioned the necessity of troops at Fort Hoskins.

With an eye no doubt on the sizeable purchase of supplies and services the army made in the area, the good citizens of Benton County protested to Governor Gibbs. Their petition painted a picture of the terrible threat posed to the whites in the area from the Indians should the army be withdrawn.[28] Gibbs forwarded the petition to Alvord, who responded that Oregon was sadly short of meeting its expected manpower contributions to the war. He suggested that the petitioners help recruit the second six companies of the First Oregon Volunteer Cavalry then under way. If they would, he would see that one company would be stationed at Fort Hoskins. Eventually, one company of the First Oregon Volunteer Infantry was stationed at Fort Hoskins.[29]

Rumors flew that Indians on the Siletz Reservation were accumulating firearms and intended to bolt the reservation and head south, a rumor that was repeated during the war.

Indian Agent James B. Condon and the army had some success fighting the liquor trade adjacent the Grand Ronde Reservation. It was illegal to provide liquor to an Indian, but getting a conviction was tough because of the courts' reluctance to accept the testimony of an Indian against a white.[30]

In spring 1863, the Nez Perce were summoned to Lapwai Agency to structure a new treaty that would legalize the mining activities of the unstoppable flood of white miners onto the Nez Perce Reservation.[31] The Indians protested they were guaranteed exclusive rights over the land by the prior treaty and the new treaty was intended to placate them.

The Nez Perce tribe had split into three factions. The Nez Perce principal chief, Lawyer, and his followers were friends of the whites. They realized the futility of resistance and favored ceding additional rights to the whites. A second faction, led by Big Thunder, another chief, was a stand-pat group. They weren't hostile to the whites, but felt that they had a treaty and it should be enforced. The third faction, the war element, was led by two minor chiefs, Joseph and Eagle-of-the-Light. They felt betrayed and were looking for a reason to drive the whites from their territory.

Lawyer and Big Thunder brought their people and their horses with them to the parley, which was held on the grounds of the mission established in 1836 by the Rev. H. H. Spalding. There were an estimated 2,000 Indians and 12,000 horses present.

The government treaty commissioners were J. W. P. Huntington, superintendent of Indian Affairs for Washington Territory; W. T. Rector, superintendent of Indian Affairs for Oregon; William H. Barnhart, agent for the Umatilla Reservation, and Robert Newell, Indian agent at Lapwai.

The treaty commissioners were not alone. To show the Indians the might of the U.S. military there were four companies of Oregon Cavalry and two companies of Washington Territory Volunteer Infantry.[32]

William V. Rinehart, a lieutenant in one of the companies, wrote that the Indians truly were impressed:

> For a month or so before, and during the treaty, our four Cavalry and two Infantry Companies were very active drilling—ostensibly for the approaching campaign against the Snakes, but really for the effect it would have upon the Nez Perce during the treaty. What most impressed them was the firing of the Howitzers that shot twice. When a shell exploded against the rocky cliff north of the Post and the sound went reverberating through the hills long after the firing, the "Ugh–Ugh" of the Indians showed plainly that the effect on them eclipsed even the flash of the long knives of the Cavalry.[33]

The treaty council took many days, much deliberation and great debate by the Indians. Toward its close, the greatly-outnumbered white participants began to fear for their personal safety. Preparations were made to defend against an Indian onslaught and extra ammunition was issued to the troops.

Again Captain Currey was called. He was given a detail of twenty men and sent to the Indian camp to discern the threat. Arriving at midnight, he found fifty-three chiefs and subchiefs of the Nez Perce tribe debating the proposals made by the white treaty commissioners.

Currey reported:

> The debate ran on with dignified firmness until near morning when the Big Thunder party made formal announcement of their determination to take no further part in the treaty, and then, with a warm and emotional manner, declared the Nez Perce nation dissolved; whereupon Big Thunder's men shook hands with the Lawyer men, telling them with a kind but firm demeanor that they would be friends, but a distinct people. It did not appear from the tone of their short, sententious speeches, that either party was meditating present outbreak. I then withdrew my detachment, having accomplished nothing but that of witnessing the extinguishment of the last council fires of the most powerful Indian nation on the sunset side of the Rocky Mountains.

The treaty was signed on June 9, 1863 only by the Lawyer faction of the tribe. It surrendered over 80 percent of the territory given the Indians by the earlier treaty, including all known gold country and the Wallowa-area lands occupied by Chief Joseph and his band.[34] This left two-thirds of the Nez Perce, along with the Modocs, Bannocks, and renegades from other tribes, ranging the area east of the Cascades.

After the Lapwai conference, the Indians trickled back to their home lands—some hopeful and some angry. The army moved on.[35]

Rinehart's account reflects the practical politics of the time. Unit commanders were charged with supplies and equipment on hand and issued while they were in command. They were obliged to either hand it over to their successors or account for what happened to it. As Rinehart's company passed through Fort Boise and up the Snake River, a loaded pack mule took a misstep and fell down a cliff. This solved a bookkeeping problem.

Rinehart wrote:

> Ferried over the Salmon River, we passed up the Little Salmon to the meadows over a very rough trail where one of our pack-mules fell over a precipice and was dashed to pieces far below. The magnitude of its load was never known until it appeared on the quarterly returns made June 30th, and if those quartermaster and company reports were true, the wonder is that the poor mule ever got half so far with such a load.

Captain William S. (Smiley) Harris, commander of Company A, First Oregon Volunteer Cavalry, had raised his company of volunteers in Jackson County. A lax disciplinarian (among other things), he proved to be one of the regiment's less successful officers. As his company and other units headed toward Fort Boise from Lapwai, Harris took leave and went to the mining camp of Bannock City to celebrate July 4. He intended to rejoin his unit at Fort Boise on July 8.

Rinehart wrote that while in Bannock City, unattended by his soldiers, a gambler, whom Harris had somehow insulted during his time at Fort Dalles, drew a revolver on him and proceeded to horse-whip him. When he returned to camp, Harris was arrested because of "lax discipline in the company. Twenty-two men deserted before the command left Fort Boise, most of them from company A."[36]

General Alvord had planned a three-pronged expedition into the Indian country of southern Idaho to protect the 1863 trains of Oregon Trail emigrants. Medorem Crawford and his Emigrant Protective Corps were en route with a number of wagons from Omaha. With his companies of infantry and cavalry from Fort Boise, Lieutenant Colonel Maury passed along the branch of the trail north of the Snake River. Colonel P. Edward Connor and his victorious California Volunteers from Salt Lake City pushed north to the less-traveled portion of the trail that ran south of the Snake River.

Crawford and the wagons arrived at Maury's summer camp near Fort Hall on August 17, 1863. Chief Pocatello and an estimated eight hundred renegade warriors had been pushed to a spot about five miles south of the camp. Maury, with his men augmented by Crawford's troopers, totaled a force of 400. They were preparing to battle the Indians when a rider from Connor's command arrived to report that Pocatello had given up and had agreed to go with Connor to treaty-grounds at Box Elder, Utah. The troops and the emigrants joined in a celebration. Rinehart reported that Captain Currey met his future wife, a member of one of the wagon trains, at the dance. Crawford broke out some champagne he had brought from the East, and the officers celebrated with a champagne supper.[37]

With the end of 1863, the war in the East was at its midpoint. In the Pacific Northwest the undermanned and underequipped army gradually was pecking away at the Indian problem, and with three years of experience behind it was developing new skills in wearing down the swift-moving native foes and forcing them onto the Indian reservations.

Chapter 10 notes

1 Carey, *A General History of Oregon*, 625.
2 Snowden, *History of Washington*, 108.
3 W.O.R., Series 1, Vol. 50, Pt. 1, 430.
4 Field, *Official History of the Washington National Guard*, 1:180.
5 W.O.R., Series 1, Vol. 50, Pt. 1, 14.
6 Bancroft, *History of Oregon*, 2:489.
7 W.O.R., Series 1, Vol. 50, Pt. 1, 462-63.
8 After the war, Mullan left the service, became a lawyer and later represented both Oregon and California in their futile claims against the federal government for unreimbursed Civil War military expenditures.
9 Edwards, "The Department of the Pacific," 51.
10 Ibid., 50.
11 W.O.R., Series 1, Vol. 50, Pt. I, 584, 656, and 1014.
12 Carey, *A General History of Oregon*, 628.
13 Ibid., 635.
14 W.O.R, Series 1, Vol. 50, Pt. 1, 30.
15 Robert Newell, an 1840 immigrant to Oregon, served as speaker of Oregon's Provisional Legislature and during the war was an Indian agent and interpreter on the Lapwai Reservation.
16 Edwards, "The Department of the Pacific," 141-142.
17 W.O.R., Series 1, Vol. 50, Pt. 1, 165.
18 Rinehart, William V., "With the Oregon Volunteers, 1862-6," Mss. 471, OHS.
19 Edwards, "The Department of the Pacific," 197.
20 Rinehart, "With the Oregon Volunteers."
21 Carey, *A General History of Oregon*, 667.
22 Hunt, Aurora, "The Far West Volunteers," *Montana, The Magazine of Western History* 12,2,(April 1962): 60.
23 Edwards, "The Department of the Pacific," 199.
24 W.O.R., Series 1, Vol. 50, Pt. 2, 156-58.
25 Ibid., 446.
26 Stone, Buena Cobb, *Fort Klamath; Frontier Post in Oregon,* (Dallas, Tex., Royal Publishing Co., 1964), 14.
27 W.O.R., Series 1, Vol. 50, Pt. 2, 318.
28 Ibid., 328-29.
29 Onstad, Preston, "A Fort on the Luckiamute, A Resurvey of Fort Hoskins," 185.
30 Barth, Gunter, *All Quiet on the Yamhill*, 241.
31 Hunt, Aurora, *The Army of the Pacific*, 232.
32 Carey, Charles H., *A General History of Oregon*, 635-37.
33 Rinehart, William V., "With the Oregon Volunteers, 1862-6."
34 Congress did not ratify the treaty until 1867.
35 The concept of achieving peace through treaty was not universally accepted among the white settlers, either. One account tells of a gathering in southern Idaho of white settlers that established a bounty for Indian scalps: $100 for that of a buck, $50 for that of a squaw and $25 for "anything in the shape of an Indian under ten." The Owyhee *Avalanche* of December 16, 1865 commented: "If some Christian gentleman will furnish a few bales of blankets from a smallpox hospital, well inoculated, we will be distributing agents and see that no Indian is without a blanket. This kind of peace is better than treaties." Fee, Chester Anders, *Chief Joseph; The Biography of a Great Indian* (New York, Wilson-Erickson, 1936) 63-64.
36 Ibid.
37 Ibid.

Chapter 11

INDIAN EXPEDITIONS 1864 AND BEYOND

T he year 1864 marked the high point of the Civil War in the Pacific Northwest. It was the year General Alvord planned for his big push. He had as many troops at his disposal as he was likely to have and figured it was his last chance. Most of his only mounted unit, the First Oregon Volunteer Cavalry, and the Washington Territory Volunteer Infantry were due to be mustered out by early 1865.

The army's principal focus was on the relatively small bands of Indians scattered throughout southeastern Oregon and southern Idaho.

They clustered in two general regions—eastern Oregon south of Canyon City and the Blue Mountains, and in the Owyhee and Snake River basins of southern Idaho.

Alvord thought that if he could send troops in strength to their usual grounds, the Indians would stand and fight and the army, with superior firepower and training, would win. He was wrong.

The army traveled by foot or by horseback, accompanied by mule trains, weapons, and sometimes herds of cattle to feed its men. The Indians traveled light.

However, for the renegade Indian there was no reliable source of supplies and equipment. He had to steal for his rations and firepower. His weapons were often inferior, his ammunition short and his aim poor.

The first Indian trouble of 1864 burst forth in February. A band of renegade Snakes raided a camp of miners at Penawawa, about fifty miles north of Walla Walla on the Snake River, burned their cabin and chased them back down the road to Fort Walla Walla.

Word got to Walla Walla the evening of February 15 in the midst of a dance being held in a vacant barracks. Two companies of cavalry were ordered to take to the trail at daybreak. Some of the officers, who were squiring women of the surrounding area, had difficulty getting their dates back home in time.[1]

Five days later the command, headed by Captain George B.Currey, came upon the Indian camp of twenty lodges. All was silent. Currey called upon the Indians to come out of their lodges. There was no response. The soldiers routed them out with a volley of rifle fire, wounding three Indians, one mortally. The chief and two others, identified by the miners as their assailants, were taken back to Walla Walla and turned over to the sheriff.[2]

Alvord laconically reported to his superiors: "This expedition of Captain Currey will have a very good effect on those Indians. They will be apt hereafter to let the miners alone."[3]

Alvord was under pressure to make his big move. Indian bands were raiding miners and settlers in the John Day area. They were interfering with travel on the Canyon City road, the main artery of commercial traffic between The Dalles and the gold country of the John Day.

On February 23, 1864, Lieutenant John A. Waymire and twenty-five men of Company D, First Oregon Volunteer Cavalry, were sent from Fort Dalles to Canyon City. On his arrival, Waymire learned that a few days before, Indians had stolen forty horses and mules from a ranch two miles south of Canyon City. A rag-tag posse of civilians, led by Cincinnatus H. (Joaquin) Miller, fiery former editor of the suppressed *Democratic Register* at Eugene City and later county judge at Canyon City, was in pursuit. Waymire followed. He found the vigilantes in camp in the Harney Valley.[4]

Leaving part of his command at a base camp, the mixed band of soldiers and civilians followed the tracks of the stolen horses and found the Indians on April 7. A pitched battle followed.

The Indians were dug in on a slight ridge. Waymire planned a charge to root out and scatter the Indians. He later wrote:

> This charge I intended should be led by the sabre and followed up with the rifles and pistols of the citizen volunteers. Just before moving forward Captain Miller advised me that this was not his way of fighting Indians and that his men must fall back to the Willow Gulch.[5]

Several Indians were believed killed. Waymire estimated the total Indian force in excess of 150.

Sergeant Robert Casteel and two soldiers, Privates Cyrus R. Ingraham and John Himber, were sent the day before the battle to investigate a sign of smoke off the trail. They never returned, and were believed to have been bushwhacked by the Indians. No bodies were recovered.

Thinking to exterminate the Snake raiders, Alvord sent two expeditions into the Indian country. Captain John M. Drake, with six cavalry officers and 160 men, left Fort Dalles April 20, 1864. He was accompanied by twenty-two Indian scouts from the Warm Springs Reservation and thirty-nine civilian quartermaster and commissary employees, eight six-mule wagon teams and ninety-nine pack mules. He carried six months rations.

Drake's job was to sweep the area of eastern Oregon north of the Blue Mountains and to protect the Canyon City road as well as the settlers of the area.

Captain Currey left Fort Walla Walla April 25, traveling with ninety-one men. He later was joined by Uma-how-lits, war chief of the Cayuse tribe, and ten warriors whom Currey described as "fine-looking fellows, well-mounted and (who) seem very anxious to return with some war trophies."[6]

Currey's orders were to operate in the Owyhee River area and the Harney basin of southeastern Oregon.

Drake's command was not a happy one. He kept a private journal in which he expressed himself freely and eloquently. He complained that the quartermaster at Fort Dalles had pushed off on him the feeblest mules and poor wagons.[7] The surgeon who accompanied the expedition, Dr. C. C. Dumreicher, showed up with the odor of alcohol about him[8] and was described by Drake as "a morbid, crusty, indolent old muggins and is of no account on such a campaign as this; cannot take care of himself much less take care of others."[9]

Drake also noted the inefficiency of his officers. This dissatisfaction evidently trickled down to the enlisted ranks. A letter was sent from "Company G" to the editor of the *Oregonian* complaining that Drake was hunting Indians where none were to be found. Currey headed south through the Grand Ronde Valley. En route he added to his expedition

Captain Edward Barry and twenty men of the First Washington Territory Volunteer Infantry who were on detached duty.

Currey's report tells not only of the Indians and his attempts to find them, but is a wonderful description of the desolate Owyhee country as he saw it:

> The region immediately opposite the mouth of Jordan Creek has a weird, antiquated look; it is one of the unusual landscapes wherein the wind has been the most powerful and active agent employed by Dame Nature to complete her exterior. The formation is of greyish red sandstone, soft, and under the capricious workings of the wind for centuries, has assumed shapes strange and fantastic. Here stands a group of towers; there is an archway curiously shaped; yonder is a tunnel running the face of a sandstone ledge hundreds of feet from the bottom. The whole catalog of descriptive antique might be exhausted in giving fanciful names to the created results of this aerial architecture. The spectacle of seeing my command wind its way through this temple of the wind was pleasing, and one that will long be remembered by the most who beheld it.[10]

On May 25 Currey and his command reached a site for a base camp. It was placed in a sheltered valley on a creek that Currey named Gibbs Creek in honor of his benefactor, the governor. The name didn't stick. It now is called Crooked Creek. The camp was named Camp Henderson after Oregon's sole congressman, J. D. Henderson. Their tents left behind to lighten the freight load, Currey's troops built wickiups of willow, sagebrush and reeds to shelter from the sun.

Camp Henderson was abandoned three weeks later. But its occupants left a memorial, a mile-long sandstone cliff into which they, and those who followed, carved their names, including those of G. B. Currey and Captain W. V. Rinehart, his adjutant, with the date of May 25, 1864. The camp site is located just south of Highway 95 where it crosses Crooked Creek midway between Burns Junction and Rome.

On June 13 and 14, men from Camp Henderson engaged in a fire fight with the Indian renegades near the camp and at least four of the Indians were killed. Rinehart, who had been on a reconnaissance to locate a camp of Indians reported by settlers, wrote that he returned to find Camp Henderson abandoned and Currey's contingent on the trail. Rinehart located the new camp after midnight and found "the Indian scouts still engaged in their scalp-dance over the scalps taken from their Snake enemies killed in Capt. Currey's engagement...."

On Tuesday, May 17, 1864 Drake's company was camped in the Crooked River Valley between what now are the hamlets of Post and Paulina. Two Indian scouts returned with the report of an Indian encampment of nine lodges and ten horses about twelve miles northeast.

For Captain Drake's command, it was to be the first Indian battle of the campaign. For Lieutenant Stephen Watson, a thirty-one-year-old native of New Brunswick, Canada and a former Jackson County representative to the 1858 Oregon Territorial Legislature, it brought the sad distinction of being the first and only officer to die of battle wounds in the Pacific Northwest during the Civil War.[11]

The Indians were camped about nine miles northwest of what now is Paulina, near what is known locally as Upper Watson Springs. They were camped against a ridge of rimrock running north and south.

Drake sent Lieutenant Henry McCall, Lieutenant Watson, thirty-nine troopers and ten scouts to make a surprise attack at dawn. They were joined a mile from the Indian camp by the eleven scouts earlier sent to the area. McCall divided the command into three elements. McCall took one group of troopers. Watson took the other. They held the two flanks. The Indian scouts, headed by Stock Whitely, a chief of the Warm Springs Indians, held the middle. As dawn broke, shortly after 4 a.m., the army force moved in upon the camp. McCall's element was delayed by swampy terrain and paused to capture the Indian horse herd.

The renegades retreated into a jumble of rocks at the foot of the rimrock.

Not visible to Watson and his men was a low wall of rocks thrown up at the base of the rimrock, which afforded the Snakes a natural fortification. A volley of rifle fire and arrows from the rocks felled Watson and two others immediately. Five more were wounded. McCall retreated to a secure position with the wounded and sent for Drake who brought additional troops. The army's total casualties were Watson, two enlisted men, Chief Stock Whitely and one other Indian scout. A civilian employee who had accompanied the group and five other soldiers were wounded. The bodies of the dead soldiers were stripped and badly mutilated. The body of the Indian scout was scalped and disemboweled.

The Snakes fled, abandoning their supplies and equipment. Drake's report estimated three dead and six wounded in the renegade camp.

Drake believed the camp had been occupied for several years and that it was from this base camp that Chief Paulina raided north to the Canyon City road.

The supply depot was named Camp Maury after Drake's colonel. The captured Snake mounts replaced army horses killed in the battle. The rest were given to the Warm Springs scouts.

The corpses of Watson and his men were rolled in their blankets and buried on a hillside overlooking the camp.[12] They were later disinterred and reburied at Camp Watson, named after Lieutenant Watson, located about five miles west of Antone.[13]

June 6, 1864 was Election Day, the day Oregon voters elected their state and local officers, as did Drake's soldiers. The civilian quartermaster packers settled into their own camp due north of Camp Maury. It was called Union Camp, likely because of the pending election.

The polls opened at Union Camp and 100 troopers and civilians voted, all but six for the Union ticket. Some soldiers did not vote. Drake explained:

> A number of soldiers declined voting, taking that plan for expressing their disgust toward Oregon and its people. They say, that as a state, Oregon has never recognized their existence, that she had done less for the country in a time of danger than any state in the Union, and has manifested no public or patriotic spirit, all of which is true to a great extent.[14]

On June 19, three days after leaving Camp Henderson, Currey's command reached a new campsite at the foot of the Steens Mountains in the Alvord Valley. Earthworks were erected.[15]

Currey and the bulk of his command set out June 22 for Malheur Lake and hoped-for rendezvous with Drake and his men. Drake seemed to realize that the Indians had fled and in his journal he bitterly criticized Alvord's order that stripped him of the freedom to go where the Indians were and instead remain in the Harney Basin until he met up with Currey.

On May 10 he wrote:

> Capt. Currey ordered to Harney Lake direct, and this command to form a junction with him there. Then what? The Indians will be on the South side of the Humboldt Mountains, and the King of France will have marched up the hill and down again. Why could the Gen. not have left each free to govern himself, after communicating all information accessible? What a blunder![16]

By August, Drake was to declare: "Neither Drake nor Currey knew where the other was." And for a time no one else knew where Currey was, either. On June 17, 1864 Alvord wrote the commanding officer of Fort Boise requesting "any information, even rumors, of Captain Currey's expedition which may come to you."[17]

Eventually the two commands met and made a new base camp which they named Rattlesnake Camp. This later was the site of Fort Harney, north and east of what now is Burns.

While Alvord had his troops galloping and hiking around the southeastern Oregon desert, the Snakes moved north, again threatening the John Day mining district and The Dalles-Canyon City Road.[18]

Alvord ordered a camp set up—Camp Watson—to protect the road. In June 1864, he also called on Governor Gibbs to recruit a company of four-month cavalry volunteers.[19]

The Dalles citizens raised bounty money to induce enlistment of these short-termers. After the briefest of training, the volunteers, commanded by Nathan Olney,[20] one-time Indian agent, was put to work supporting Captain R. C. Caldwell's men from Fort Watson patrolling the road.[21]

There was considerable pressure on Alvord to make the road safe. Portland mercantile interests controlled the market for supplies to the Canyon City area as well as the thriving mining camps of southern Idaho. The Canyon City road was a vital commercial link.[22] Competitors from Red Bluff, California were trying to crack the market, contending that a more reliable source of supplies could be provided overland from the south.

Poorly trained, badly disciplined, and indifferently led, Olney's forty-man cavalry unit proved at best of cosmetic effect.

Drake noted in his journal:

> Olney pays no attention to, and will not obey his orders, and Caldwell threatens to put him and all his men in the guardhouse. He has written to the general recommending the disbanding of Olney's detachment as utterly worthless and unmanageable. I would not be surprised if they were turned over to me; however, I hope not.[23]

On a separate occasion he referred to Olney's short-timers as "Olney's Forty Thieves."[24]

After receiving a copy of *The Dalles Mountaineer* containing a windy letter to the editor from Alvord, Drake's ill will toward Alvord spilled over into white fury. The *Mountaineer* editor, no friend of the military, on July 1 criticized the Currey and Drake expeditions as "a wild goose excursion up Crooked River." Alvord responded with a defense that Drake interpreted as blaming him for missing the Indians and not on Alvord's order to meet Currey at Harney Lake.

Drake wrote:

> Gen. Alvord in his efforts to retain or acquire a popularity with the people, has belittled himself to publish in the 'Mountaineer' a whole column of correspondence in which he endeavors to show how much he has done to secure the safety of the Canon (sic) City road, but says not one word of the orders...which sent me flaking toward Lake Harney. On the contrary, he endeavors to shift the responsibility,...thus shoving the responsibility for these Indian outrages upon my shoulders.[25]

A month later he was to tersely comment: "In my judgment Genl. Alvord is superannuated and ought to be retired."[26]

Alvord ordered Currey to head north to defend the John Day mining area. Alvord, who had the rank but not the experience, gratuitously offered Currey, who had the experience but not the rank, advice on how to dig the Indians out of their fortifications.[27]

Currey's men swept much of the John Day River Basin, with little Indian contact. His frustration and exasperation in chasing groundless rumors of Indian presence was reflected in his letter to Fort Vancouver August 1, 1864:

> You will see by this and my former reports that since I took command of the two expeditions the country has been pretty well scouted from the head of Malheur River, on the east, to the west bank of the Des Chutes on the west, thus familiarizing our troops with a region hitherto unknown to our arms and filled by the fertile imagination of a panic-stricken people with hordes of savages strongly posted in the impregnable fastness of trackless mountain and yawning canyons.[28]

Indian troubles in 1864 were not confined to the area patrolled by Currey and Drake. In March, a small band of reservation Indians fled the Alsea sub-agency on the Oregon Coast. Lieutenant Louis Herzer and ten men of the California Volunteer Infantry company stationed at Fort Hoskins were sent to bring them back.

The Indians had reason to leave. The supply of game was poor, the rations and supplies promised them by their treaties often were indifferently provided, and the climate on the Siletz Reservation was wetter than they were used to.[29]

The detail was out twenty-one days and went as far south as Coos Bay, traveling much of the way on the ocean beach. It returned with thirty-two Indians, some of whom had left as much as two years earlier, while there were others who had never been confined to the reservation. Another group of seventeen returned voluntarily.

Herzer, in his report, commented bitterly that he would have accomplished more except white settlers in the vicinity of both the Umpqua River and Coos Bay "always took the part of the Indians, assisting them to hide or escape to the hills, where pursuit was impossible."[30]

The preceding December a settler named Cook had been killed by a group of Quileute Indians near Grays Harbor, Washington. The Indian Department demanded the tribe surrender all of the murderers. The tribe refused, but offered to surrender the leader of the band that did the killing.

Alvord asked for a company of infantry from California to chase down the killers. In September, General Irvin McDowell's aide de camp wrote back, directing Alvord to accept the surrender of the ring leader, commenting:

> There are so many complaints from officers of that (Indian) department of the unpunished murder of Indians by white men that the general feels a repugnance to exact the extreme penalty of our law on the red man, when the white man goes so constantly unwhipped of justice.[31]

This contention was supported in the report of Lieutenant Colonel C. S. Drew of the First Oregon Volunteer Cavalry. Drew wrote from a camp in the Sierra Nevada Mountains 100 miles east of Fort Klamath, recounting that a band of armed white men had attacked a group of unarmed Indians.[32] The expressed purpose: To steal two Indian horses to get even for the loss of livestock by one of the members of the white group a year earlier. The unarmed Indians were joined by a group of Indians who were armed. They fought back. One of the attacking whites was killed, and Drew turned the horses back over to their Indian owners.[33]

A mixed detail of cavalry and infantry commanded by Colonel Reuben Maury left Fort Boise July 20 to pursue a band of renegades who had raided whites near Boonville (Ruby City), Idaho Territory.

After twenty-eight days on the march through rough terrain and deep canyons, the worn out troops returned with minimal Indian contact. Maury reported: "On inspection of the Infantry, I found them all quite or nearly barefoot, having worn out two pairs of shoes each in twenty-days' march."[34]

The civilian vigilante posse that set out before the army found their Indians. They lost two men. But they tracked down a part of the band. Maury reported:

> The party killed and scalped according to their own account thirty-five. The scalps were brought in. The number of men killed is stated by different parties 2 to 7, remainder women and children.... Infants were thrown against the rocks and killed.[35]

Another detail from Fort Boise went in August to the Salmon River area in pursuit of Indians who raided cattle and horse herds and stole flour from the white settlers. The detail was out five weeks and claimed several Indian lives.

After an autumn of chasing after Indians they could not find, Captains Currey and Drake, with their trail-worn troops and horses, returned to their home stations.

The six months expedition produced no real victories. But it served to wear down the Indian renegades. Faced with bitter winter weather and short of supplies, Paulina, whose band was only a part of the problem, surrendered at Fort Klamath in November.[36]

On October 20, 1864 General McDowell directed Oregon Governor Addison Gibbs to recruit one thousand men for a regiment of Volunteer Infantry.[37] On November 23 McDowell, responding to reports not only from the District of Oregon and from other commands in his department, issued a general order prohibiting the indiscriminate killing of the renegade Indians:

> ....Hereafter no officer or soldier will execute or aid in executing any indian prisoners on any pretext whatever. If an indian commits any crime, the military may hold him under guard until the civil authority can take charge of him.[38]

1865 AND AFTER

On January 11, 1865 six Indians (four armed with rifles and two with bows and arrows) tried but failed to ambush two travelers near the Cottonwood stage station on the Canyon City road. The same band of Indians was believed responsible for rustling thirteen head of horses later in the month.[39]

On March 7 a posse of twenty-four civilians went in search of those who had stolen the stock. According to their story, nineteen warriors, five women and four children were induced to surrender. Lieutenant William M. Hand's report stated:

> The citizens intended to bring in the whole band, the chief agreeing to the plan and apparently perfectly satisfied, but instead of doing as he promised, at the first opportunity he gave a signal when they all broke and ran. The citizens then commenced firing on them, killing 12 and wounding nearly all of the rest. Two squaws were accidentally killed besides.

On April 18 three white men were killed nearby, their bodies scalped and mutilated.

Three times troops from Fort Hoskins were sent to return Indians to the Siletz Reservation. They rounded up forty from Linn County, ten from the Corvallis area and seventy-nine on an expedition that lasted more than a month and went as far as Crescent City, California.

In February, troops from Fort Boise killed seven Indians and recovered stolen horses in the Bruneau Valley. The detail captured several Indian women and children. The captive Indian dependents were supposed to be returned to Fort Boise. But the army had been feeding destitute immigrants and was running low on supplies. So Captain Frederick Seidenstriker, then in command at Fort Boise, directed his field detachment to turn the Indians loose rather than keep them and feed them.

Later, a band of about eight Indians was found dressing out the carcasses of steers they had slaughtered. Thirty warriors were killed and an estimated thirty more were wounded.[40]

On May 23, 1865 General Alvord was summarily relieved from duty and ordered to turn over his command "to the senior officer on duty under him," and to report to Washington, D.C.

The reason for Alvord's dismissal appears to have been two-fold:

Secretary of War Edwin Stanton, in private correspondence to General Grant, acknowledged that "frequent complaints have reached the Department in respect to General Alvord." Prior to the Civil War, as a lieutenant, Grant had served under Alvord who was then a captain, in the Oregon Country. Grant grew unhappy, resigned his commission and returned to Illinois. He wrote Stanton, saying:

> I know Alvord well. I do not think that he is fit for command, and he ought to be called East. He is a good man in his intentions and would do well to place on any kind of a board, but I know of no other duty he is eminently suited for...."[41]

Grant suggested that the District of Oregon required no replacement for Alvord.

Colonel Reuben Maury of the First Oregon Volunteer Cavalry assumed temporary command of the District of Oregon. But Maury was a volunteer and General McDowell gave him little authority.

Maury, who understood the dynamics of the Indian campaign, recommended stationing additional troops throughout the Indian country. Because things were then relatively quiet, McDowell refused. When the Indian raids resumed, the army was unable to respond.[42]

On June 27, General George Wright assumed command of the army in the Pacific Northwest. The District of Oregon became the Department of the Columbia which meant that its commander ran things and reported to Washington, D.C. and not to San Francisco.

On July 28, 1865 Wright, his wife, and his staff officers boarded the *Brother Jonathan*, the side-wheel steamer that regularly ran between San Francisco and Portland. The cargo was heavy. It even included two camels, intended as pack animals, and General Wright's huge Newfoundland dog. There also was $200,000 in gold—payroll for the troops, locked in the ship's safe. This was in the days before the Coast Guard and the Plimsoll line that marked the loading capacity of ships.

The captain was Samuel J. DeWolf, an experienced mariner. He protested that the ship was overloaded. The shipping agent told him that the ship and its cargo would sail and that if DeWolf didn't want to skipper the ship, there were others on the beach who cheerfully would.

A nor'wester was blowing hard as the ship left the San Francisco Bay.

Off Crescent City, California, the ship speared itself on what later would be called Jonathan Rock. Five of the six lifeboats foundered and sank, and the ship followed. DeWolf told a departing crewman who survived, "Tell them that if they had not overloaded us we would have got through all right and this would never have happened." Only 19 of the 232 passengers and crew survived. General Wright and his wife, were among the casualties.

Although the sea was rough and the wind heavy, it was a clear day. Much of Crescent City stood impotently on the headlands as the ship sank in forty-five minutes.[43]

Officers of the soon-to-be-discharged First Oregon Volunteer Cavalry had been promoted and commissioned in the new First Oregon Volunteer Infantry. One of them was Captain-now-Colonel George Currey, its new regimental commander. Now the direction of the Oregon-Idaho Indian wars was in the hands of local field commanders who had long chafed at the army's policy of fair-weather campaigning.

Currey became commander of the new Department of the Columbia. This was a position of prominence for an officer of volunteers. But, as Grant had told Secretary of War Stanton in his letter urging Alvord's removal, Oregon didn't really need a general anyway.

Currey and other command officers had been sitting around campfires grousing about the army's Indian War policies for three years. It was enough that in March 1864 five company grade officers—John Drake, William V. Rinehart, W. V. Spencer, H. C. Small, and Stephen Watson—wrote the Secretary of War asking that a board of officers be convened in Oregon to examine them for commissions in the regiments of Colored Troops being formed from freed slaves in the East. They wrote that they wished "to engage in active service, and believe that we can do a greater amount of good than by remaining on this coast—where there is little probability if any of more than garrison duty."

William V. Rinehart, Captain-turned-Major, wrote in his memoirs:

> From the earliest Military occupation of the Oregon country, it had been the settled policy of the War Department to send troops into the Indian country only in summer, withdrawing them to Fort Walla Walla, The Dalles and Fort Vancouver for winter quarters. The excessive cost of transporting supplies across the Blue Mountains from the Columbia River, about ten cents per pound even in summer, had been urged as the principal reason for such a course.[44]

Currey sent troops to six separate temporary posts in eastern Oregon and two in southern Idaho. In Oregon; Camp Polk near the mouth of the Crooked River, Camp Logan on the road between Colfax and Canyon City, Camp Lyon in Jordan Valley, Camp Alvord on Horse Creek in the Alvord Valley, a camp on Silvies River north of Malheur, and Camp Colfax at the Willow Creek crossing of the Canyon City-Boise road. The Idaho camps were at Old Fort Hall and Camp Reed near Salmon Falls.[45]

Currey told the troops to erect winter shelters for themselves. It was his theory when winter came and snows hardened, troops in the eastern Oregon posts would start for the Harney Basin, where Currey believed the renegades historically holed up for the winter. He believed that the Indians could be routed out of their winter diggings and forced to stand and fight or flee the territory.

Hearing of the plan, the War Department scotched it and ordered Currey mustered out along with most of the volunteers. But the word came too late for some of the troops. Too far from civilization to be recalled, they spent a miserable winter.[46]

Yet the winter campaign was carried out under command of Colonel Currey and Lieutenant Colonel John M. Drake, his successor, from the remaining posts. And it worked. On November 20, 1865 a twenty-man detail of Oregon Cavalry from Camp Watson tracked down a band of twenty-five to thirty Indians. The detail's leader, First Sergeant George Garber, was mortally wounded. Several Indians were killed, several more wounded and, most importantly, nearly three tons of dried meat and other provisions intended to carry the renegades through the winter was destroyed.[47]

After the battering his band had taken in 1865 and with the prospect of a hungry winter campaign, Chief Paulina decided to surrender again, for the second time. Paulina had given up to Lieutenant Colonel R. E. Drew at Fort Klamath in 1864 but later changed his mind and fled back into the wilderness.

Rinehart wrote:

> As evidence that (Colonel Currey's) camps had been properly selected, namely in the Indian winter homes, Chief Paulina, the terror of the whole frontier, came in with his tribe and surrendered to me at Fort Klamath before Christmas. They were in a starving condition and were fed by me from Government stores.

But Paulina couldn't confine himself to the Malheur Reservation. The story is that Paulina had been raiding cattle herds and was shot and killed northwest of what is now Ashwood by Howard Maupin while feasting on a roasted ox in 1867.

After his release from duty August 10, 1866, Rinehart was appointed Indian Agent of the Malheur Reservation where he served for six years, supervising the Indians he had fought across eastern Oregon for four years.

The last Pacific Northwest volunteer companies were mustered out of service in 1866 and 1867, and were replaced by the 14th Infantry Regiment, whose commander was Lieutenant Colonel (formerly Major General) George Crook. Most of the men were seasoned Civil War veterans who had decided they liked the military life. These veteran soldiers took over the frontier posts. They had plenty of equipment and even a twenty-six member regimental band, which played get-acquainted concerts up and down Oregon's Willamette Valley. It was the first music other than bugle, fife, and drum that the army in the Pacific Northwest had known since the Fourth Infantry Band was bundled up with the rest of the regulars and shipped out from Fort Vancouver at the start of the war.

Acting under new federal legislation, the army also mustered two companies of troopers recruited from the Warm Springs Indian Reservation, thus doing what Captain Drake and others had long encouraged—fighting the renegade Indians with soldiers recruited from friendly tribes.[48] Gibbs' replacement as governor, George L. Woods, argued long with the War Department over the chivalry of war. Woods believed in a war of extermination against the renegades without regard to sex. Woods pointed out that the Indian women were reported to have taken the lead in devising fiendish tortures of women and children in the Van Orman massacre in 1860.[49]

Crook took to the field and followed Currey's winter campaign formula. Rinehart told of Crook's campaign:

> [Crook] began at once a vigorous campaign against the Snake Indians who occupied, in marauding bands, the country bounded on the West by Deschutes River, on the North by the Blue Mountains, and on the South by the Steens Mountains and Goose Lake...He followed the Indians almost incessantly whenever he found them (in large or small parties) and when they surrendered to him they were found to be completely starved out and absolutely afoot. They had subsisted upon their horses and exhausted their resources before accepting the hard condition of unconditional surrender.

But after more than three years of desperate resistance they finally sued for peace and were collected at Camp Harney in 1870.

Only a scattering of renegade Modocs and Shastas remained at war. The whites and these small bands battled each other until the Modoc War broke out in 1873. The hanging of Captain Jack and the other leaders of the Modocs in October 1873 marked the real end of the Indian struggle in the Pacific Northwest.[50]

Chapter 11 notes

1 Rinehart, "With the Oregon Volunteers," 1862-6.

2 Ibid.

3 W.O.R., Series 1, Vol. 50, Pt. 2, 308.

4 W.O.R, Series 1, Vol. 50, Pt. 2, 309.

5 W.O.R, Series I, 50, Pt. 1, 310-15.

6 W.O.R., Series 1, Vol. 50, Pt. 2, 317.

7 Knuth, Priscilla, ed., "John M. Drake, 'Private Journal,'" OHQ, 65(1964):17.

8 Dumreicher, who held the rank of surgeon, was brought before a court martial board on grounds of insubordination, but was acquitted when the eight-officer court martial board tied 4-4. Rinehart, William V., With the Oregon Volunteers, 1862-6, mss. 471, Oregon Historical Society.

9 Ibid., 16.

10 Fuller, "The First Oregon Cavalry," 148.

11 Rinehart, "With the Oregon Volunteers," 1862-6.

12 W.O.R., Series 1, Vol. 50, Pt. 2, 329-31.

13 Kenney, Judith Keyes, "The Founding of Camp Watson," OHQ, 58(1957): 5-16.

14 Knuth, "John M. Drake" 48.

15 W.O.R., Series 1, Vol. 50, Part 2, 320.

16 Knuth, "John M. Drake," 56.

17 W.O.R., Series 1, Vol. 50, Pt. 3, 867.

18 Knuth, "John M. Drake," 63.

19 W.O.R., Series I, Vol. 50, Pt. 2, 863.

20 Nathan Olney served as a rifleman in the Oregon Regiment of Riflemen during the Cayuse War and commanded the short-lived Wasco County Volunteers (August-September 1855) sent to the relief of a wagon train attacked near Fort Boise. He served as county judge and Indian sub-agent. As was accepted practice for the time, he believed in patronage. Commissioned for the term of service as a first lieutenant, he appointed his younger brother, Orville Olney, a second lieutenant and his second-in-command. An older brother, Cyrus Olney, served as an associate justice of the Oregon Territorial Supreme Court.

21 Knuth, "John M. Drake," 63.

22 Edwards, "The Department of the Pacific," 260.

23 Knuth, "John M. Drake," 88-89.

24 Ibid.

25 Ibid., 77.

26 Ibid., 84.

27 W.O.R., Series 1, Vol. 50, Pt. 2, 901.

28 W.O.R., Series 1, Vol. 50, Pt. 1, 324.

29 Schablitsky, "Duty and Vice," 53-54.

30 W.O.R., Series 1, Vol. 50, Pt. 1, 353-354.

31 W.O.R., Series 1, Vol. 50, Pt. 2, 971.

32 As mentioned previously, some on the frontier did not wait for the army. They exercised self help. The Boise Rangers and their Idaho Territory successors operated under some formalized structure. Others just went out and—right or wrong--killed the Indians they felt had it coming.

33 W.O.R., Series 1, Vol. 50, Pt. 1, 911.

34 Ibid., 384-85.

35 Ibid., 1068.

36 Ibid.
37 Oregon Legislature, Journal of the House of Representatives, 1864 Session, Special Message of the Governor, 33-34.
38 Department of the Pacific, General Orders No. 53, November 23, 1864.
39 W.O.R., Series 1, Vol. 50, Pt. 1, 396.
40 Ibid., 400.
41 bid., 592.
42 Edwards, The Department of the Pacific, 280.
43 Lomax, Alfred L., "Brother Jonathan," Pioneer Steamship of the Pacific Coast," OHQ, 60(1959):331-347.
44 Rinehart, "With the Oregon Volunteers, 1862-6."
45 Carey, History of Oregon, 641.
46 Carey, A General History of Oregon, 674.

Chapter 12

AN ARRAY OF THREATS

Put yourself in the position of a resident of the Pacific Northwest in the early 1860s. The United States is engaged in a war that has torn the nation apart. You are far from the population and political centers of the country. Communication with the rest of the country is slow and uncertain. What news there is of the war appears in the local newspapers, much of it a mixture of fact, rumor and political polemic.

Lonely and seemingly ignored by a federal government—whose principal interest seemed to be the streams of gold beginning to trickle from the young mines east of the Cascade Mountains—is it any wonder that events remotely connected to the sparsely populated Pacific Northwest portended, to some anxious souls, a threat and at the worst an imminent invasion?

To some, the threat of invasion seemed to lurk from the Mormons of Utah Territory, from the British colonies in Canada, from the sea, and from Mexico. And there were some homegrown distractions as well.

THE PUGET SOUND CUSTOMS HOUSE FIGHT

Perhaps the most bizarre event of the Civil War in Washington Territory occurred in early August 1862, when the federal Collector of Customs for Puget Sound threatened to blow up Port Townsend. This wasn't an outside threat exactly, but it certainly put local nerves on edge.

Victor Smith, a former newspaper editor from Cincinnati, was the U.S. Collector of Customs. Like many of President Lincoln's early political appointees, Smith was of help to the Republican Party during the 1860 elections and reportedly also was a distant cousin of Secretary of the Treasury Salmon P. Chase.[1]

Smith and his family arrived at Port Townsend July 30, 1861. The Collector of Customs office was about all there was at Port Townsend. In a letter to his boss Chase, Smith complained that Port Townsend lacked "...a Schoolhouse, a church, a Black-Smith shop or an Industry of any kind."[2]

The Collector of Customs had a real job. At the start of the war, a significant part of the federal government's revenue was from customs duties. Smith collected this federal tax on foreign goods shipped to Puget Sound ports. In addition, Smith managed the hospital that the government maintained for the benefit of ailing seamen. He also managed funds for the Lighthouse Service's new lighthouse at Cape Flattery.

To assist him in collecting these duties he had two revenue cutters that served not only Puget Sound but the Columbia River entry as well: the *Joe Lane,*[3] a sailing vessel that didn't sail very well unless the wind was astern[4] and the *Shubrick,* a 140-foot side-wheel steamer.[5] Armed with cannon installed at the start of the war, these two ships were the Pacific Northwest's "navy." The *Shubrick* also served as a lighthouse tender and as the mail boat, connecting Puget Sound communities with Victoria, B.C. and the twice-monthly mail boat that served it from San Francisco.

An opportunist, Smith wanted to move the customs house and its attendant payroll and purchases, from Port Townsend to Cherburg (later renamed Port Angeles). Smith owned an interest in the Cherburg town site and contracted to buy a controlling interest in the local newspaper, which he promised to devote "to the national recognition of Salmon P. Chase."[6]

In the early weeks of 1862, fearing that he was about to be removed from office, Smith left Port Townsend for Washington, D.C. When he left, Smith appointed J. J. Van Bokelin as deputy collector in his absence. What happened to Van Bokelin is not reported. In June, Captain J. S. S. Chaddock of the *Joe Lane* installed his lieutenant, J. H. Merryman, as acting collector.

One August afternoon, the *Shubrick* showed up, carrying the returning Victor Smith as a passenger. Smith had not been fired.

Moreover, his boss, Secretary of the Treasury Chase, had convinced the Congress to move the port of entry from Port Townsend to Cherburg.[7]

Smith entered the customs house and demanded that Merryman turn over the records to him. Believing that Smith had been fired, Merryman demanded evidence that he still held the office. Smith either could not or would not. He returned to the *Shubrick*. Shortly thereafter an armed guard from the revenue cutter entered the customs house and delivered a discomforting message to Merryman. Smith had ordered the *Shubrick*'s twelve-pounder cannon loaded with explosive shells. Merryman had fifteen minutes to turn over the customs office papers and files or the *Shubrick* would shell the building. This caused concern in the tiny village.[8] The customs house was on the waterfront and immediately behind it was the main street of Port Townsend. Bombarding the customs house meant blowing up the town.

Merryman handed over the files. Smith and the *Shubrick* steamed off to Port Angeles and the locals called for help. Word was sent to Territorial Governor William Pickering at Olympia. Pickering, a sixty-year-old of British birth (sometimes called William the Headstrong), gathered up his personal secretary, the local U.S. Marshal, and Henry M. McGill. McGill previously was acting territorial governor.[9] He had been appointed most recently U.S. Commissioner, which meant that McGill had the power to act in the absence of the nearest federal judge, whose office was in Portland. The group boarded the steamer *Eliza Anderson*. They stopped at Fort Steilacoom to pick up Major G. W. Patten, the post commander and ranking army officer in the Puget Sound country. Patten's correspondence with his superiors in San Francisco gives a report of the affair.[10]

The *Eliza Anderson* got to Port Townsend to find the *Shubrick* gone. Merryman had gone to Victoria. Pickering and his assistant went with the *Eliza Anderson* to interview Merryman there.

McGill took testimony of some of the townsfolk and decided to issue a warrant for the arrest of Smith and one Wilson, commander of the *Shubrick*.[11]

That night the *Shubrick* steamed into view, but stopped a mile offshore. A ship's boat came ashore with the mail from Olympia. McGill sent the marshal to arrest Wilson and Smith. The marshal returned and said that Wilson refused to acknowledge the warrant and that he had been refused access to Smith, who was in the cabin below. McGill instructed the marshal to go back and take the two by force.

There then followed a comic chase as the marshal tried to seize Smith and Wilson. The marshal and his men were in a rowboat. The *Shubrick* had its steam up. Every time the oarsmen got near the boat, the *Shubrick* moved away.

The *Shubrick* then put a tow rope on the *Joe Lane*, anchored nearby, and steamed off to Port Angeles.[12] Patten and Pickering gave up and went home. Smith and Wilson were indicted by a grand jury at Olympia. Testimony was taken in a hearing. Upon order of the Secretary of the Treasury, all charges were dismissed.[13]

Smith later built a house for himself and his family at Port Angeles and erected a building that he rented to the government as a customs house. Both were near the bank of Valley Creek, which flowed through the town. On December 16, 1863, the stream was blocked upstream by a landslide. That night the dam burst and a wall of water fifteen feet high swept over the customs house and the Smith residence. Two customs service employees were killed. Smith's wife and their four children narrowly escaped death. Smith lost both home and fortune, and subsequently his job.[14]

In 1865, Washington's Territorial Delegate, Arthur A. Denny, got Congress to move the customs house back to Port Townsend.[15] It was still there in 1869 when Harvey W. Scott, the editor of the *Portland Oregonian*, reported it as being: "...[A]bout as poor an apology for a building to be occupied for such a purpose as could well be imagined. It is small, mean, rickety, unpainted and unfurnished, and, for the credit of the country, should be replaced with something better."[16]

In 1865, Smith drowned in the sinking of the *Brother Jonathan* off the Northern California coast.[17]

THE UTAH THREAT

The Mormon residents of Utah Territory caused concern to the Union government. There were unsubstantiated fears that Utah would leave the Union, and that it would join in the formation of the Pacific Republic.

At the start of the Civil War, Utah Territory was 98 percent Mormon. Brigham Young and his followers had settled Utah after terrible abuse. To some, the opening of the Civil War seemed a fulfillment of Joseph

Smith's 1832 Christmas Day prophecy, when he accurately predicted that a revolution would begin in South Carolina. He said this revolt would grow into a sectional war that would pit brother against brother and result in the uprising of the slaves and their admission into the military service of the Northern states. He said it would bring death and destruction unparalleled in the history of America.[18]

Had they wished to, the Utah Mormons could have found reason to side with the South. In 1860, the winning Republican political campaign included a pledge to abolish polygamy, then an accepted practice in Utah. Utahans also fervently believed in states rights, a hallmark of the Confederacy. But they did not favor slavery. The 1860 census showed only nineteen slaves in the territory. Also, most Mormons hailed from Northern states and believed that God divinely inspired the United States, and its Constitution. So Utah determined to sit out the war.

Brigham Young vowed that Utah would send no troops to fight. In a July 4, 1861 speech, Apostle John Taylor summed it up: "Shall we join the North to fight against the South? No. Shall we join the South to fight against the North? As emphatically, no! Why? They have... brought it upon themselves, and we have no hand in the matter."[19]

Utah held a constitutional convention and elected a slate of state officers, with Brigham Young as governor. He would serve if and when Congress approved statehood.[20]

The 500 federal troops in Utah at the start of the war were relocated to other, threatened posts.

The Overland Mail route, the Pacific Coast's principal connection to the East, had been moved north to Utah from New Mexico, which had been invaded by the Confederates. The transcontinental telegraph line also passed through Utah. The federal government saw the Pacific Coast's only direct links with the rest of the nation threatened by Indians and in uncertain Mormon hands.

In April 1862, Brigham Young ordered a detachment of Utah's militia to escort an eastbound wagon train. That same month, at the request of Adjutant General Lorenzo Thomas, a 100-man cavalry company was mobilized to guard stage and telegraph lines in what now is southeast Wyoming until federal troops could be sent in.[21]

In October 1862, Colonel P. Edward Connor and 700 troopers of the Third California Volunteer Infantry Regiment were sent to Utah to secure the communications links for the Union. Connor and his men moved into a new post, called Fort Douglas, on a plateau above Salt Lake City, a position that permitted defense against the Indians. It also allowed the army to keep an eye on what was going on in town.

Connor, who later was promoted to brigadier general, desperately wanted to break the theocratic control of Utah by the Mormon Church. He railed continually against Young and the church leadership. He sponsored his own anti-church newspaper. He advocated non-Mormon immigration as a means of diluting the control of the church, and explored the territory's mineral resources in hopes of attracting non-Mormon immigrants.[22]

Lincoln defused the situation partially by firing the anti-church Territorial Governor Stephen S. Harding, his third appointee to the job. James Duane Doty, an Indian agent who enjoyed the confidence of the Utah leaders, was appointed in his place.[23]

Connor's superior, General Irvin McDowell, told Connor to worry about the Indians and to forget about reforming the Mormon Church. He wrote: "The object of troops being at this time in Utah is to protect the overland route and not to endeavor to correct the evil conduct, manifest as it is, of the inhabitants of that Territory...."[24] Friction between the military and the church authorities gradually eased.[25]

Indian troubles continued through the end of the war. To flesh out his units, Connor enlisted Confederate parolees, the so-called "Galvanized Yankees" who elected to join the Union Army to serve in the Indian country.[26]

There is no real evidence that Brigham Young and the church leaders ever seriously thought of proclaiming independence, of joining either the Confederacy or the Pacific Republic, or of allying with the Indians against the Union. Utah stayed out of the war. But the conflict between the civilian and military authorities in Utah justified concerns in the West.

THREAT FROM THE NORTH

There was concern that Great Britain would use the distraction of America's Civil War to take back the Oregon Territory that it gave up fifteen years earlier.

Some British officials were likewise concerned. They feared that with its military swollen to meet the challenge of the Confederacy, the

United States might overwhelm the few troops that Britain maintained in its North American possessions, and make British America a part of the United States.

Indeed, Secretary of State William H. Seward, a man who evinced little statesmanship in his early dealings with the Crown, publicly suggested at the start of the war that Canada ought to be brought into the United States. The jingoist *New York Herald* proposed a two-year truce between the United States and the Confederacy to allow the occupation of Canada, Jamaica, Cuba, and Central America.[27] Seward's injudicious statements turned considerable sentiment in Canada (which generally was pro-abolitionist before the war) against the North.

These concerns weren't totally unfounded. Scarcely fifty years before, the United States had fought the War of 1812 with England on American soil. Although he gave up his command early in the Civil War, the Army Chief of Staff, General Winfield Scott, made his spurs as a soldier while he was a brigadier general fighting the British during that war.

Early in 1862, President Lincoln appointed Allen Francis as the first U.S. consul in western British Canada. The current British Columbia was then two colonies, Vancouver Island with its capitol at Victoria, and mainland British Columbia with its capitol at New Westminster. Sir James Douglas of the Hudson's Bay Company was governor of both.

Francis set up office on April 14, 1862 in the former harbormaster's office on the waterfront in Victoria. His monthly reports to Secretary of State William Seward provide a riveting view of the progress of the war as viewed from the Canadian West.

Victoria was a remote posting for Francis. Mail came via San Francisco twice a month.[28] But Francis, in addition to his normal duties of looking after the needs of destitute U.S. merchant mariners and collecting impost duties for the U.S., also became the point man and military intelligence agent for the U.S. on the western end of America's vulnerable international border.

Francis was one of myriad consular agents appointed by Lincoln. As publishers of the *Illinois State Journal* at Springfield, he and his brother, Simeon Francis (the new U.S. Army paymaster at Fort Vancouver), were old friends of the new president.[29]

At the start of the war, British Columbia was host to hundreds of men from the Southern states who had flocked to the new gold fields of the Fraser River. Americans of varying political persuasion made up half the business community of Victoria. The resident Wells Fargo agent, a Southerner, made the first political statement of the secessionist element when he pulled down the American flag that flew over his business and substituted the Union Jack.[30]

Early in the war, Francis said he believed that the bulk of English citizens in Pacific Canada favored the Confederacy. A number, he said, openly rejoiced at early Confederate victories.[31]

Governor James Douglas wrote the Duke of Newcastle at the Colonial Office in December 1861, outlining a plan to invade the undefended Puget Sound and seize the Oregon Country north of the Columbia River. He believed American settlers would accept the invaders because they would provide protection against the Indians.[32] But Britain had already declared its desire to stand neutral.

Others weren't that certain. In an 1863 report to his superiors on the military defense of British America, Lieutenant Colonel W. F. D. Jervois recommended that in case of war with the United States, the western possessions be abandoned and British troops retreat to the more defensible East.[33]

Lieutenant John Adair, son of Oregon's former collector of customs and the first Oregon graduate of the U.S. Military Academy, left his duty station in Washington Territory and fled with his father to the gold fields of British Columbia. One newspaper claimed the Adairs intended to join in efforts for the Pacific Republic.

On November 13, 1862 the Prince of Wales came of age and the city of Victoria celebrated. Secessionists joined in the celebration by flying the Confederate flag on Victoria's principal street.

Fifty-odd resident Southern sympathizers formed a "Southern Association" and made their headquarters at J. S. Shepard's appropriately named Confederate Saloon.[34]

Lord Lyons, Britain's representative at Washington during the war, did much to keep relations between the U.S. and Great Britain on an even keel.[35] On November 8, 1862, the U.S. Navy breached international law by capturing two Confederate diplomats who were traveling to London aboard the British ship *Trent*. This caused a flurry of diplomatic notes. Great Britain dispatched additional troops to British America.[36] Lord Lyons' reports to London soothed official suspicions that the U.S. had territorial designs upon British North America.

Britain's realization that it had a military leviathan on its Canadian border was one of several factors that led to the Act of Confederation in 1867 that welded its separate possessions into the Dominion of Canada.

During the war, Britain had four naval vessels based at Esquimalt north of Victoria. They were the steam frigate *Topaze*, the survey ship *Hecate*, the gunboat *Grappler* and the gunboat *Forward*, which, although carried on Great Britain's list of ships, was not seaworthy.[37] Britain's total ground forces on the Pacific Coast were a company of Royal Marines in the San Juan Islands and a detachment of army engineers at Esquimalt.[38]

The U.S. had no navy ships stationed north of San Francisco.

Both Francis and General Alvord repeatedly pleaded for naval support. In retrospect, federal hand-wringing over the possibility of a British attempt to retake the Oregon country seems ludicrous. The U.S. had 2,400,000 men under arms at one time or another during the war while Britain's army in North America never numbered more than 17,000.[39]

In their personal dealings, the Americans and the British military got along famously. In 1845, while the U.S. and Britain were wrangling over who should own the Oregon Country, Britain sent the twelve-gun armed sloop *Modeste* to Fort Vancouver. It moored at the Hudson's Bay Company dock on the Columbia and stayed until the treaty settling the dispute was signed in 1846.

The American settlers welcomed the *Modeste*. The British and the Americans hosted each other at social functions. Best of all, the Crown sent in a barrel of silver dollars to be used to pay the officers and crew. In a day when the taxes of the Provisional Government were payable in wheat and debts were settled by a trading of due bills drawn on Hudson's Bay Company and the proprietors of the mill at the Willamette Falls, this was a godsend, giving cash-poor Oregon an infusion of real money.

At the start of the war, army headquarters in San Francisco stationed one of the Pacific Northwest's two companies of regular army infantry in the politically sensitive San Juan Islands. Through the war, the U.S.

Army and a company of British Marines maintained a presence on opposite ends of San Juan Island while diplomats waited until the end of the war to arbitrate whether the San Juan Islands were a part of Washington Territory or British America.

The U.S. presence (one company of regular army infantry) was located at what is known as American Camp. The semi-annual army manpower reports referred to it as "Camp Pickett" through 1864, long after its peacetime commander, Captain George Pickett, resigned, joined the Confederacy, and suffered historic ignominy by leading the South's suicidal charge at the battle of Gettysburg. Pickett superintended the removal of clapboard buildings from Fort Bellingham, abandoned at the start of the war, to the San Juan Islands installation.

Britain and the U.S. argued whether the boundary agreed to in 1846 lay to the north or the south of the San Juan Island group, which left the San Juans and its British, American and native inhabitants in a political no-man's land. A joint occupation agreement was signed March 13, 1860 and it continued in force until 1871 when Kaiser Wilhelm of Germany, acting as arbitrator, awarded the San Juans to the United States.

The two major conflicts were over the sale of liquor to Indians (prohibited by the laws of both countries) and title to land. The Hudson's Bay Company claimed a twenty-acre parcel of land in the islands, as did two competing American settlers.

While these worthies argued over whose set of laws applied, other settlers took advantage of the confusion by paying taxes to neither Washington Territory nor Canada. And the drinking community was awash with untaxed whisky.[40]

Captain Lyman Bissell, commander of the U.S. troops, and his British counterpart, Captain George Bazalgette, got along well.[41] On July 4, 1863, the English and American garrisons on San Juan Island held a track meet and a joint banquet to celebrate Independence Day. Later in the summer, 100 men and women from Victoria paid a social call on both posts and a huge picnic was held.

The unsettled issue of land title resulted in an attempted prosecution for trespass of a British citizen in the Washington Territory Justice Court. The defendant refused to appear. A brief trial, conducted in a barroom while spectators drank and played cards, resulted in an in absentia conviction of the absent Briton.

Major General Irvin McDowell, accompanied by Territorial Governor William Pickering, traveled to the San Juans to resolve the dispute. Pickering agreed to appoint no more justices of the peace there. McDowell told his officers to enforce the laws against American citizens and let the British Marines take care of their people.

CONFEDERATE ACTIVITY IN EASTERN CANADA

The Confederacy plotted a series of diversionary attacks on the North from Quebec and Ontario. All but one failed.[42] But the great distress and distraction that resulted from those attempts washed over into the Pacific Northwest.

Jacob Thompson, who had served as Secretary of the Interior in the Buchanan administration, was the key player in the Canada operations of the Confederacy. In April 1864, armed with a letter from Jefferson Davis giving him authority to take such actions "as shall seem most likely to the furtherance of the interests of the Confederate States of America," Thompson and C. C. Clay, an ex-senator from Alabama, headed for Toronto, carrying $600,000 in Confederate funds to finance their operations.[43]

Thompson financed an insurrectionist with the melodious name of Minor Major, who proposed to (and apparently did) sink steamboats on the Mississippi. Thompson also advanced funds to a group of would-be arsonists who proposed to burn Cincinnati, but never did. He bankrolled Charles H. Cole, who promised to capture and sink the U.S.S. Michigan, the only Union gunboat on Lake Erie. Cole dispatched a crew of twenty-odd men armed with a trunk full of revolvers who high-jacked the lakes steamer Philo Parsons, sank another steamer, the Island Queen, and then gave up the effort. Thompson also contracted with a Colonel Martin to set a series of fires in New York City. Nothing happened there, either.

In November 1864 Thompson bought—for twice its value— the steamer Georgiana, apparently to convert it into a Confederate gunboat. His plans were discovered and foiled.[44]

He also concocted two plans to invade Chicago from Canada, and to free and arm Confederate prisoners held in the North's infamous prison at Camp Douglas.

The one Confederate thrust that accomplished something was done without Thompson's participation or knowledge. With twenty-five Confederate soldiers (most of them escaped prisoners) Lieutenant Bennett H. Young rode across the international border and robbed three banks in St. Albans, Vermont. One man was killed, four were wounded and $15,000 was taken.[45]

Overall in Canada, sentiment was strong for the Union. An estimated 48,000 Canadians crossed over the line to serve in the Union Army.

CONFEDERATE ACTIVITY IN BRITISH COLUMBIA

Confederate activity in British Columbia never got much beyond the shouting and flag-waving stage. Consul Francis recruited a cadre of faithful Unionists who infiltrated the ranks of the secessionists and reported their secrets. On February 14, 1863, Francis reported that a Confederate agent named Manley was in Victoria negotiating for the purchase of an eight-gun English steamer, the *Thames*, to be outfitted as a privateer.[46]

The same letter reported a rumored plan to seize the U.S. Revenue Cutter *Shubrick*, on one of its periodic mail calls at Victoria. Francis told his suspicions to one Lieutenant Selden, the *Shubrick*'s second in command, known to be a firm Unionist. While the ship's captain and most of the crew were ashore, Selden and six members of the crew cast off and returned to Port Townsend.

Author David William Higgins wrote that he was told by John Jeffreys, a leader of secessionists in British Columbia, that Jeffreys held a letter of marque from the Confederacy and intended to capture the *Shubrick* and use it as a privateer to capture an American gold ship.[47] In response to this rumored take-over plan, the *Saginaw* visited Victoria and showed the flag in April 1863. The *Naragansett* paid a visit in 1864. These were the only two ventures by the U.S. Navy north of San Francisco during the war.

As 1865 began, the Southerners in British Columbia sensed the approaching defeat of the South. In February, Consul Francis reported that the local Confederates had organized to emigrate to the north of Mexico. Some, he said, already had left by ship via San Francisco for a new life in Mexico.[48]

Threat from Mexico

No one really believed that Mexico would try to take back the vast territories it lost to the United States in the 1846-48 Mexican war. However, things were a mess in Mexico. France had invaded and set up a puppet government. A leading Confederate secessionist was promoting France's attempt to make a colony out of the Sonora, on the southern border of Arizona and New Mexico.[49] A nervous U.S. military feared that France might invade the Southwest.[50]

This prompted a continuing competition between the Pacific Northwest, California, and the Southwest for scarce men, equipment, and navy ships. As always, the Pacific Northwest lost.

General Henry Sibley's failed attempt to take New Mexico and what later became Arizona for the South was launched in part upon the hope that Mexican President Benito Juarez could be convinced to cede some of Mexico's northern states to the Confederacy.[51]

When a California-built steamer, the *Colon*, was sold to the government of Peru, tensions were further heightened. Fearful of offending the French, President Lincoln stopped the export of ships or war-related marine supplies from the U.S. and especially from the West Coast. Built in San Francisco, the *Colon* was considered war material and was held in port six months, until March 1865 when it finally was released to its Peruvian buyers.[52]

In April 1864, President Juarez sent his general, Placido Vega, to San Francisco to purchase arms and other military supplies for the Republican forces at Mazatlan. Vega visited with Thomas Brown, U.S. Treasury agent at San Francisco and others, received clearances, then loaded part of his supplies aboard a ship headed for the Mexican port.

Major General Irvin McDowell, commander of the Department of the Pacific, learned of this after the ship sailed. He ordered the ship seized and returned its cargo to storage at the Benecia arsenal. Another stockpile of arms and ammunition was seized at Half Moon Bay near San Francisco. Vega howled that he had paid for the goods and their shipment and had done what he thought was necessary to effect their export. McDowell stuck by his orders.[53]

There was considerable sentiment in southern California to stay out of the war. Some proposed separating California from San Luis Obispo to the south into a separate state to be called Central California.

In January 1859 the California Legislature passed a memorial to Congress asking for the division. A referendum in the southern counties approved the plan by a two-thirds vote, but Congress rejected the idea.[54]

Meanwhile, France wanted Mexico to cede to it the state of Sonora, which France would hold as a colony. With its extensive and valuable gold deposits, Sonora was a prize.[55]

The commander of the Department of the Pacific, General George Wright, realized this and wrote to Washington in March 1864:

> With Sonora, a State on our Southern border, and in close proximity to one of our finest harbors on this coast, in possession of a foreign Government, which has given the most unmistakable evidence of its sympathy with the rebellion, what might we expect but a bold attempt to seize the glittering prize of California, the bright occidental star of our Union.[56]

William M. Gwin, a former U.S. senator from California and early supporter of an independent Pacific Republic, now appeared as an agent of France's Emperor Napoleon III. Gwin went to France in 1863 and worked for French recognition of the Confederacy. He convinced the Emperor of a scheme to colonize Sonora for France. A fair hand at international politics, Napoleon III knew what Sonora's gold deposits would do for his embarrassed national treasury. He also knew that the Austrian Archduke Ferdinand Maxmilian had been denied any role in the Austrian imperial government by his brother, Emperor Francis Joseph. Napoleon III wanted to found a Mexican empire. Maximilian, who had some government reform ideas of his own that he wanted to try out, was persuaded to accept the crown as Emperor Maximilian of Mexico. He sailed for Mexico with his wife Carlotta in 1864.

Gwin went to Sonora but accomplished little because of the chaotic political and economic conditions there. Yet his presence there was noticed in the North. Rumors spread that he was organizing rebels for raids over the border into California like the Confederate guerilla leader William Quantrill was in the East.

General U.S. Grant, in a letter to McDowell of January 5, 1865, warned that Gwin might invade. He directed McDowell to defend such an attack, and if attacked, to counterattack into Mexico. If such was the case, Grant said that McDowell should seize and hold part of the Mexican territory, which would leave the U.S. in a position of strength come treaty time.[57]

McDowell was not the only one concerned about the perceived French threat on the southern boundaries. On March 17, 1865, on the eve of his departure from command of the Military District of Oregon, General Alvord wrote his headquarters in Washington to warn again of the rebel underground he believed was stockpiling weapons and waiting to rise up against the Union in Oregon. He wrote, "I am satisfied they hope and expect complications on the Southern Coast of California, anxious to embroil us in collision with the French Government."[58]

Chapter 12 notes

1 Bancroft, *History of Washington, Idaho and Montana* (San Francisco, The History Company, 1890), 221.

2 Scott, *History of the Oregon Country,* 5:61.

3 The ship was actually named the *Joseph Lane,* but was referred almost uniformly as the *Joe Lane.*

4 McCurdy, James G., *By Juan de Fuca's Strait,* (Portland, Or., Binfords & Mort, 1937) 69.

5 Wright, E.R., *Lewis & Dryden's Marine History of the Pacific Northwest*, Portland, Or., Lewis & Dryden Printing Co. 1895), 84.

6 Salmon P. Chase Letters, quoted in "Lincoln-Time Letters," *Pacific Northwest Quarterly*, 16: 269.

7 Bancroft, *History of Washington, Idaho and Montana*, 220-21.

8 W.O.R., Series 1, Vol. 50, Pt. 2, 70-73.

9 Field, Virgil F., *The Official History of the Washington National Guard*, (Tacoma, Wash., Washington Military Department, 1961), I:200. "Lincoln-Time Letters," supra.

10 W.O.R., Series 1, Vol. 50, Pt. 2, 70-73.

11 Ibid., 117.

12 Ibid., 70-73.

13 McCurdy, James G., *By Juan de Fuca's Strait,* (Portland, Or., Binfords and Mort, 1937) 57.

14 Ibid., 54-57.

15 "Lincoln-Time Letters," 266.

16 Scott, *History of the Oregon Country*, 61.

17 Campbell, Patricia, *With Pride in Heritage; History of Jefferson County* (Port Townsend, Wash., Jefferson County Historical Society, 1966), 119.

18 Waters, Gary L., *The Western Territories in the Civil War*, (Manhattan, Kan., Sunflower University Press, 1971),45-46.

19 Ibid., 47.

20 Ibid., 48.

21 Colton, Ray C., *The Civil War Years in the Western Territories*, (Norman, Okla., University of Oklahoma Press, 1959), 161-62.

22 Josephy, *The Civil War in the American West*, 262-63; Edwards, "The Department of the Pacific," 247-56.

23 Josephy, *The Civil War in the American West*, 262.

24 W.O.R., Series 1, Vol. 50, Pt. 2, 909-10.

25 Edwards, "The Department of the Pacific," 187-95.
26 Athearn, Robert G., "West of Appomatox," *Montana, The Magazine of Western History*, 12:2, (Spring 1982), 9.
27 Winks, Robin W., The *Civil War Years: Canada and the United States,* (Montreal, McGill University Press, 4th Ed., 1998), 57.
28 Consulate of the United States, Victoria, Vancouver Island, Correspondence Files, 1861-1865, National Archives Branch, Seattle, Wash.
29 McLarney, Donald F., "The American Civil War in Victoria, Vancouver Island Colony," mss, (Des Moines, Wash., Highline Community College, 1972), 8.
30 Winks, *The Civil War Years*, 158.
31 Consulate of the United States, Victoria, Vancouver Island, supra.
32 Governor James Douglas to the Duke of Newcastle, December 28, 1861, Vancouver Dispatches, mss., Provincial Archives, Victoria, B.C., quoted in McLarney, Donald F., "The American Civil War in Victoria, Vancouver Island Colony," mss., 4.
33 Winks, *The Civil War Years*, 283.
34 W.O.R., Series 1, Vol. 50, Pt. 2, 1061.
35 Gallas, Stanley, "Lord Lyon and the Civil War, 1859-1864: A British Perspective," (PhD diss., University of Illinois at Chicago, 1992).
36 Winks, *The Civil War Years*, 73.
37 Gilbert, Benjamin Franklin, "Naval Operations in the Pacific, 1861-1866," (PhD diss., University of California, 1951), 67-68.
38 Winks, *The Civil War Years*, 158.
39 In 1860 Britain had 4,300 troops in British America. By 1861 there were 7,000. In 1862 there were 17,000 and by spring 1865 there were 8,200. Winks, Robin W., *The Civil War Years; Canada and the United States* (Montreal, McGill University Press, 4th Ed., 1998), 281.
40 Ibid., 281.
41 Field, *The Official History of the Washington National Guard*, 1:216-20.
42 W.O.R., Series 1, Vol. 50, Pt. 1, 435.
43 Some say it was as much as $3,000,000, but in any event it was a lot of money for the time.
44 Schweninger, Joseph Michael, "'A Lingering War Must Be Prevented': The Defense of the Northern Frontier, 1812-1871," (PhD diss., Ohio State University, 1998).
45 Bovey, Wilfrid, "Confederate Agents in Canada During the American Civil War," *The Canadian Historical Review, New Series*, 2(1921): 46-57.
46 McLarney, Donald F., "The American Civil War in Victoria, Vancouver Island Colony," 24-28.
47 Higgins, David Williams, "The Mystic Spring: And other Tales of Western Life," 1908, quoted in Gilbert, Benjamin Franklin, *Naval Operations in the Pacific,* 76-78.
48 Consulate of the United States, Victoria, Vancouver Island, supra.
49 Hunt, *The Army of the Pacific*, 304-5.
50 Edwards, "The Department of the Pacific," 265.
51 W.O.R., Series 1, Vol. 50, Pt. 1, 1012-13.
52 Hunt, *The Army of the Pacific*, 317-18.
53 Ibid., 315-317.
54 Wang, "The Mythical Confederate Plot in Southern California," 14.
55 Dustin, Charles Mail, "The Knights of the Golden Circle," *Pacific Monthly Magazine*, November 1911, 498.
56 W.O.R., Series 1, Vol. 50, Pt. 2, 788-89.
57 Edwards, "The Department of the Pacific," 265.
58 U.S. Army, District of Oregon, Correspondence book, National Archives, Washington, D.C., 274-75.

Chapter 13

THE THREAT FROM THE SEA

L ong before the Oregon Country became a part of the United States, there was agitation to protect the coast—and particularly the Columbia River—against invasion from the sea. As times changed, the reasons for concern also changed. But the demand for fortifications and warships was constant.

Several theories developed about why fortification was necessary:

1. At a time when both the United States and Great Britain laid claim to the Oregon Country, if the U.S. built forts at the mouth of the Columbia it would help secure the U.S. claim to the Oregon Country.

2. It would keep Great Britain, which ceded title to the lands south of the forty-ninth parallel in 1846, from taking back what became known as the Pacific Northwest.

3. It would guard against a fear that with the U.S. involved with the Civil War in the East, foreign powers might try to invade to seize control of the Oregon Country and its valuable gold deposits.

4. It would guard against invasion by Confederate privateers, who, in fact, never threatened the Oregon-Washington Coast and made themselves felt in the Northern Pacific only after the war ended.

5. The United States had decided it should defend all of its principal harbors. This decision had marginal military merit after the end of the Civil War and continued until the last of

151

the coastal forts were decommissioned at the end of World War II.

Representative John Floyd of Virginia made the first effort to establish a fort on the Pacific Northwest's mightiest waterway. In 1820, and again in 1821, 1824, 1827, and 1828 he agitated in Congress to occupy the Oregon Territory and establish a fort at the mouth of the Columbia River. After a ten-year lull, Congress was asked repeatedly from 1838 on to erect and man the fort.[1]

In the aftermath of the Whitman massacre, in the winter of 1847-48, beleaguered Oregonians sent Joe Meek and J. Quinn Thornton to Washington, D.C. to plead for territorial status for Oregon. They also asked for a ship of war on the Columbia River.[2]

These early efforts to establish a military presence on the Columbia were aimed at securing the Oregon Country from Britain. However, when the U.S. and Britain entered into the joint occupation agreement in 1818 and renewed it in 1827, this dampened the zeal of those who wanted to use the army to stake a claim to the Oregon Country. In 1842 Engineer Colonel Joseph G. Totten recommended erection of a fort. In 1855 Secretary of War Jefferson Davis urged fortification of the Columbia.

Britain, nervous about losing its claim to the Oregon country, sent two British officers, incognito, to examine the mouth of the river. They recommended that Britain build three batteries of ten guns at Cape Disappointment at the north headlands of the river's entrance, a six-gun battery and blockhouse at Point Adams to the south, and additional fortifications at Tongue Point, three miles upstream from Astoria. Their report was dated at Fort Vancouver June 16, 1846, the day after Britain signed the treaty surrendering forever its claim to the Oregon country.[3]

PROTECTING THE COLUMBIA RIVER

On February 26, 1852, President Millard Fillmore signed an executive order that withdrew land at Point Adams and Cape Disappointment from settlement and made each a military reservation.[4] Thereafter, efforts to build a fort at the mouth of the Columbia were aimed not at claiming the Oregon Country for the United States, but at keeping Britain from taking it away.

152

There was arguable reason for this concern. The Oregon gold rush, starting in the 1850s, had made Portland Oregon's major metropolitan center. In September 1860, Colonel George Wright, then commander of the Department of Oregon, plaintively wrote General Winfield Scott, the army's commanding general, noting that the shoreline frontier was without any defense.

> [O]ur main artery, the great Columbia river, navigable for steamships one hundred and fifty miles from its mouth, with many thriving towns on its banks, the military post of Fort Vancouver, the arsenal, and the beautiful city of Portland, at the head of steamship navigation, on the Willamette, all are at the mercy of a single hostile steamer. The state of things demands the immediate and serious attention of the government.[5]

Nine months later, after the start of the war, Wright wrote his departmental commander:

> At this moment a single hostile steamer could enter the Columbia River and lay waste all the settlements to the Cascades, 150 miles, as well as the large and flourishing city of Portland,[6] twelve miles up the Willamette. Even this post and the ordnance depot are not prepared for defense against heavy guns.[7]

The start of the war finally triggered congressional action. Oregon's Senator James Nesmith was newly elected and a member of the Senate Military Affairs and Militia Committee. He got $100,000 included in the military appropriation bill passed February 20, 1862 for use in fortification of the mouth of the Columbia "if in the judgment of the President the same shall be advisable."[8]

President Lincoln already was on record in favor of the development of new coastal forts. In December 1861 Secretary of State William Seward wrote the governors of the Pacific Coast. He asked the states to help put all harbors in a "condition of complete defense." He promised the states to help finance the cost of new forts. He said the federal government would reimburse them.

Oregon's legislature took no action.[9]

When General Benjamin Alvord assumed command of the now-District of Oregon in July 1862, he almost immediately started agitating for defense of the Columbia. He asked General James W. Ripley, Chief of Ordnance, for fifty rifled cannon. Pointedly commenting that Britain had "several war vessels" constantly stationed at Esquimalt Harbor on Vancouver Island, Alvord wrote Secretary of the Navy Gideon Wells asking for two "iron clad vessel(s) of the character of the *Monitor*," one for the mouth of the Columbia River and the other for Puget Sound.[10]

Lieutenant George H. Elliot was sent to locate the forts. He recommended two forts, one at Cape Disappointment and the other two miles above Point Adams on the Oregon side of the river.

Folks in the Pacific Northwest—and in Washington, D.C.—were getting nervous about the defense of the Columbia River. And things were happening to justify this apprehension. At the start of the war the U.S. Navy had only six ships in its Pacific Squadron, headquartered at Mare Island in San Francisco Bay. Two of them were sailing vessels of indifferent tactical value. Two more ships finally were added in 1863.[11] These ships were responsible for protecting American interests throughout the Pacific from the Pacific Northwest Coast to China.

The Pacific Squadron's primary concern was protecting the five passenger and freight steamers of the Pacific Steam Ship Company that carried gold mined from the western gold fields to Panama for transshipment to the east.[12] Loss of these ships would be a serious blow to the U.S. economy.

As the war progressed, other nations moved their fleets into the Pacific. France's ships backed its occupation of some Mexican Pacific Coast ports. Spain made an abortive effort to regain its former colonies in South America. Seizing on the murders of expatriate Spanish national farm workers in Peru, Spain sent a fleet of warships into the Pacific and seized the guano-rich Chincha Islands offshore Pisco, Peru, and precipitated intermittent war activities against Peru and its ally, Chile.[13] Britain moved its nine warships from the China Sea and the Indian Ocean into the Pacific.

The French fleet paid a courtesy call to San Francisco. Admiral Alexander A. Popov, worried that the revolt of Poland might explode into a full-out war, kept Russia's Pacific fleet at anchor in San Francisco harbor from September 1863 to August 1864.[14]

These visits made San Francisco's social set and waterfront saloon-keepers happy, but it worried the army.

General McDowell reported ruefully to his superiors that he possessed not a single gun "fixed or afloat, bearing or that can be brought to bear on" the Russian, English and French warships that were scattered over the harbor.[15]

PRIVATEERS

One of Confederate President Jefferson Davis' first acts was to propose that the Confederacy contract out its naval activities to the private sector, just as the United States and its predecessor colonies did during the Revolutionary War and the War of 1812. The Confederacy issued commissions to privately owned ships that made them and their crews, essentially, a part of the Confederate navy.[16]

A vessel operating as a Confederate privateer under a letter of marque was authorized to seize U.S. flag vessels, take them to a Confederate or neutral port, and after proper forfeiture proceedings, have them sold. The owners of the privateer and the crew were to get the lion's share of the proceeds.[17] The Confederacy also agreed to pay a lump sum to the owner and crew for the sinking of any U.S. war vessel. Possession of a letter of marque meant that, if captured, the master and crew of a privateer were to be treated as prisoners of war and not as pirates.

The Treaty of Paris of 1856 made the use of privateers illegal. But the U.S. did not sign that treaty, and the Confederacy didn't exist at the time. So it really did not apply. Southern ship owners muscled cannon aboard their ships and set out to hunt down and capture U.S. flag vessels.

Panic gripped the U.S. merchant fleet. Insurance rates covering cargo in U.S. merchant vessels skyrocketed.

Some Union vessels were captured. But generally, privateers were not that successful. The system worked only if a profit could be made. In order to make a profit, the captured ships had to be sailed to a neutral foreign port or a Confederate port and sold there. British ports, among others, refused entry to the captured ships.

There were at least three outright attempts to sail Confederate privateers in the Pacific.[18] At least two were aimed at capturing treasure ships sailing out of San Francisco. All failed.[19]

In March 1863, Asbury Harpending, a Kentuckian living in California, and Ridgeley Greathouse, a secessionist banker from

Yreka, California, obtained a letter of marque, bought, armed and manned the ninety-ton schooner *J. M. Chapman,* then in San Francisco harbor.[20]

But it is hard to keep a secret. With Greathouse as the captain, they attempted to leave the pier under cover of darkness. It was low tide. The vessel ran aground. The next morning they tried again. The wind died and two boat loads of sailors from the U.S. sloop-of-war *Cyane* anchored nearby boarded the *Chapman.* Its crew was captured. Three of the ringleaders, Greathouse, Harpending, and Alfred Rubery, were imprisoned but later freed, Rubery by pardon, the other two as a part of a general act of amnesty.[21]

A year later, Thomas Egerton Hogg, who later became famous as the organizer of the spectacular and expensive failure, The Yaquina Bay and Willamette Rail Road Company which attempted to build railroad over Oregon's Santiam Pass,[22] organized a plan to seize the Panama Railroad Company steamer *Salvador* on its run from Panama to San Francisco. Again, someone talked. Hogg and his six accomplices boarded the *Salvador* at Panama. When the ship reached international waters, the Confederates were seized. Their captors found uniforms, firearms, a Confederate flag and a letter of instructions from Stephen Mallory, the Confederate Secretary of the Navy, in their luggage.[23] Hogg and his crew were tried by a military commission and ordered hanged. General Irwin McDowell commuted Hogg's sentence to life in prison and his accomplices to a term of ten years. All were freed as a part of a general amnesty given Confederate prisoners in May 1868.

On January 16, 1865, the *Oregon Statesman* at Salem reported that police and "two secret detectives" in San Francisco had arrested a Michael Hayes who bore a letter of marque from the Confederacy, thwarting his plan to purchase and arm a small schooner as a raider.

Editor Asahel Bush thundered:

> Death would be too merciful a penalty for the wretch who could seek to aid the rebel cause and enrich himself by disturbing the tranquility of this coast and destroying the property of peaceful citizens....
>
> A small vessel armed with a single gun, and manned by a pirate crew, afloat on the waters of the Pacific, would make us feel as we never have the effects of this war.[24]

No account of Michael Hayes and his alleged attempt at privateering appears in the published consolidated army and navy records published after the war.

Fearful of additional high-jacking efforts, General McDowell, in July 1864, ordered the screening of all passengers on American Pacific Coast vessels. Each passenger was required to turn over any weapons to an officer of the ship and all hand luggage was searched for weapons. The steamers' officers were required to be armed.[25] Toward the end of the war, passengers arriving at San Francisco were screened for passports. If they had none, they were refused entry. Passengers direct from New York and from Oregon were admitted without screening. Off Cape Disappointment on the Washington Territory coast, officers boarded ships bound from Victoria to U.S. ports to check passports of passengers.[26]

BUILDING THE FORTS

Lieutenant George Elliott, the engineer charged with locating the site of the Columbia River forts, said that the only feasible site for cannon at Fort Cape Disappointment was about 200 feet above sea level and almost directly above the main shipping channel, which came close to the north shore. Fort Stevens was named after General Isaac Ingalls Stevens, former Washington Territory governor killed at the Battle of Chantilly September 1, 1862. It was to be placed on the south side of the entrance.

Elliott recommended rifled cannon for Cape Disappointment.

The army's basic artillery piece at the time was a cannon similar in design and operation to those used during the War of 1812. It was a muzzle-loader and a smoothbore. It fired round shot and was called a Rodman.

But round shot in a smoothbore barrel didn't work well while pointed downhill.[27] The shot would roll out, or at best lose both force and accuracy in firing. A newer design, the Parrott gun, had a rifled bore. Named after its inventor, Robert Parrott of the West Point foundry in New York, the Parrott gun was more difficult to manufacture, and in short supply.

The $100,000 appropriated in 1862[28] didn't get the Columbia River forts much past the planning stage, so on February 20, 1863, Congress appropriated another $200,000 for defense of both the

Columbia and Puget Sound.[29] One month later the Chief of Engineers ordered Lieutenant Colonel Rene DeRussy, the engineering officer for the Pacific Coast, to begin construction.

On July 13, 1863, now-Captain George Elliott arrived to follow up on his earlier work and superintend the construction at Cape Disappointment. Things went slowly. Local help was hard to find because many workmen had gone to the newly opened gold fields in eastern Washington and Idaho. Those who remained wouldn't work for what Elliott could pay.

Elliott finally raised the pay. The army helped by sending a handful of court-martialed soldiers under sentence of confinement to work out their sentences at Cape Disappointment.[30] One battery of five guns, called the Tower Battery or Lighthouse Battery, bracketed the Cape Disappointment lighthouse. Another was slightly inland.

On April 5, 1864 General Alvord ordered Captain William H. Jordan and his Company A, Ninth U.S. Infantry from Fort Vancouver to man and complete Fort Cape Disappointment.[31] [32]

By November 1864 Fort Cape Disappointment was in business. But with its smoothbore cannon and the front-pintle carriages on which they were mounted, the cannon were designed to point out, not down. The main channel of the Columbia ran below the bluff on which the guns were mounted, which gave the infantry-turned-artillerymen cannon that could be brought to bear only as the enemy ships approached the bar, or long after they left it.[33]

Construction of Fort Stevens started in July 1863, but things went more slowly than at Cape Disappointment.

Fort Stevens was a so-called Star Fort—a nine-sided fortress.[34] It was built so that guns could be brought to bear upon vessels in the south channel, and also allow sweeping fire to be directed sideways at any foot troops that might try to mount its walls. Designed to hold forty-three cannon, Fort Stevens was surrounded by a ditch that held up to three feet of water part of the time. Only twenty-six guns were ever mounted.

Earlier U.S.-built forts were of masonry construction, but the damage done to the brand-new Fort Sumter in Charleston Harbor at the start of the war taught the army that exploding shells could shatter brittle walls of brick and stone.[35]

158

Fort Stevens was designed as an earthen structure. The theory was that an incoming shell would bury itself in the twenty-foot tall mound of earth in front of the gun emplacements, and the shock of the explosion would be absorbed by the soil. Unfortunately, Fort Stevens was built where there wasn't much soil. So sand was taken from the surrounding ditch and mounded to form the walls of the fort. The manmade sand dunes were tied together by huge timbers and covered with a thick layer of dirt hauled in from off site.[36]

Captain Elliott also had charge of the construction of Fort Stevens and suffered the same manpower problems as at Cape Disappointment. It took his crew nearly a month to clear the pile of huge, fallen trees that blanketed the site. By November 1864, Elliott's crews had finished digging the ditch around the earthwork and had completed gun platforms for seventeen cannon. The gun platforms were of wooden timber and plank laid on top of the sand.[37]

In April 1865 the engineers proclaimed their work at Fort Stevens done. The walls, four support buildings, and twenty-nine gun platforms were completed. Eight smoothbore cannon with barbette carriages were on hand, but unmounted. On July 4, 1865, a company of the Eighth California Volunteer Infantry raised the flag and declared Fort Stevens ready to defend the Columbia.

By then the war was over.[38]

But the end of the war did not mean the end of worry to those in the Pacific Northwest.

C.S.S. SHENANDOAH

One of the Confederacy's most successful military ventures started late and had its greatest success after the Civil War had ended. It also caused great apprehension in the Pacific Northwest, which feared that it might become a target.

Confederate agents in London bought the *Sea King*, a British merchant ship powered both by sail and steam, in October, 1864. It was sent to a remote corner of the Spanish Madeira Islands where it was renamed the *C.S.S. Shenandoah,* outfitted as a cruiser and sent by the Confederacy to raise havoc with the United States merchant fleet in the Pacific. In eight short months on a voyage through the South Atlantic, around Cape Horn and through the south Indian Ocean and the Pacific, the *Shenandoah* captured thirty-eight American flag vessels, sank thirty-four of them and paroled four to carry prisoners. The value of the ships and their cargo was estimated at $1,361,583. It also captured 1,033 American crewmen and sent a number of U.S. warships on a world-wide chase.[39]

The *Shenandoah*, by then in the Bering Sea and months from its last civilized port of Melbourne, Australia, fired the last shot of the Civil War on June 22, 1865, seven weeks after General Dick Taylor, in Alabama, surrendered the last Confederate army.[40]

The day-to-day events of this classic voyage are recounted in a lyric, forty-seven-page report written at the close of the voyage by its Captain, James Waddell, a six-foot one-inch, 200-pound ex-U.S. Navy officer from North Carolina.[41]

On April 13, 1865, the *Shenandoah* left its last port of call, the South Pacific island of Ponape, and sailed north to find and sink the American whaling fleet.

The *Shenandoah* sailed through the Russian Sea of Okhotsk, then north of the Aleutians into the Bering Sea in search of the American whaling fleet. Between June 22 and 28, 1865, the *Shenandoah* captured and sank or paroled twenty-four American ships.

Then the ship turned south.

The privateers decided to capture the treasure ships that carried gold from San Francisco to the Isthmus of Panama for reshipment to the eastern states.

On August 2, 1865, the *Shenandoah* was west of the southern tip of Baja California. The sails of the British bark, the *Barracouta,* were spotted thirteen days out of San Francisco. Waddell order a cannon fired. He sent his sailing master to board her and inquire of the progress of the war. The conversation was recorded as this:

"What is the news of the war?"
"What war?"
"The war between the United States and the Confederate States."
"Why, the war has been over since April. What ship is that?"
"The Confederate steamer *Shenandoah*."
"Good God almighty. Every navy in the world is after you."[42]

The *Barracouta*'s captain brought out the San Francisco newspapers, which told of the end of the war. The *Shenandoah*'s crew rowed silently back to their ship. Waddell ordered the cannon dismounted and stowed below.

After some debate with his officers and over the protests of a number of the crew, Waddell ordered the *Shenandoah* on a two-month voyage around Cape Horn and up the Atlantic to Liverpool.

On November 6, 1865 Waddell entered the Mersey River at Liverpool and surrendered the ship and its crew to the commander of the British Warship *Donegal*.[43]

After some delay, the Admiralty set the crew free. The Confederacy's naval agent in London, James A. Bulloch, who originally engineered the purchase and outfitting of the *Shenandoah,* still had some of the Confederate government's funds on hand. He used them to pay the *Shenandoah's* officers and crew part of the wages due them.

AFTER THE WAR

The *Shenandoah's* Captain, James Waddell, returned to his family in Annapolis. He became a ship's captain for the British-owned Pacific Mail Line. In 1877 his ship struck an uncharted rock along the Mexican Coast and sank. Waddell then became commander of the Maryland State fleet policing the state's oyster beds. He died in 1886.[44]

Fort Stevens and Fort Cape Disappointment remained active army installations after the Civil War and were manned until the end of World War II, with the exception of the period 1884-1898 when Fort Stevens was placed on inactive status and its troops withdrawn.[45]

In March 1875, Fort Cape Disappointment was renamed Fort Canby after General Edward R. S. Canby, killed in the Modoc Indian War April 11, 1873.

The original Civil War cannon were removed from the two forts and replaced between 1887 and 1904 with breech-loading rifled cannon in concrete emplacements.

A third fort, Fort Columbia, was built across the river and upstream from Fort Stevens. It was in service from 1898 to 1945.

All three fort sites are now state parks.

Chapter 13 notes

1 Hanft, Marshall, *Fort Stevens, Oregon's Defender at the River of the West* (Salem, Or., Oregon State Parks and Recreation Branch, 1980) 4-9.

2 Tobie, *No Man Like Joe,* 148.

3 Hanft, *Fort Stevens,* 17-18.

4 Ibid., 21, 27.

5 Ibid, 9.

6 At the most recent census in 1860, what Wright described as the "large and flourishing city of Portland" had a population of 2,874. University of Oregon, Bureau of Population Research and Service, *Population of Oregon Cities, Counties and Metropolitan Areas, 1850 to 1957,* Information Bulletin No. 106, April 1958.

7 Hanft, *Fort Stevens,* 2-3.

8 Ibid., 10-11.

9 Hagemann, *Lincoln and Oregon,* 48-49.

10 Field, *The Official History of the Washington National Guard,* 1:202.

11 Hunt, *The Army of the Pacific,* 301-302.

12 Gilbert, "Naval Operations in the Pacific, 1861-1866," 148-70.

13 Guano, the accumulated droppings of sea birds, was a valuable ingredient in the manufacture of gunpowder.

14 Gilbert, "Naval Operations in the Pacific, 1861-1866," 171-95.

15 W.O.R., Ser. 1, Vol. 50, Pt. 2, 929-30.

16 Robinson, William Morrison, Jr., *The Confederate Privateers* (New Haven, Conn., Yale University Press, 1928) 1, 2, 18-19, 25-26, 321, 327.

17 Union sailors also got a share of the proceeds from the sale of Confederate ships caught smuggling goods. Lt. Roswell Lamson, Oregon's first Naval Academy graduate, wrote in 1864 that he expected to receive $3,000 or $4,000 from the condemnation and sale of the rebel steamer *Little Ada,* captured while smuggling lead and drugs from Bermuda to South Carolina. McPherson, James M. and McPherson, Patricia R., *Lamson of the Gettysburg, The Civil War Letters of Lt. Roswell H. Lamson, U.S. Navy* (New York, Oxford University Press, 1997) 193.

18 Although Confederate privateers were numerous on the East and Gulf coasts, there were hardly any in the Pacific. Confederate President Jefferson Davis insisted upon hewing strictly to the statute that created the Confederate privateer fleet. No letter of marque could be issued unless the applicant had his ship in hand. With the ship in the Pacific and President Davis in Virginia, this made it difficult to get a commission. Toward the end of the war, some letters of marque were issued in blank, which made it possible for at least two of the three attempts known.

19 Plans were laid twice in British Columbia to outfit privateers. One was the proposed capture of the U.S. Revenue Cutter *Shubrick.* The other was a proposal to purchase and outfit of the steamer *Fusi Yama* in 1863. Neither got beyond the talking stage.

20 Edwards, "The Department of the Pacific," 153.

21 Hunt, *The Army of the Pacific,* 305-11 and 314-15.

22 Scott, Leslie M., *The Yaquina Railroad,* OHQ 16(1915):228-43.

23 Robinson, *The Confederate Privateers,* 275.

24 *Oregon Statesman,* January 16, 1865.

25 W.O.R., Series 1, Vol. 50, Pt. 2, 912.

26 Hunt, *The Army of the Pacific,* 320.

27 Hanft, Marshall, "The Cape Forts, Guardians of the Columbia," OHQ 74(1973):7.

28 Hagemann, *Lincoln and Oregon,* 53-55.

29 Hunt, *The Army of the Pacific,* 234.

30 U.S. Army, Headquarters, Department of the Pacific, General Orders No. 60, December 28, 1864.

31 Hanft, *"The Cape Forts,"* 21.

32 During the Civil War, no separate branch of the army was specifically trained for coastal defense. Artillery was artillery. It was not until after the Spanish-American War that a separate Coast Artillery branch was established. General Alvord's dispatch of one of his two companies of regular army infantry to finish up and man Fort Cape Disappointment showed that he, like other army commanders, preferred the regulars, rather than the war-time volunteers, for difficult chores.

33 Hanft, *Fort Stevens,* 18.

34 Hagemann, *"Lincoln and Oregon,"* 54.

35 Hanft, "The Cape Forts," 15.

36 Hanft, *Fort Stevens,* 38.

37 This caused problems. The sand underneath soon shifted and dry rot invaded the untreated timbers, rendering some platforms unusable.

38 Hanft,"The Cape Forts," 30-35.

39 A most complete and fascinating account of the *Shenandoah* is contained in Morgan, Murray, *Confederate Raider in the North Pacific,* Washington State University Press, 1995.

40 W.O.R.(N), 832.

41 Ibid., 785-836

42 Morgan, Murray C., *Confederate Raider in the North Pacific,* (Pullman, Wash.: Washington State University Press, 1995), 262.

43 W.O.R.(N), 832-35.

44 Morgan, *Confederate Raider in the North Pacific,* 330-31.

45 Hanft, *"The Cape Forts,"* 30, 35, 49.

Chapter 14

RAISING THE TROOPS

At the start of the war, the army pulled most of its regular army troops in the Pacific Northwest south to California and the East. Oregon and Washington Territory then had to raise the volunteer troops necessary to deal with any possible Confederate sympathizers and the Indian difficulties.

This was no easy task. For men who were establishing farms or searching for gold, military service held little appeal. And, as Oregon Adjutant General Cyrus Reed commented at the end of the war, the vast majority of a soldier's duties in the Pacific Northwest were "a farmer's and a wood-chopper's work."[1]

THE WASHINGTON TERRITORY VOLUNTEER INFANTRY

The first volunteers in the Pacific Northwest came from Washington Territory. A majority of Washington Territory's voters were Democrats and supported the Union. But still numb from the lengthy and widespread Indian wars of the 1850s, as a whole, Washington Territory was unenthusiastic about the prospect of war.

The territory had no governor. Richard Gholson, President Buchanan's appointee as territorial governor, left the territory upon Lincoln's election and returned to the South for service with the Confederacy. William H. Wallace, a prominent Washington Territory politician and Indian War veteran, was appointed governor. Two other Easterners were earlier appointed but turned down the job. Almost immediately after taking office, Wallace was elected Territorial Delegate to Congress and resigned to go to Washington.[2] Then John Evans of Illinois was appointed. He refused the job because of Washington's remoteness.

The job of recruiting Washington Territory's volunteers fell to Territorial Secretary Henry McGill who was acting governor.[3]

In compliance with President Lincoln's call for volunteers, on May 10, 1861, McGill issued a call for volunteers to take up arms in defense of the Union, but there was no real response.[4]

When the legislature met later that year, resolutions were introduced in both houses pledging the support of the territory to the Union. Neither was adopted, but the legislature did vote to pay the $7,755.33 direct tax levied on Washington Territory by Congress to help pay for the war.[5]

In October 1861 Justus Steinberger, prominent politician and a former agent of the Pacific Mail Co. and Adam Co.'s Express, was commissioned by General George Wright to organize a regiment of ten infantry companies from Washington Territory. The 1860 census showed 11,594 in Washington Territory (which then included Idaho and western Montana). This number was significantly reduced by the exodus to the new mines in Canada in 1861. At the time the territory had about 6,000 men between the ages of eighteen and sixty.[6] But because the territory was still recovering from a lengthy Indian war and new gold discoveries in the region made mining more attractive to its male population than army service, enlistments lagged.[7]

After arriving in the Puget Sound country, Assistant Secretary of War Colonel Thomas A. Scott soon determined that Washington Territory could never hope to raise its quota of troops.[8] Eventually, General Wright authorized Colonel Steinberger to recruit the balance of his men in California where men were available and willing to serve.[9]

Unsuccessful California miners viewed Oregon and Washington— and the new gold fields of the Pacific Northwest—as a place of true adventure. Flooding in the Sacramento Valley had done serious damage to industry and agriculture and many men joined the Washington Regiment because they needed the work.[10] Of the ten companies of the Washington Territory Volunteer Infantry, one was mustered into service at Fort Vancouver (many of its recruits from Oregon), one at Fort Steilacoom and the rest in California.[11]

There are few remaining original records of the Washington Territory Volunteers,[12] but in 1961, Colonel Virgil F. Field, in his *Official History of the Washington National Guard*, compiled a summary of service by men of the Washington Territory Volunteers from records held by the Washington Historical Society. Of the 1,059 enlisted or commissioned Washington Territory volunteers, 264 were from Washington Territory and 125 from Oregon.[13] Of those serving in the Washington Territory regiment, 209 were listed as deserters, nine were dishonorably discharged and fifteen died of various causes during service.[14] Army records at the end of the war showed 964 served in the Washington Territory regiment.[15]

The Washington Volunteers served only in Washington, Oregon, and Idaho. They manned forts in the dusty Indian country east of the Cascades and participated in the difficult Indian campaigns. The last of the Washington units was mustered out December 11, 1865. Regiment organizer Steinberger stayed in the service and held the rank of major. He was serving as paymaster at Helena, Montana when he was thrown from his horse and killed October 14, 1870.[16]

OREGON'S FIRST ATTEMPT TO RAISE TROOPS

Oregon tried to raise troops for federal service on five separate occasions during the Civil War. The first failed attempt occurred early in the war. The other four were: Colonel Thomas Cornelius' initial call for the First Oregon Volunteer Cavalry Regiment in November 1861; a call for an additional six companies of cavalry in November 1863; a call for ten companies of the First Oregon Volunteer Infantry Regiment in October 1864; and a January 1865 call for additional recruits to fill out the depleted ranks of the First Oregon Volunteer Cavalry Regiment.

In June 1861, roughly seven weeks after the opening shot of the Civil War and just over two weeks after President Lincoln called for 75,000 volunteers to put down the rebellion, Oregon Governor John Whiteaker issued a long address to the people of Oregon from his farm home at Pleasant Hill, near Eugene. He suggested that Oregon stay out of the war. Whiteaker contended that Oregon was so far removed from the site of actual battle that it would not be expected to provide troops for the war. He urged that Oregon involve itself only if necessary for its own defense.[17]

In July 1861 Congress passed the peculiarly named Volunteer Employment Act which called for mustering in army volunteers who would serve six months to three years and have the same standing, pay, and allowances of members of the regular army.[18] The federal government waited for Oregon's government to start recruiting. But nothing happened.

Oregon and Washington Territory had been stripped of regular army troops called back to the battlefields of the East. Soon there were fewer than 700 officers and men left in the Pacific Northwest.[19] Among those recalled were the three companies of dragoons previously stationed at Fort Walla Walla. The miners' invasion of the Nez Perce reservations in eastern Washington brought an immediate and pressing demand for army troops.

In early 1860, the Superintendent of Indian Affairs headed off potential war between the Nez Perce and the invading hordes of miners. Miners would be allowed to work parts of the Nez Perce lands, but they would not be allowed to settle there. In return, the government would protect the Indians against the miners and would enforce the treaty.

The commanding officer of Fort Walla Walla notified Colonel George Wright that he could not protect the Indians against the trespasses of the whites. Without more troops, he warned, the Indians were likely to start war.[20]

In June 1861, Colonel Wright asked Governor Whiteaker to organize one company of volunteer cavalry for the service in the Indian country.[21] Each man was to be paid the regular wage of a soldier. The army, ever anxious to avoid the expense of purchasing the horses upon which to mount this frontier cavalry, directed each recruit to provide his own horse, for which he would be paid extra. There was precedent for this. In 1856, the Oregon Territorial Legislature agreed to pay its militia in the Rogue River wars $2 a day for the use and risk of their horses. This was a lot of money for a horse, but it was payable only when the federal government made the funds available.[22]

Governor Whiteaker called for eighty-eight volunteers. He appointed A. P. Dennison as recruiting agent. Dennison was a good Peace Democrat who had been Indian agent during the Buchanan administration and delegate to the 1860 Democrat National Convention.[23] Dennison appointed five assistant recruiting officers. Their combined efforts brought twelve recruits.[24]

Headquartered at The Dalles, Dennison's spectacular failure as a recruiter may not have been totally his fault since most of Oregon's population was in the Willamette Valley. As a Peace Democrat, he got no editorial support from either the Copperhead or Unionist press. Not wanting to give Whiteaker the power to appoint the volunteer company's officers, Unionist editors urged would-be soldiers to stay away. Whiteaker's authority to enlist was revoked October 23, 1861.

Although poor at raising troops, Dennison was prompt at sending in the bill. He submitted a claim to the federal government for $1,985.25, including $365 for his own services and $273 for the services of his assistants.[25]

THE FIRST OREGON VOLUNTEER CAVALRY

The army made a second and unusual try to raise troops in Oregon. On September 24, 1861 Adjutant General Lorenzo Thomas bypassed Governor Whiteaker and issued a direct commission to three Oregon men, directing them to enlist twelve companies of volunteer cavalry for federal service.

The commissions went to Thomas Cornelius, Reuben F. Maury, and Benjamin F. Harding. Cornelius was a veteran of the Yakima and Rogue River Indian Wars. He was commissioned a colonel and was designated recruiting agent. Maury was a lieutenant colonel and his deputy. Harding was appointed quartermaster and mustering officer.

The recruitment effort not only bypassed Oregon's state officials, but it also avoided the regular army chain of command. The order for the muster said: "Unless otherwise ordered you will be governed by directions sent to you by Col. E. D. Baker."[26]

This shows that Oregon's Republican U.S. senator and President Lincoln's long-time friend Baker had picked the First Oregon Volunteer Cavalry's principal officers just as he had chosen most of the men Lincoln appointed to federal office in Oregon.

The order appointing Harding shows the need for speed in recruiting Oregon's cavalry unit and getting them into action. It also shows the thin staffing of the District of Oregon. It directed that Harding be "mustered into the service immediately upon receipt of this letter by an army officer in his vicinity." If no army officer was handy, Harding was authorized to "muster himself into the service by taking the oath of allegiance before a civil magistrate."[27]

Cornelius set about filling up his staff. Charles Drew, quartermaster of the Oregon militia during the Indian wars, and

Jacob S. Rinearson were appointed majors on November 6, 1861.[28] Richard S. Caldwell was appointed adjutant November 15. William B. Watkins was commissioned as surgeon December 11. David W. Porter, quartermaster, and David S. Bolton, assistant surgeon, were commissioned early in 1862.[29]

Cornelius ordered recruiting activities throughout the state. Companies were planned at Jacksonville, Salem, Portland, Canyonville, The Dalles, Oregon City, Kirbyville, and Vancouver. The structure was that of the Sixth Regiment of Cavalry of the regular army. Its manpower requirements were approximately 1,200 men and included, among other positions, chief buglers, battalion hospital stewards, battalion saddler-sergeants, battalion veterinary sergeants, musicians, farriers and blacksmiths, saddlers, wagoners, and 864 privates.[30]

Training camps were established near Phoenix—then called Gasburg (Camp Baker)—Salem, and Oregon City (called both Camp Barlow and Camp Clackamas).[31] The organization of the First Oregon Volunteer Cavalry was, at best, a "teach yourself" project.

John M. Drake, a first lieutenant appointed in November 1861, was mustered in at Camp Baker. His memoirs noted that most of the officers knew absolutely nothing about military matters. Someone picked up a copy of the *Army Regulations of 1841* and a copy of Hardee's *Infantry Tactics*. With those instructional materials, four muskets and two cavalry sabres left over from the Rogue River War, they began to learn art of war. Fortunately officers found men in the area who had served in the regular army. These veterans taught the recruits the manual of arms and rudimentary sabre exercises.[32]

The First Oregon had no uniforms and no weapons. Eight months after the order creating the First Oregon Cavalry was issued, Colonel Justus Steinberger, then commanding the District of Oregon, reported to his superiors at San Francisco that he had enough uniforms to partially outfit only two of the regiment's six companies.[33]

In early spring 1862 the officers trained their squads of recruits. Drake's memoir noted that the men were trained marching as best they could. He described their drilling as "obtaining education under difficulties you may be sure. In the course of a few weeks we were able to go through the ordinary garrison duties with some degree of proficiency."

Recruiting continued on a one-on-one basis and through advertisement in the state's newspapers. Cornelius appointed civilian recruiting officers but most of the actual recruiting was accomplished by would-be officers who knew that they would be commissioned as leaders of men in the U.S. Army only if they could find volunteers willing to serve under them.

One of these hopefuls was George L. Woods who attempted and failed to raise a company at Lafayette. Woods advertised in the *Oregon Statesman* in early December 1861:

VOLUNTEERS WANTED.

95 MEN ARE WANTED at Lafayette, Yamhill County, Oregon, to enlist in the Cavalry Service of the United States army, for three years, unless sooner discharged. Each man to furnish his own horse and horse equipments. The pay will be $31.00 a month for man and horse. Clothing and arms furnished the men, same as in regular army, and $100 bounty at the expiration of enlistment.

GEORGE L. WOODS, Recruiting Officer Lafayette, Nov. 30th, 1861.

Recruiting went slowly. As stated in the order authorizing its organization, the principal mission of the First Oregon Volunteer Cavalry was to meet all exigencies, especially in protecting the Oregon frontier. But gold had been discovered in Idaho, and money could be made in the mines.[34] In all of eastern Oregon, only forty men were enlisted.

The prospects of army service in the Indian country weren't attractive.[35] Recruiting officers posted broadsides asking for volunteers to soldier at $31 a month while labor-starved private companies posted advertisements next to them, offering $5 a day for experienced miners.

Yet, Oregon recruits did sign up. For those without a horse, men with more than one sold their extras. Recruit Hobart Taylor at Camp Baker said in his diary that he got $125 for one horse and $180 for another.[36] Cornelius and his men succeeded in mustering only six companies who finally were assembled in May 1862.[37] The bulk of them were members of established families.[38] Historian Hubert Howe Bancroft referred to them as the "Puritan Regiment" because of their habits of temperance. Of fifty-one desertions from the Oregon

Volunteer Cavalry, Bancroft's research claimed there were only three from established pioneer society and the rest from "the floating population of the country."

Wright, indicating that the recruiting effort was costing too much money, ordered a halt to further recruiting. Much of the lackluster response to army service may be attributed to delay. Oregonians were asked to enlist after the initial enthusiasm for the war had waned.

Senator Baker had promised the First Oregon Volunteer Cavalry eventually would serve in the East.[39] But with his death at the battle of Ball's Bluff, Virginia on October 21, 1861, his promise died with him. Historian Charles Carey suggests that Baker's death discouraged enlistments.

William V. Rinehart, one of the original company officers of the First Oregon Volunteer Cavalry, later claimed the implied promise of service in the East was a deliberate deception designed to lure rough-and-tumble miners to the two companies initially recruited in southern Oregon. In an 1874 letter to historian Frances Fuller Victor, Rinehart said this implied promise allowed recruitment of companies A and D in a matter of days. It helped, he said, to "fill up the ranks with a far better class of men than would have enlisted for frontier service on this Coast." The broken promise, if there was one, he noted, contributed to the desertion of twenty-eight men in a single week from Fort Boise in July 1863, when gold mining reached peak fever in the Boise Basin.[40]

This promise is accounted for by historians in the report of James A. Waymire of Polk County. Waymire enlisted as a private in Company B on January 1, 1862 and was promoted to lieutenant April 13, 1863. At the end of the war, in a report to Oregon Adjutant General Cyrus Reed he wrote:

> I will say here that from my personal knowledge I know that a great majority of the men who composed the First Oregon Cavalry were young men acting from a conviction of patriotic duty. They left pleasant homes and profitable occupations to take up arms, not only in defense of our frontiers against the Indians, but also to assist in preventing or countenancing any movement on the Pacific Coast in favor of the attempt to dissolve the Union; they also hoped that should the war prove a long one, and should there be no serious difficulty here they

171

would, after being drilled and disciplined, be ordered East to engage in some service there. That they have fought no great battle, nor won any important victories, is the misfortune and not the fault of the Oregon volunteers.[41]

In his report at the end of the war, General Reed listed fifteen deaths in the First Oregon Volunteer Cavalry. Of these, Lieutenant Stephen Watson and five enlisted men were killed in battle with the Snake Indians on May 1, 1864 near the Crooked River. Three died of disease and six died of non-combat violence.[42]

THE THIRD ATTEMPT TO RAISE TROOPS IN OREGON

By early 1863 official Washington was beginning to question Oregon's indifferent contribution to the war. Well into the second year of the war, Oregon had volunteered only six undermanned companies of cavalry which amounted to one-half of a regiment. Maybe, some thought, it was because Oregon was so far removed from the battlefields of the East. But California, equally distant though admittedly more populated, had contributed nine full regiments.

However, a new political climate in Salem gave hope to the quest for further military support from Oregon. Addison C. Gibbs, a thirty-seven-year-old Unionist, was sworn in as governor on September 10, 1862. Less than two-and-a-half months later General Wright, commander of the Department of the Pacific, relayed a call. Washington wanted six more companies to fill out the First Oregon Volunteer Cavalry Regiment.

This time, with a governor the army thought it could trust, that call was issued through state government rather than through the federal government. Oregon would appoint the officers and recruit the men. As each company was filled it would be mustered into service.

On January 10, 1863 Gibbs issued a flowery and patriotic proclamation asking for six companies of men, about five hundred in all. The proclamation trumpeted:

> They will be needed on the frontiers of this state and Washington Territory, and for the expeditions against the Snake Indians, who have so long been mercilessly engaged in robbing our fellow citizens. I cannot doubt that the citizens of Oregon, who have always responded to any demand for

their military services, will in like manner respond to this call, thereby showing their loyalty to the Government and aid in chastising marauding bands of Indians which infest our frontiers.[43]

Gibbs appointed political friends as recruiters and told them to emphasize the ongoing war against the Snake Indians. With the challenge issued, Gibbs and Oregon sat back and waited for the enlistments to roll in. And waited.

General Benjamin Alvord didn't think the recruiting effort would work and he was right.[44] A collateral issue Alvord complained about was the government's practice of paying its troops in Oregon with paper money—greenbacks that traded at a deep discount to gold.[45]

Young Oregon was not interested in army service on the frontier. Even the rumor that Oregon troops might be sent to Texas didn't spur enlistments.[46] An Oregon correspondent wrote in the *San Francisco Bulletin*:

> ...The progress in this respect may be well illustrated by the following anecdote: Not long since a little son of Gov. Gibbs was met on the street by an acquaintance of his father's, and was asked what the Governor was doing. The lad promptly replied that he was trying to raise volunteers. "With what success?" says the patronizing friend. "Oh," says Willie, with a face full of juvenile irony, "He is doing very well; he has one captain and thinks he knows where he can find another."[47]

Officers already serving with the First Oregon Cavalry were sent back to their home communities to recruit the reluctant. One recruiter was now Lieutenant James Waymire of Polk County. In a letter dated April 11, 1863, from Mount Hood, Yamhill County,[48] he wrote to Oregon Adjutant General Reed:

> During the past week I have canvassed most of Yamhill and Polk Counties and obtained no recruits. With much exertion I have made use of all fair means to induce enlistments, and am convinced that, without drafting, no valuable acquisitions can be made to the army from this part of the country. Indeed, but few men could be spared from the farms here.

After seven months effort on August 10, 1863, fifty-seven men were finally sworn in. Most had been enlisted by Lieutenant John F. Noble at Portland. A smaller group, enlisted by Lieutenant Henry C. Small at Eugene City, was consolidated with Noble's company.[49] Both were commissioned officers. This was Company G. Other officers given temporary commissions by the state to assist in recruiting were sent home.

There was some thought given to recruiting the rest of the companies in California, as the Washington Territory Infantry Regiment had done, but it never got past the talking stage.

General Alvord reported to his Department of the Pacific Headquarters that the failure to meet recruiting quotas was linked to "the mining excitement and temptations on this coast, in the depreciation of legal tender notes, and the absence of war stimulus. The first six companies of the First Oregon Cavalry were raised under the war stimulus of 1861." He noted that the earlier regiment "was raised during the fervor of the Union sentiment....When the effort to raise the other six companies was made last year all that excitement had died out."[50]

Beset by a desperate lack of troops in June 1864, forty volunteers with Nathan Olney serving as first lieutenant were mustered in as a temporary detachment of cavalry to serve a term of four months.[51] Orville Olney, appointed as second lieutenant, was Nathan Olney's assistant, as well as his younger brother. An older brother, Cyrus Olney, formerly was an associate justice of the Oregon Territory Supreme Court. These men participated in that summer's expedition into the Canyon City area, with indifferent results.[52] Like the First Oregon Volunteer Cavalry, each man furnished his own horse.

RECRUITING THE FIRST OREGON VOLUNTEER INFANTRY

Things looked tough for the army in the Pacific Northwest as the winter of 1864-65 approached. In November 1864 members of the First Oregon Volunteer Cavalry Regiment would be eligible for discharge, their three-year hitch completed. Already thinned by desertion, the ten companies of the First Washington Territory Volunteer Infantry also were due for discharge.

There were, of course, men in both regiments who signed on after the original muster and had time yet to serve. But not many volunteers would reenlist. This was especially true in the Oregon Cavalry. The men had originally enlisted under the impression—justified or not—that they would be sent east to the scene of real battle. Instead they spent their time on garrison duty in the Pacific Northwest and the futile chasing of unfriendly Indians.

Oregon's cavalrymen had a second reason for disgust with government service. Oregon's cavalry troopers were recruited with the promise that if they brought along their own horses, they would be paid not only for their own services, but extra for the use of their mounts. However, on May 20, 1864 Congress voted to stop paying rent for the troopers' privately owned horses, deciding to purchase and provide government animals instead. It was the end of the summer before Oregon troopers found out that they would be paid only for themselves and not their animals. By this time, most had spent the summer in the Indian Country of eastern Oregon, leaving them with no pay and horses that were pretty well clapped out, worth little on the market because of a tough summer.

In August 1864 General McDowell came to Oregon and visited with Governor Addison C. Gibbs. They jointly requested approval to raise companies of both infantry and cavalry in Oregon, and in Washington and Idaho territories. The War Department approved, but for some reason McDowell asked only that Gibbs raise a regiment of Oregon infantry.

The Oregon Legislature was in the final day of its biennial session. McDowell had asked for one thousand men. Gibbs asked the legislature for a bonus to bring in the recruits. The legislature passed a bounty law. The sum of $50 was to be paid at enlistment, and $100 more at discharge.[53]

The $50 enlistment bonus was not paid in cash. It was in the form of a bond, payable plus interest in twenty years. Diarist William Hilleary said these enlistment bonds were sold by enlistees to speculators and others for up to $28 each. He said he bought one for $2.50 cash and his pocket watch.[54] After his discharge on March 19, 1866, Private Anderson H. Brown wrote that he went to Salem, got his end-of-service bond worth $100 in the future and immediately traded it for $20 worth of corn.[55]

In 1865 the Oregon Legislature passed another act allowing a $50 bounty to those who would enlist for one year. In addition the federal government granted warrants, payable in the future, of $300 for each enlistee.[56] Many local communities raised cash to encourage enlistment. Polk County conducted a serious campaign, hiring the Monmouth Brass Band for eight days to play at a series of fund-raising rallies throughout the county. The Polk County committee raised $1,139.50 to be divided among its fifty-three volunteers.[57] Josephine County raised $2,500 and Marion County took in over $1,000. The Multnomah County Commissioners gave each Multnomah County volunteer $10 at enlistment and the promise of $20 upon discharge. Clackamas County also raised local bonus money. Individual bounties ranged from $21 to $100.

The threat of a draft that never was to come provided a great stimulus in enlisting Oregon volunteers.[58]

Gibbs' proclamation dated October 24, 1864 declared:

> The State will be divided into districts, according to the number of persons in each district liable to do military duty. When each district has furnished its quota of men, there will be no draft in the same, under this call – Each District will furnish one company.[59]

Quotas also were set for each county.[60] Gibbs' proclamation laid on county officers the obligation to promote enlistment, saying: "The men are needed promptly and every consideration of patriotism and of State, local and personal pride requires that you commence promptly, and prosecute vigorously the business of obtaining volunteers."

The officer commissions offered to successful recruiters were attractive. Gibbs granted conditional commissions to those he considered worthy. If they could recruit enough men to fill the ranks, they got to command them as real army officers.

The first company to be sworn in was Company A, First Oregon Volunteer Infantry of ninety-eight men from Polk and Benton counties, mustered December 15, 1864. This company had as its officers Captain Charles LaFollett, First Lieutenent W. J. Shipley and Second Lieutenant W. R. Dunbar.

Company A was known as the "Puritan Company." Its fifty-three Polk County recruits showed their hearts were pure as well as patriotic by signing a pledge published in the *Oregon Statesman* on "our word and sacred honor that we will not drink any intoxicating liquors or play any game of cards during our term of service to the United States army."[61]

Some signed up locally. Others traveled a distance to enlist. Anderson H. Brown, the Roseburg-area farmer, wrote in his diary that on January 22, 1865, he "heard some speaking for the enlistment of soldiers." He left Roseburg with three other men who walked three days to Eugene to enlist. Brown reported that the foursome spent their nights in private homes en route and "had to wade some streams and sloughs."[62]

The First Oregon Volunteer Infantry was mustered at the State Fairgrounds at Salem. The army called it Camp Reed, naming it after Oregon Adjutant General Cyrus A. Reed. After the first of the year 1865, correspondence refers to it as Camp Russell. It then was named after General David Allen Russell, commanding officer of Fort Yamhill 1857-1861 who was killed at the battle of Opequan, Virginia on September 19, 1864.[63]

It wasn't much of a camp, but at least the men weren't under canvas. One recruit, William M. Hilleary, said the army took over the pavilion building.

> One wing of the old pavilion was fitted up for the squad room, in which were our bunks. It was our sitting room, parlor, bedroom, hall, all in one. Another wing of the pavilion was occupied by the kitchen and culinary department, which was dubbed "Hotel de Russle" for it was here that we, with an eye on the main chance, "rustled" for our grub.[64]

Jonathan M. Drake, the disconsolate captain of the First Oregon Volunteer Cavalry who commanded one wing of General Alvord's unsuccessful campaign against the Snakes in eastern Oregon that year, was placed in charge of the recruiting depot. Drake was shortly to become a lieutenant colonel of the volunteer infantry regiment.

Things did not move smoothly at Camp Russell. Drake wrote to his boss, Lieutenant Colonel T. C. English, Provost Marshal and Superintendent of the Volunteer Recruiting Service at Portland:

December 5, 1864: Requesting authority to hire a civilian physician to tend the troops. "The weather is extremely inclement— aining constantly—the buildings are cold and damp, and the men have generally left comfortable homes; heavy colds and chills are the result."[65]

December 6, 1864: Requesting more blankets, bugles and uniforms that fit.[66] "The trousers, boots and flannel coats are all small sizes—the accumulation of several years at the warehouse at Fort Vancouver."[67]

December 7, 1864: Request for arms, at least enough for a guard detail. "A large number of men will be on my hands in a few days and I know of no means of keeping them together, or managing discipline amongst them, without a guard. The town of Salem is close at hand, and the disposition amongst this class of men to hunt out neighboring places of resort, render some means of discipline necessary."[68]

One company was recruited in Lane County by Stephen A. Rigdon. For some reason, a different set of officers was proposed. The aggrieved would-be recruits hired a local lawyer to get the original set of officers reinstated, but failed.[69]

The troops remained at Camp Russell only until their companies achieved full strength and were mustered in. Then they were immediately shipped out. Alvord had proposed leaving all units at Camp Russell until the full regiment was mustered. Among other things, he felt "the magnetism of numbers" would aid in the recruiting effort. He was overruled. There were facilities available at permanent installations, and the muddy conditions at the Salem Fair Grounds mandated getting the troops elsewhere as soon as possible.

While waiting, the new troopers drew their blankets, uniforms, and two-man bed sacks which they shared with a "bunkee" and learned basic drill movements.[70]

Company A from Polk and Benton counties shipped out aboard the steamer *Reliance* December 18. After an overnight campout in the courthouse at Oregon City, Company A shipped again for Portland, and after another change of boat, steamed through heavy ice to the dock at Fort Vancouver.[71]

Fort Hoskins had been vacant, except for a three-man caretaker detail, since October 7, 1864. Company B left Camp Russell and its muddy grounds December 27, and arrived at Fort Hoskins after a two-day march.[72] Company F spent three days on the road, arriving January 21, 1865.[73]

Oregon never did field a full ten companies. Recruiting went as slowly as it had for the cavalry three years before. The war was nearly over and civilian jobs paid more. Chasing after recalcitrant Indians did not appear that romantic. Eventually, eight companies were recruited.[74]

Oregon's infantry volunteers didn't get into action until the war had ended in the East. They served on garrison duty and pounded after the elusive Snake Indians until they were replaced by regular army units shipped in from the East. The last company was discharged in August 1867.[75]

None of Oregon's infantry volunteers was killed in action. Two died of disease. One died of "non-combat violence."

The record of the First Oregon Volunteer Infantry is incomplete. Many of the records were lost. Much of what we know today about the First Oregon Infantry was compiled by Adjutant General Reed, who consolidated the state's bounty records with unit histories volunteered by some of the regiment's former commanders in a report in 1866.[76]

Chapter 14 notes

1 Oregon Adjutant General, "Report for the Year 1865-1866," cited in Barth, Gunter, *All Quiet on the Yamhill* (Eugene, Or., University of Oregon Press, 1959), xi.

2 Hansen, "Public Response," 18-19.

3 L.J.S. Turney of Illinois was appointed to take McGill's place as territorial secretary. Turney served as acting governor until Governor William Pickering arrived in June 1862.

4 Snowden, *History of Washington,* 104-5.

5 Hansen, "Public Response," 18-19.

6 Richter, "Washington and Idaho Territories," 27.

7 Edwards, "The Department of the Pacific," 135.

8 Hansen, "Public Response," 18-19.

9 Recruiting Washington Territory troops out of state was not unique. Colonel Edward D. Baker, then a U.S. senator from Oregon, recruited the 1st California Infantry Regiment in Pennsylvania. This regiment later was renamed the 71st Pennsylvania Infantry and Baker, still Oregon's senator, was its commander at his death October 21, 1861. (Platt, "Oregon in the Civil War," 101-103.)

10 Edwards, "The Department of the Pacific," 135.

11 W.O.R., Vol. 50, Pt. 2, 896-99.

12 Records of the Washington State Military Department, Record Group 82, Historical Record Notes, Washington State Archives, Olympia, Washington, cited in Schablitsky, Julie M., "Duty and Vice: The Daily Life of a Fort Hoskins Soldier, 28-20 [check page numbers].

13 Field, *The Official History of the Washington National Guard,* 1:239.

14 A 20 percent desertion rate is astonishingly high, but probably can be attributed to the fact that the majority of the regiment's enlisted men were recruited in California and had little ties with the Pacific Northwest.

15 W.O.R., Series 3, 4:1269.

16 Snowden, History of Washington, 121-2.

17 Carey, Charles H., *General History of Oregon*, 1922, 626-627.

18 Hunt, "The Far West Volunteers," *Montana the Magazine of Western History*, 12,2(1962):49.

19 Hansen, "Public Response," 21.

20 Edwards, "Oregon Regiments in the Civil War," 86.

21 Hageman, "Lincoln and Oregon," 39.

22 Victor, "The First Oregon Cavalry," 130-31. Bancroft, *The History of Oregon*, 2:414.

23 Carey, *History of Oregon*, 626-27.

24 Josephy, *The Civil War in the American West*, 265.

25 Carey, *History of Oregon*, 626-27.

26 Hageman, "Lincoln and Oregon," 40.

27 Edwards, "Oregon Regiments in the Civil War," 133-34. Hageman, "Lincoln and Oregon," 39-40.

28 At the close of the Indian wars, Drew sold the left-over militia supplies. Oregon had bought them originally with scrip issued by the territorial government that had never been redeemed. Drew refused to accept scrip for the surplus supplies he sold at the end of the war and incurred the wrath of Oregon businessmen who were stuck with Oregon Territory's near-worthless paper. Oregon's canny territorial government did not obligate itself to pay the debt. The scrip was redeemable only when the Legislature appropriated funds to pay it, a practice followed in earlier Indian conflicts. Scrip sold for 30¢ on the dollar in 1856. There were charges it sold for as little as 10¢. Thomas Dryer, Republican editor of the *Oregonian*, charged Democrat territorial officials had speculated in the scrip and had pocketed $78,000 in sale proceeds. Clark, "Military History of Oregon, 1849-1859," *OHQ*, 36(1935):46-47.

29 Oregon Adjutant General, "Report for the Year 1863," Exhibit, House of Representatives Journal, Oregon Legislative Assembly, 1864 Session.

30 Heitman, Francis B., *Historical Register and Dictionary of the United States Army, from its Organization, September 29, 1789, to March 2, 1903*, 2:598-601, cited in Kittell, Allan, Ed., *Bear Bravely On: Letters from Sergeant John Buel Dimick, First Oregon Volunteer Cavalry to Almira Eberhard, 1862-1865*, (Portland, Or., Lewis & Clark College archives, 1983).

31 Rinehart, "With the Oregon Volunteers," 1862-6, mss. 471, OHS Library.

32 Drake, John M., "The Oregon Cavalry in the Indian Country," *OHQ*, 65(1964):396.

33 W.O.R., Vol. 50, Pt. 1, 1073.

34 Hunt, "The Far West Volunteers," 53-54.

35 Maxwell, Ben, "Oregon Proved Apathetic to Arms Raising Efforts During Civil War," *Salem Capital Journal*, January 3, 1961 (Installment 2) 1, 3.

36 Taylor, Hobart, *Diary*, mss., Southern Oregon Historical Society, Medford, Oregon.
37 Alvord complained that the first 12 companies could have been filled had more time been available for recruiting. After Baker's death, management of the recruiting effort was left in limbo. Bancroft, *History of Oregon*, (San Francisco, The History Co., 1888) 2:508.
38 Platt, "Oregon in the Civil War," 99-100.
39 Ibid.
40 Rinehart, "With the Oregon Volunteers, 1862-6," Mss. 471, OHS.
41 Victor, "The First Oregon Cavalry," 134-35.
42 Oregon Adjutant General, "Report for the Year 1865-1866," Exhibit, House of Representatives Journal, Oregon Legislative Assembly, 1865 session.
43 Carey, *History of Oregon*, 667.
44 Edwards, "The Department of the Pacific," 197.
45 W.O.R., Vol. 50, Pt. 2, 399-400.
46 Carey, *History of Oregon*, 635.
47 *San Francisco Bulletin*, February 25, 1863, quoted in Young, F.G., *Financial History of Oregon*, OHQ, 9(1910):404.
48 Mt. Hood was a post office two miles north and west of the hamlet of Hopewell. McArthur, Lewis L., *Oregon Geographic Names*, (Portland, Or., Oregon Historical Society, 4ᵗʰ Ed., 1974), 513.
49 W.O.R., Vol. 50, Pt. 2, 897; Carey, Charles H., *History of Oregon*, 1922, 635.
50 W.O.R., Vol. 50, Pt. 2, 897-99.
51 W.O.R., Vol. 50, Pt. 2, 863-64, 879.
52 Drake, John M., "The Oregon Cavalry," 88-89.
53 Carey, *History of Oregon*, 1922, 633, 639-41.
54 Hilleary, William M., *A Webfoot Volunteer*, 56.
55 Brown, Anderson H., unpublished diary, Justine Jones collection.
56 *Oregon Statesman,* November 14, 1864.
57 *Oregon Statesman,* December 19, 1864.
58 In his draft proclamation of October 17, 1863, President Lincoln exempted Oregon from the draft. Hageman, *Lincoln and Oregon*, 57. As we've already learned, the state was canvassed by mustering officers and a list of all men eligible for the draft was created.
59 Oregon Legislature, Journal of the House of Representatives, 1864 Session, 33.
60 The quota for each county gives an interesting tally of where military-age men were located at the time: Jackson 55; Josephine 25; Curry 5; Douglas 50, Coos 12, Lane 64, Linn 100, Benton 44, Polk 40, Marion 98, Clackamas 49, Yamhill 46, Tillamook 3, Multnomah 122, Washington 43, Columbia 7, Clatsop 11, Wasco and Grant 120, Umatilla 35, Baker and Union 58. *Oregon Statesman,* November 7, 1864.
61 *Oregon Statesman,* December 19, 1864.
62 Brown, Anderson H., unpublished diary.
63 District of Oregon, U.S. Army, Special Order No. 168, December 7, 1864, quoted in Hilleary, *A Webfoot Volunteer*, 33.
64 Hilleary, William M., "Recollections of the Service by a Linn County Volunteer," Harrisburg, Oregon *Disseminator,* 1883, quoted in Hilleary, William M., *A Webfoot Volunteer*, 33.
65 District of Oregon, U.S. Army, Correspondence file, Recruiting Rendezvous, National Archives Branch, Seattle, Washington, 3.
66 Uniforms were issued in three sizes only. If it didn't fit, you had to make the alterations yourself. Hilleary, William M., diary, quoted in Kittell, Allan (Ed.), *Bear Bravely On, Letters from Sergeant John Buel Dimick, 1862-65,* (mss., Lewis & Clark College archives), I-1-5.
67 W.O.R, Series 1, Vol. 50, Pt. 2, 1020-22.
68 District of Oregon, U.S. Army, Correspondence file, Recruiting Rendezvous, 4.
69 Ibid., 43.
70 Hilleary, *A Webfoot Volunteer*, 42.
71 *Oregon Statesman,* January 7, 1865.
72 Fort Hoskins Post Returns, microfilm, University of Oregon Library.
73 Hilleary, *A Webfoot Volunteer*, 38-39.
74 Platt, "Oregon in the Civil War," 108.
75 Oregon Military Department, "Civil War Era," mss., 10. Report of the Adjutant General of the State of Oregon for 1868, 43-45.
76 Oregon Adjutant General, "Report for 1865-1866."

Chapter 15

CIVILIAN LIFE

O regon and the Pacific Northwest were far removed from the scene of Civil War conflict. Its citizens were both fascinated and apprehensive as battle after battle was reported during the four years of the war. Crowds gathered in front of newspaper offices to see telegraphed dispatches of action in the East posted for public view. Public sentiment soon jelled with the bulk of it favoring the Union.

PATRIOTISM

A contemporary analysis came from Ira F. M. Butler, a founder of Monmouth, Oregon and the speaker of the Oregon Territorial House of Representatives in 1859. On December 29, 1861 Butler wrote to relatives in Monmouth, Illinois:

> There is another excitement here that is even painful to talk about. I mean the rebellion going on against the best government that the sun ever shined on. A large majority of the people of Oregon are for the Union, but there is a class of men here that styles themselves Peace Democrats that are opposed to the war and always talking about its unconstitutionality, and say the people of the South can't be conquered. Such stuff is all moonshine and proceeds from a traitor's heart.[1]

There were frequent accounts of fraternal friendship extended on the eastern battlefields by members of the Masonic Lodge to those who otherwise would have been enemies. Masons and their families took special care of wounded lodge members found on the battlefield and provided food to hungry prisoners who were Freemasons.[2] Oregon Freemasons in their 1862 annual meeting decided to the contrary.

They resolved that they would not extend the hand of fellowship to those who opposed the Union.[3]

Citizens expressed their support for the Union in a variety of ways. They displayed the flag, held meetings, formed parades, made patriotic speeches, and denounced those who thought otherwise.

July 4, 1861 was celebrated in Salem with ceremonies that were solemn and well-attended. From the distance of almost fifty years, writer T. W. Davenport recalled the event:

> The gloom was thick upon us and there was no thought of trifling. The people had gathered in from far and near, came in wagons and carriages with their families, on horseback, afoot, every one holding a flag as though it were the ark of his refuge, all moving in procession this time from a sense of duty, and as silent as Spartan soldiers going into battle.[4]

Union victories were celebrated. When news of the Union victory at Gettysburg and the capture of Vicksburg reached Portland, citizens poured into the streets. The volunteer fire companies and citizens paraded, carrying torches, banners, and flags. Illuminated transparencies of patriotic symbols were cast on building walls. Fireworks were set off. Crowds gathered in the public square and cheered patriotic speeches by the leather-lunged and eloquent. Cannon were fired in celebration.

Victories were celebrated and Independence Day observed by the firing of cannon, which could be a dangerous diversion. The July 20, 1863 *Oregon Statesman* reported a premature discharge of cannon that wounded two at Vancouver, Washington Territory, and killed one and wounded another at Florence, Idaho Territory. It said California papers reported similar accidents.[5]

At Eugene City, where the presence of Southern sympathizers was suspected throughout the war, the Fourth of July celebration in 1864 was an orgy of patriotism. Cannon fire rocked the town. Part of Eugene watched while the rest of the town performed the celebratory parade, 2,500 were served supper and a grand ball closed the day at the St. Charles Hotel.

The *State Journal* rightfully proclaimed: "The day and its pleasures long will be remembered by those present."[6] Citizens joined the military in its celebration of Independence Day.

Stephen Staats, a pioneer of the Monmouth area and later a Polk County commissioner, wrote of his visit to Fort Yamhill on July 4, 1862:

> ...I availed myself of an invitation to be present at the celebration of the Anniversary of the birth of our National Independence at Fort Yamhill, the Fourth....At about noon, a national salute of thirty-four guns were fired; thus ignoring the idea of a dissolution of the Union,...After the salute and a review of the troops stationed there, all repaired to a place in front of the quarters of Captain Scott, where the Declaration of Independence was read....
>
> After the oration, the people were invited to participate in the refreshment of their physical frames from the hospitable board spread for the occasion....
>
> At night a splendid ball was given. The hall, in which the festivities were to take place, was tastefully decorated with evergreens, some of them forming appropriate mottoes. All went harmoniously....
>
> The Flag of our country is floating on high,
> Stand firm by that flag till you conquer or die.[7]

SOUTHERN SENTIMENT

In the summer of 1861, as the nation headed toward division, Southern sympathizers raised a so-called "Rattlesnake Flag" on the pole in the Jacksonville town square in southern Oregon.[8] Townsfolk watched silently. No one made a move. Dr. Lewis Ganung, the local physician, and his wife, Zany, were returning to their home. Zany Ganung, a statuesque woman of firm belief, spotted the flag, went to her house, returned with a hand ax and chopped down the flagpole. She then cut the flag loose, took it to her house and burned it in the stove. No one interfered.[9]

At Silverton, Oregon Southern sympathizers rode through town shouting "Hurrah for Jeff Davis." Fist fights followed arguments over the merits of the war.[10]

Newspapers printed inflammatory articles intended to champion one side or the other in the war. The *Oregon Statesman* reported that rebel soldiers had dug up the bones of Union dead at Bull Run and sawed them into rings which they proudly wore on their fingers.[11]

Newspaper editors cheerfully and frequently insulted colleagues of opposing political view. The *Oregon Statesman*, one of the more vitriolic of Union publications, on March 14, 1864 characterized the editor of the Copperhead *Eugene Review* as a reptile driven from Ireland by St. Patrick.[12]

Sometimes common sense avoided conflict. South and North feuded verbally at the frontier gold camp of Florence in Washington (later Idaho) Territory. As July 4, 1862 approached, the likelihood of true battle loomed.

To defuse the conflict, several reasonable citizens talked Charles Ostner, a local of artistic bent, into preparing a work of art. Snow was brought in and piled on Main Street. At night as temperatures lowered to freezing, water was poured on the snow and it formed into a block of ice.

Shrouded by a screen of canvas, Ostner set to work.

On Independence Day his ice sculpture, George Washington on horseback, was unveiled. All cheered. No one fought.[13]

The Pacific Northwest was frustrated by the delay in news from the eastern battlefields. Phoebe Judson Goodell, who lived near Olympia, wrote: "In our anxiety for news, the lagging wheels of time moved slowly between our once-a-week mail carried by Captain Finch on the Steamer *[Eliza] Anderson*."[14] In Oregon, the newly-elected Unionist 1862 legislature moved to secure Oregon against dissident thought. It passed an act requiring that every person having a claim for money against the state to subscribe an oath of fealty to the Union before getting paid. Secretary of State Samuel E. May, who was the disbursing officer, had doubts he could legally withhold payment if the oath was refused. Governor Addison C. Gibbs vetoed the bill. He said he didn't think the secretary of state should have the power to override a creditor's rightful claim. The House of Representatives failed to override the veto.[15]

PUSHING THE LIMITS

Salem's Congregationalist community was troubled by politics. Obed Dickinson who, with his wife Charlotte, was sent by the Missionary Society to launch Salem's first Congregational Church, followed the Congregational credo, which held that the pulpit should be denied those who owned slaves or were sympathetic to slavery.

185

Dickinson was an avowed abolitionist. He preached against slavery and invited Negroes of the community to participate in church affairs.

By 1863 Dickinson's anti-slavery fulminations had made him enemies. Church attendance fell. Isaac N. Gilbert, deacon and principal financial supporter of the church, failed to make his sizeable annual tithe. The church's ten-year effort to finance and build a new sanctuary foundered. The work was only partially completed, and money ran out.

In January 1863 the congregation voted to ask Dickinson to stop preaching abolitionism—to refrain "from presenting these exciting topics (slavery, etc.)"—in his future labor with the church. Dickinson resigned. The congregation accepted.

Six months later, after a renewed flow of contributions allowed the completion of the new church, Dickinson was invited to return. By a split vote, his contract was renewed for another year. However, Dickinson soon gave up. In 1867 he quit the pastorate, remaining in Salem as a seed merchant and nurseryman. In 1879, Dickinson left the Congregational Church and devoted his religious efforts to the Seventh Day Adventist Church.[16]

The racial issues raised by the Civil War had a side effect in Oregon. Oregonians became less tolerant of Indians and other non-whites.[17] This included the mixed race descendants of early Hudson's Bay settlers.

MONEY PROBLEMS

In early 1864 residents of the Abiqua basin northeast of Silverton, Oregon, held a precinct meeting. After choosing a chairman and secretary, they passed a resolution. First, they formally supported the reelection of President Lincoln. Then they got down to the real issue. They decried the decision of the Oregon Court that allowed state and county tax collectors to refuse greenbacks at par in payment of taxes and allowed them to require payment in gold only.[18]

Oregon's Republican legislature decided that it was not going to be stuck with the task of paying the cost of state government with depreciated paper dollars. Because the bulk of state revenues came from a state property tax levy collected by the counties, the legislature required that all state and local taxes be paid in gold. Former Governor John Whiteaker and his neighbors sued the Lane County sheriff, who also served as the county tax collector. They asked the court to order the state to allow tax payments in the form of federal "legal tender" notes. The Circuit Court and later the Oregon Supreme Court refused his demand.[19]

THE SANITARY COMMISSION AND THE POWER OF WOMEN

The men who stayed at home talked about the war. The women did something about it.

At the start of the war, the army's medical department was headed by an octogenarian veteran of the War of 1812. The medical department was under-equipped, understaffed and hopelessly unorganized. The army's bungled handling of the wounded at the first Battle of Bull Run brought out women activists. Looking to the model of Florence Nightingale, who helped bring order to the British system of military medicine during the recent Crimean War, women decided to do the same. Nationally, the Sanitary Commission was organized. It was headed by men, but run by women.

The Sanitary Commission essentially invaded the medical department's turf. It collected private funds and provided bandages, medicine, and nursing care for ill and wounded soldiers. Powerful political leaders backed the Sanitary Commission's good works. President Lincoln, who muttered something about "a fifth wheel," concurred, and the Sanitary Commission and its relief workers were grudgingly granted access to the troops.

The first Sanitary Commission group formed in Oregon was at McMinnville in 1863. That group's minute book shows that it organized, adopted bylaws and a constitution, then set about raising money that was delivered to Governor Gibbs who headed Sanitary Commission activities in Oregon and forwarded the funds to the East. Members at McMinnville knitted socks that sold for 50 cents a pair; made quilts for $21.50, and held public dinners. McMinnville raised $1,620.55 during the war, notwithstanding the grumbling of some "gentlemen of the village," who felt such actions were not ladylike.[20]

Soon Sanitary Commission groups sprang up throughout the state. Newspapers listed individual contributions to the Sanitary Commission, even those as little as 25 cents.[21]

Oregon's branch of the Sanitary Commission formally organized in August 1864. On March 9, 1865 it boasted that it had collected

$6,231.22 in coin and $3,422 in greenbacks. In a broadside, the Oregon Commission urged formation of more local chapters. The Oregon committee was the business aristocracy of the state: C. H. Lewis, president; E. D. Shattuck, secretary; Henry Failing, treasurer, and Committeemen P. C. Shuyler Jr., Z. B. Gibson, A. M. Starr, and H. W. Corbett.[22]

The Sanitary Commission was active also in Washington Territory. The first group was organized at Vancouver and a territorial headquarters was established at Olympia. A partial list of contributions indicates local organizations at Port Madison, Port Gamble, Monticello, Boisfort Prairie, Port Angeles, Claquato, Yelm, Whidbey Island, Chehalis, Grand Prairie, and Clallam.[23] Historian Arthur A. Denney claimed Washington Territory produced more contributions per capita for the Sanitary Commission than any other state or territory.[24]

DISEASE AND NATURAL DISASTER

Disease and extreme weather added to the burden of the Civil War in the Pacific Northwest. In October and November 1861, heavy snow fell over the Willamette Valley, followed by three days and nights of unremitting rain.

In early December, three families in the Mission Bottom area north of Salem were flooded out of their homes. Soon marooned families were being plucked from attics and rooftops throughout the Willamette Valley. Pioneer Champoeg and the town of Independence were flooded.[25]

The Columbia River also was flooded. The Willamette River backed up at Oregon City and almost flooded the Willamette River Falls there. At least one downstream-bound steamboat reportedly steamed without damage over the falls.[26]

The flood also swept away the portage railroad and bridges at the Cascades of the Columbia which delayed the dispatch of troops the following spring to Fort Colville.[27]

Families in the Mission Bottom area took a year to rebuild and return to their devastated homes. One, the family of Jimmy Harpool, returned to live in their house, which had not floated away. But they "suffered so from mosquitoes and malaria that in time they moved away and made a permanent home near Turner."[28]

The summers were hot and the winters unseasonably cold. The *Oregon Statesman* reported that the temperature at Salem on July 26, 1863 reached 106 degrees.[29]

In a letter dated February 15, 1862, the commanding officer of the District of Oregon reported that the departure of Company C, Ninth Infantry, from Fort Vancouver to Alcatraz Island was delayed because of ice blockades in the Columbia River.[30]

At Seattle during the winter of 1861-62, temperatures plummeted to four degrees below zero on two consecutive days and ice on Lake Union was six inches thick.[31]

Scarlet fever and smallpox raged in the Willamette Valley during the summer of 1863. Almira Eberhard wrote her beau, John Buel Dimick, that there were two or three funerals a week in the Salem area.[32] A newspaper correspondent from Boise reported an epidemic of typhoid fever and measles and one case of smallpox in December 1863.[33]

But while the day-to-day lives of the average citizen went on as normal, life changed indeed for the young men who enlisted in the three under-sized regiments of army volunteers that provided protection to the remote Pacific Northwest frontier during the war years.

Chapter 15 notes

1 Butler, Ira F. M., Letter, December 29, 1861, Butler Family letters, Oregon State Library, Salem, Oregon.

2 Roberts, *House Undivided*, 337-39.

3 Grand Lodge of Free and Accepted Masons of Oregon, Annual Proceedings, 1862, 231. The Masonic fraternity had powerful adherents during the war. Former President James Buchanan was a past master of a Pennsylvania lodge. Vice President Andrew Johnson was a member of Greenville Lodge No. 119 in Tennessee. Three Union Army generals, George B. McClellan, Rufus Ingalls, and Henry C. Hodges, were members of Willamette Lodge No. 2 at Portland, Oregon. All became members while serving in the pre-war army in the Pacific Northwest. Roberts, *House Undivided*, 337-39.

4 Davenport, "Slavery Question in Oregon," 363.

5 *Oregon Statesman,* July 20, 1863.

6 *State Journal,* July 8, 1864.

7 *Oregon Statesman,* July 14, 1862.

8 Some accounts say it was the Stars and Bars, but this was before a formal flag was adopted by the Confederacy. There is some dispute as to whether this actually occurred. Southern Oregon historian Ben Truwe says the first published account of this event was in the Portland *Oregonian* June 11, 1931. But folk tales, if they are interesting enough, easily become history.

9 Haines, Francis D., *Jacksonville: Biography of a Gold Camp,* Medford, Or., Gandee Printing Center, 1967, cited in Truwe, Ben, "In Search of Zany Ganung," unpublished research manuscript, Southern Oregon Historical Society, Medford, Or.

10 Hoblitt, Flora F., "When Silverton was Young," *Silverton Appeal-Tribune*, June 25, 1954.

11 *Oregon Statesman,* June 30, 1862.

12 *Oregon Statesman,* March 14, 1864.

13 Richter, "Washington and Idaho Territories," 26.

14 Goodell, Phoebe Judson, *A Pioneer's Search for an Ideal Home*, (Tacoma, Wa., Washington Historical Society, 1966), cited in Hansen, "Public Response to the Civil War in Washington Territory and Oregon, 1861-1865.

15 Carey, *History of Oregon,* 665.

16 Oliver, Egbert S., *Obed Dicksinson's War Against Sin in Salem, Oregon,* (Portland, Or., Hapi Press, 1987) ii-iii, xvi-xxxiii.

17 Tobie, *No Man Like Joe*, 254.

18 Oregon *Statesman*, March 12, 1864.

19 *Whiteaker et al v. Haley*, Oregon Reports, Vol. 2, 128 (1865).

20 Case, Victoria, "It Began With McMinnville Ladies Sanitary Aid Society," *Sunday Oregonian,* February 19, 1961.

21 *Oregon Statesman,* February 22, 1864.

22 Oregon Branch, U.S. Sanitary Commission, Circular, *To the Friends of the Sanitary Commission,* March 9, 1865, University of Oregon Library.

23 Snowden, Clinton A., *History of Washington*, 113-14.

24 Kittredge, Frank A., "Washington Territory in the Civil War," *Washington Historical Society Quarterly,* 2(1907):39.

25 Hubbard, Cora, "Early Settlement of Independence," mss., Independence, Or. Public Library, 3.

26 Steeves, Sarah Hunt, *Book of Remembrance of Marion County, Oregon, Pioneers, 1840-1860,* (Portland, Or., The Berncliffe Press, 1927), 324.

27 W.O.R., Series 1, V. 50, Pt. 1, 1150.

28 Steeves, *Book of Remembrance,* 322.

29 *Oregon Statesman,* July 27, 1863.

30 French, *History of the Washington National Guard,* 1:194.

31 Dorpat, Paul, "Now & Then: Snowbound", *Seattle Times*, January 28, 2001, Magazine section, 22.

32 Dimick Papers, Oregon Historical Society, Portland, Oregon, cited in Kittell, Allen (Ed.), *Bear Bravely On, Letters from Sergeant John Buel Dimick,* Lewis and Clark College, Portland, Oregon, 1983.

33 *Oregon Statesman*, December 21, 1863.

Chapter 16

THE LIFE OF THE SOLDIER

T
he daily life of the Civil War soldier in the Pacific Northwest was dull and tedious, but occasionally it was downright interesting. We know this from contemporary news accounts and official correspondence. But much of the relevant information comes from diaries, letters written home from soldiers in the field, and late-in-life memoirs of the young men who enlisted to defend their country but never saw the real war.[1]

WHO WERE THEY?

Statistics exist for some of the 1,810 men who served in the two Oregon regiments, which, though far under strength because of the reluctance of many Oregonians to enlist, served the interests of the nation in the Pacific Northwest. They were compiled after the war by Benjamin Apthorp Gould as a part of a national survey of American soldiers.[2] Few detailed records survive of the 964 men who served in the Washington Territory Volunteer Infantry.[3] But most were recruited outside the territory.

In Gould's compilation, there were 875 Oregon enlisted men in the First Oregon Volunteer Cavalry. Almost half, 427 (48.8 percent) were farmers, 155 (17.7 percent) were laborers and forty-four (5.03 percent) were miners. The list of recruits included attorneys, a dancing master, a druggist, a medical student, and eleven teachers.

Army regulations restricted enlistment to those aged eighteen to forty-five, but these limitations were ignored in Oregon. One, listed as a drummer boy, enlisted at twelve. There were 107 enlistees under eighteen and six over forty-five. The oldest was fifty-four.

The average age of these Oregon volunteers was just under twenty-six. This was consistent with an after-war survey of records of thirty northern states that showed an average age at enlistment of 25.8083 years.

Of the Oregon Regiment enlistees, 89 percent were born in the United States. Among the rest, one was born at sea, one was born in Sri Lanka, and another claimed his place of birth as Kur Hession (likely the German settlements in the Kur River basin of southern Russia).

Of those 778 born in the United States, 27 percent were from states that later joined the Confederacy, most from so-called Border States. Only seventeen Oregon enlistees were born in the Deep South.

The average height of Oregon enlistees was five feet, eight inches. The shortest was the twelve year-old drummer, who was four feet, five inches tall. One older recruit was four feet, eight inches tall. The tallest was six feet, five inches.[4]

PAYING THE TROOPS

At the start of the war, army privates and corporals were paid $13 a month. Pay day was every other month. The army didn't simply send the money. The paymaster, an officer assigned to each military district, came around with his escort, lined the troops up, and paid them off.

Despite the regulations, pay didn't arrive as scheduled. Company D, Fourth California Volunteer Infantry served five months at Fort Hoskins before getting paid. Royal Bensell wrote in his diary: "Glory to God...anxiously expected Pay-Master Maj. Benj. Alvord arrives. We are to receive our pay tonight."[5]

When payday came, gambling and drinking followed. Many men were soon broke.

The soldier's salary too often was paid not in gold but in devalued paper legal tender notes. At the start of the war, there was no central banking system. The U.S. government collected its taxes and paid its bills in gold. By February 1862, the federal government was already deeply in debt for the cost of the war. It had two choices, borrow the money from the state banks, or print its own paper money.

Congress authorized $150,000,000 in legal tender notes. By 1865 there was $450,000,000 in paper money outstanding. These legal tender notes were to be redeemed, when Congress authorized it, in gold. They were supposed to be equal in value to gold. But they traded at a discount to gold.

In February 1863 Oregon Adjutant General Cyrus Reed relayed to Alvord the complaints of the Oregon Volunteers. They were being paid in legal tender notes, which, he said, was the same thing as a pay cut, effectively reducing their pay up to 50 percent.[6]

Alvord responded that, in fact, all Oregon troops were being paid in gold. But Bensell in his diary in July 1864 complained that greenbacks were issued as pay and worth only 38 cents to the dollar in trade.[7]

Soldiers got extra pay for extra duty. Bensell earned $21 extra one pay period for working as an expressman. Other soldiers moonlighted as tailors, cobblers, and barbers and were paid by their fellow soldiers. Pacific Northwest troops were not, as were their compatriots in Nevada, Utah, and Arizona, allowed to take time off to work as miners.[8] At some Pacific Northwest posts, army bakeries sold bread to the locals and used proceeds to buy fresh beef on the local market.

Poor pay was one of the Pacific Northwest soldier's greatest complaints. The June 14, 1864 *Boise Daily News* commented: "The greatest incentive to soldiers for desertion from their posts was the difference between their meager wages—$16 per month for an infantryman—and the possible daily return from local mining claims—$150 to $200."[9]

OUTFITTING THE TROOPS

Civil War soldiers were issued uniforms at enlistment. Made of thick woolen cloth called "kersey," they were worn at all times, and came in only three sizes. If the uniform didn't fit, it was the soldier's responsibility to get it altered or to trade for something more his size. Shirts were of white "domet flannel," an itchy cloth of wool and cotton. Soldiers often substituted cotton civilian shirts, although regulations said they weren't supposed to.[10]

The uniforms were manufactured at the army's arsenal at Schuykill, Pennsylvania, and issued to Pacific Northwest units from the quartermaster warehouse at Fort Vancouver.

Since the uniforms didn't fit well and were never pressed, Civil War army units were not dashing in appearance.

At the formation of the First Oregon Volunteer Infantry at Camp Russell in Salem, Captain Jonathan Drake complained to his headquarters that most of the uniforms he received for issue were leftovers in size small.

While uniforms were in short supply at the start of the war, by the end, the army had a huge inventory of blue jackets and trousers. The army kept its blue woolen uniforms until late in the century when it ran out of trousers. Then the units had blue jackets and khaki trousers.

In 1917 at the start of World War I, Oregon organized its own Home Guard. Arthur Ward, then a high school student at Independence, enlisted. He recalled he was issued a blue uniform jacket left over from the Civil War. His weapon was a 45.70 single shot rifle from the 1870s.[11]

The initial issue of uniforms to the First Oregon Volunteer Infantry was the dark blue wool dress tunic with thigh length skirts. A portrait of a Company A private taken shortly after his induction in Portland shows a soldier with full dress tunic and a leather collar stock, designed to keep the head in an upright position, which was great for a parade but uncomfortable to a soldier pursuing Indians on the frontier.

Army trousers were sky blue until 1858 when they were changed to the same dark blue as the tunic. The army changed back to light blue at the start of the war. Since it used less dye, light blue was cheaper to manufacture.[12]

Once they had their uniforms, soldiers wore nothing else, on duty or off. At Salem's Camp Russell, when recruits were issued their new uniforms, some traded their discarded civilian clothing to "pie women"—women of the community who baked pastries in exchange for the cast-off civilian wear.

After original issue, soldiers were required to buy replacements from the army. Soldiers had a clothing allowance of $8.44 a month for the first year of service and $5.24 a month thereafter.

New issue was charged in 1864 at the following prices:

Overcoat with cape $14.50
Dress coat $8.75
Pair pants, light blue $3.50
Forage cap $1.00
Pair drawers, knitted $1.75
Shirt $1.50
Pair shoes, sewed $2.70
Pair stockings $0.48
Hat and dress hat trimming $1.25

Pair suspenders $1.33
Plain hat $1.25
Knit shirt $2.25
Pair boots, sewed $4.65
Blanket, single $7.00
Blouse $4.00
Pair drawers, plain $1.30
Pair cavalry pants $5.90
Pair heavy infantry pants $4.75 [13]

Clothing wore out rapidly under field conditions. Some remote units lacked replacement shoes, drawers, shirts and trousers.

FEEDING THE TROOPS

Early in the war, Army Surgeon General William A. Hammond claimed that the U.S. soldier was the best fed of any soldier in the world.[14] On paper, and given the limitations of the science of nutrition as it was then known, he may have been right. But there is a difference between plan and execution.

The quartermaster system was creaky at best. The era's food preservation was mainly intended to keep the food from rotting before it was eaten, with taste and nutrition a secondary consideration. Consequently, the Union Army soldier was often not well fed, which made him susceptible to disease and slowed his recovery from illness and injury.

Army regulations in 1863 prescribed the daily ration for soldiers:

12 oz. of pork, or 20 oz. of fresh or salt beef.
22 oz of soft bread, flour, or corn meal.

In addition, for every 100 men, the daily issue of:

15 lb. of peas or beans (dried).
10 lb. of green coffee or 8 lb. of roasted coffee or 1 lb., 8 oz. of tea.
15 lb. of sugar.
4 qt. of vinegar.
3 lb. 12 oz. of salt.
4 oz. of pepper.
30 lb. of potatoes (when available), and
1 qt. of molasses.[15]

Companies could sell unused rations back to the quartermaster and then purchase fresh goods as they were available on the local market.[16] Troops at permanent installations were expected to raise their own vegetables. In 1858, before the war, troops at Fort Hoskins reportedly harvested 800 bushels of potatoes from their own farm.[17] The additional food was a necessity rather than a luxury.

In season, wild fruits and berries were a welcome addition to the everyday military diet. With their meager wages soldiers bought eggs, apples, and potatoes from nearby farmers, sometimes going to town for a better price.

Private Royal Bensell and his comrades in the Siletz Blockhouse pooled their money and paid two Indian women $1 each to pick and carry 180 pounds of fresh oysters from the Yaquina Bay oyster beds to the blockhouse. Farmers traded produce for coffee, vinegar, and condiments in military stores.

On at least one occasion, Oregon volunteers paid to feed their government mounts. In October 1863 Captain William V. Rinehart's company ran short of feed in the Powder River Valley and used their own money to buy grain for their undernourished horses.[18]

Scurvy, caused by the lack of vitamin C, was a constant threat. Before it developed the classic symptoms of bruising and loose teeth, scurvy caused what was called "scorbutic diathesis" or incipient scurvy. Its myriad symptoms baffled most doctors. They classified it as "chronic diarrhea," rheumatism, and debility. Scurvy led to poor blood coagulation and slowed recovery from wounds and injury.

After March 1859, War Department Regulations required local commanders to purchase and issue anti-scorbutics to their troops.[19] But the question of what was a good anti-scorbutic remained somewhat iffy. Contractors produced and sold to the army "desiccated" or dried vegetables and potatoes. The British in the Crimean War had used desiccated potatoes: potatoes, finely cut and dried. One Civil War veteran who lived well into the twentieth century likened them to Grape Nuts cereal in texture. The army wrongly thought they were an anti-scorbutic. The minimal content of vitamin C in fresh potatoes was reduced when the potatoes were dried.[20]

Desiccated vegetables were a mix of vegetables dried and pressed into sheets or large round cakes about two inches thick. Depending on the contractor, it was sometimes heavily peppered in a further attempt at preservation. When cooked, desiccated vegetables tasted as bad as they looked.

The Civil War soldier's basic field ration was hardtack or hard bread, a dry land version of ship's biscuit. It was made of unleavened flour, a bit of salt and water, and was designed to be nutritious and indestructible. It was mixed in a thick solution, rolled into half-inch thick sheets, cut in squares slightly less than three inches in size, and baked hard. A daily ration was nine or ten biscuits.

Hardtack was truly hard. Troops would gnaw on it, if they had to. Otherwise, it was broken up and fried in fat, or mixed with coffee to make a sort of slurry. If hardtack got damp, it bred weevils and worms. The troops called it, among other things, "worm castles."[21]

In some permanent installations there were designated cooks, usually men not fit for general duty. In the field and in most of the smaller frontier posts, rations were issued to each man and it was every man for himself. Men partnered up to form groups called messes. They pooled their rations and shared cooking chores.

The young men who formed the frontier army were poor cooks. Left on their own, they did not swiftly adopt good household skills. Poor sanitation and the tendency to fry everything in grease made for gastric distress.

Simple cooks used simple rations to make simple meals. The meat they received was often heavily salted in an effort to preserve it. The goal was to keep it unspoiled for two years. Salt beef, also known as "pickled" beef or "salt horse," might be left to soak in a running stream overnight to wash out the salt. Or it was boiled. Either got rid of the salt, but also much of the taste. Preserved pork and bacon was heavy with fat. Some camps had cook stoves. Fort Hoskins had only open fireplaces. In the field, an open fire sufficed.

Meat was served boiled, fried, or combined with what vegetables were available to make a stew of sorts.

Beans were a staple. When put in a kettle with meat and buried overnight in a hole filled with hot coals, it made a dish that was palatable if not nutritionally balanced. One easily made but generally loathed dish was minute pudding—three cups of flour and two-and-a-half gallons of milk mixed together and cooked. It fed about fifteen.[22]

A company of Oregon Volunteer Infantry arrived at Fort Hoskins in 1864 and found barrels of salt pork dated 1852. The cooks bravely tried to cook this ancient meat, but it smelled so bad they threw it out.[23]

In March 1862, Royal Bensell complained: "Our pork is spoiled, our flour damaged, makes miserable bread. Complaints long and bitter, no vegetables either fresh or desiccated issued."[24] Hilleary also noted that on occasion the meal served up consisted solely of bread and coffee.[25]

Things were no better at Camp Baker in southern Oregon. Hobart Taylor, a recruit in the First Oregon Volunteer Cavalry, noted in his diary: "Supper in great varieties. First: bread and meat and water, spoiled by adding some coffee to it. Second: meat, coffee and bread; Third: coffee, bread and meat."

In the Pacific Northwest, soldiers hunted wild game and harvested wild fruits and berries in season. They also raided farm orchards and gardens when they could get away with it.[26]

A neighbor of Fort Hoskins said what he made selling eggs and milk to the army, he lost on pigs.[27] Diarist William Hilleary, then stationed at Fort Hoskins, noted that on several occasions the night guards reported being attacked by a bear, which was slain, butchered and provided ample steaks that tasted like young pork. This was referred to as "slow bear."[28]

Hilleary also wrote of "fishing" for chickens. A baited fishhook was thrown in front of a neighbor's chicken. The chicken swallowed the hook and lay quiet and in pain until taken by the soldier to the barracks for slaughter.

In January 1866, the quartermaster's monthly report at Camp Curry in central Oregon listed the following rations and supplies issued to the eighty-seven soldiers and eight civilian employees during one month's time:

Pork 471 lb.
Bacon 168 lb.
Pickled fish 415 lb.
Dried fish 149 lb.
Fresh beef 2174 lb.
(6 beef of the camp herd of 31 were slaughtered)
Flour 3072 lb.
Corn meal 31 lb.

Hard bread 91 lb.
Beans 227 lb.
Rice 73 lb.
Rio coffee 285 lb.
Costa Rica coffee 17 lb.
Tea 4 lb.
Brown sugar 427 lb.
White sugar 40 lb.
Vinegar 28 gal.
Candles 63 lb.
Soap 113 lb.
Fine salt 106 lb.
Coarse salt 34 lb.
Pepper 8 lb.
Desiccated potatoes 71 lb.
Mixed vegetables 3 lb.
Tobacco 16 lb.[29]

The camp also used ten-and-a-half tons of hay and 3,300 pounds of oats fed to the livestock.

DISEASE

During the war, disease killed twice as many soldiers as the wounds of battle. In the Pacific Northwest, where there wasn't much gunfire, disease was the chief medical challenge.

Troops in the Pacific Northwest generally enjoyed better health than the soldiers of the eastern battlefields. There was good reason for this. The soldiers who served in the District of Oregon lived better than their eastern contemporaries, who spent considerable time in the mud and dust of the battlefield.

Soldiers in the Pacific Northwest were stationed at remote posts away from the epidemics of the crowded East. Generally, troops recruited in the East had all been exposed to measles, mumps, chickenpox, and the like. Many of the men recruited to western (actually midwestern) theater armies came from rural areas and were more susceptible to those maladies.

Army doctors did a better job of screening recruits for medical infirmities in the Pacific Coast states. Through the first half of the war, commanders in the East complained that their ranks were clogged with men physically unfit for the rigors of military service. Surgeon Charles S. Tripler, medical director of the Army of the Potomac, complained early in the war that some communities apparently viewed the army as a "grand eleemosynary institution" to care for defectives who otherwise would be public charges in their home communities.[30]

Because bad diet led to a weakened immune system and left a man more susceptible, disease was often fatal to the Union Army soldier.[31] Sanitation was also a problem. Inadequately trained volunteer officers did not require prudent sanitary efforts in the camps. Garbage often was left where it fell. Manure and debris lay on the grounds, or if it was removed, lay in open piles near at hand.

At permanent installations, the latrine was a pit privy. In the field, it was supposed to be a straddle trench thirty feet long, into which a covering of dirt periodically was shoveled. Many men did not use them. For some, it was a matter of modesty. For others, it was slothfulness or habit.

A farm boy who relieved himself behind a bush at home was likely to do it in camp. On the farm, it created no hazard. But when it was done hundreds of times by hundreds of men it was something else entirely.

Army regulations required that hands and faces be washed daily, feet twice a week and complete baths once or twice a week.[32] Most Pacific Northwest posts had little if any facilities for bathing. The regulations were, at best, ignored.

All sorts of peculiar medical beliefs governed actions by soldiers. On patrol in eastern Oregon, John Buel Dimick wrote: "I have not washed my face since we started. Alkali dust will (make) a person's face sore if he washes. So I have concluded not to wash mine."[33]

Contaminated drinking water caused much of the disease. Purification methods were unknown. Boiling drinking water was considered a waste of time and firewood.

The average Civil War doctor didn't know how to effectively treat most of the diseases and injuries of his patients. His knowledge of anatomy was thorough. But physiology, the science that tells doctors what the various parts of the body do, was almost unknown. Bacteriology was unknown. It was not until the 1870s that the work of Louis Pasteur taught a surgeon to wash his hands, sterilize his surgical tools before using them, and keep the wound clean.

The origin of most diseases was unknown. The most prevalent army diseases were respiratory and diarrhea. Popular theory was that a primary origin of these diseases was a "malignant miasma," arising from decaying vegetable and animal matter.

Amputation was a common but radical treatment of serious wounds of the arm or leg. Infection was bound to follow the surgeon's poking around the wound with a contaminated finger or probe.

In light of today's medical knowledge, the list of medicines commonly used by Civil War doctors was mostly useless. Quinine was effective for treatment of malaria. But doctors used it indiscriminately for diseases against which it has no effect.[34] Digitalis, belladonna, opium, and a handful of other medicines that worked were included in a pharmacopoeia with hundreds of others that did not. Surgeon General William A. Hammond was sacked after he prohibited the use of mercury-based medicines.

A frequent cure-all was a good purge to clear the bowels.

Many relied on folk medicine. On August 12, 1864 Captain George Currey and his expedition arrived at the site of Camp Alvord in southeast Oregon. They had been on the trail since April 20. Of Currey's 134 men, 106 were ill with dysentery—referred to in his report as the "bloody flux." The surgeon with the group, Dr. Horace Carpenter, was ill with the rest, and had long since run out of what medicine commonly prescribed for this malady. The ever-creative Currey sent the troops out to dig up the roots of the wild geranium, fed the ill a tea made of it, and later claimed that it worked.[35]

A good study of medical care at Fort Hoskins was done by Timothy D. Trussell, a graduate student at Oregon State University. Almost three-quarters of the cases treated at the Fort Hoskins hospital fell into one of six categories of disease. These, together with like classifications for the pre-war (1849-59) army as a whole, were:

Disease	Civil War	1849-59 (percent)
Trauma	11.68	18.9
Sexually transmitted disease	4.25	16.8
Respiratory disease	11.3	114.8
Disease of the digestive tract	25.5	113.6

Fevers	19.6	77.4
Alcohol-related	1.9	3.5[36]

The army in the Pacific Northwest relied on military surgeons, often recruited locally, and contract surgeons who continued their private practices. Some posts did not have surgeons. They relied upon hospital stewards who were enlisted men with on-the-job training.

Some hospital stewards were fairly competent, while other men were given the job because they were not fit for general service. Some were experienced, like Edward Colmache, an army hospital steward who was stationed at Fort Hoskins before the war, and who stayed as a member of the volunteer companies at the start of the war. It was unusual for a regular army enlisted man to stay on the job as a member of a volunteer company. A factor for Colmache was likely his marriage of some years to an Indian woman.[37]

When stationed at Fort Hoskins, Royal Bensell wrote of Colmache in his diary on July 8, 1864:

> Edward Colmache receives commission as Surgeon in the 1st Oregon State Cav. He is an old soldier, an excellent Doctor, but a most indolent man. Has kept a squaw for the last seven years. His system is so thoroughly impregnated with syphilitic disease as to show itself in its most loathsome form in his face, on his neck, &c., &c., yet this man will soon dictate etiquette, manners, &c., to his moral superiors.[38]

Some doctors were respected. Some were not. Bensell said Dr. E. Y. Chase at Fort Hoskins was so little respected that ailing soldiers would go to Corvallis and pay for care from private physicians. Colonel Thomas Cornelius, when he moved part of the First Oregon Volunteer Cavalry to Fort Walla Walla, was told to take his surgeon with him because the post surgeon there was an alcoholic.

The best record of the military medical system in the Pacific Northwest was at Fort Hoskins, as recounted in Trusell's master's thesis. That Fort Hoskins was a healthy post may have been due in part to the water which was piped from a cased spring above the post. The clean water avoided many of the water-borne diseases.[39] The original army-installed pipes were of lead, but no one stayed there long enough to suffer lead poisoning.

The records of the Fort Hoskins hospital, 1857-1865, show the most common complaints were respiratory disease, gonorrhea, and syphilis.

Respiratory disease came from exposure to the cold and wet and to other people who already had it. A small camp of Indians who were allowed to live off the reservation just below the Fort Hoskins post boundaries were thought to be a common source of venereal disease.

THE TEDIUM OF DUTY

For the soldier in the Pacific Northwest, there was no enemy but the weather, the military system itself, and the occasional warring Indian, when he could be found.

Soldiering was little different for the Civil War soldier on the nation's westernmost frontier than it was before the war. It was described by one old sergeant as "either a very lazy, tedious sort of life, or one that demands the last ounce of physical strength and such as only an iron constitution can stand."

The good months were for patrol. But even that was tedium. When the troops were on patrol, the cavalry rode. But only one of the three undermanned regiments in the Pacific Northwest was cavalry. The other two were infantry. Infantry is best for guard duty and for assault and defense against a traditional massed enemy. But there was little to guard on the frontier, and renegade bands of Indians were the only enemy. This foe was not a traditional soldier and for the most part was mounted on a fleet-footed horse.

Getting from one place to another took some doing. When two companies of Oregon Infantry transferred from the muster grounds at Camp Russell in Salem to their first duty station at Fort Hoskins, the march took the better part of three days. Travel between Fort Hoskins and the blockhouse on the Siletz Reservation was a two-day march through the woods of the Coast Range.

When the weather was poor, army policy kept the troops in their permanent stations. Garrison duty consisted "mostly of drill, guard duty, care and feeding of horses, repair and maintenance of the facilities and policing the post."

The soldiers chafed at confinement to post limits. At Fort Yamhill, Bensell recounted: "Courtwright said, the nearest he had been over the 'Limits' was 'he got on the fence and S—t over.'"[40]

Soldiers also were expected to raise much of their own food and their own livestock. Anderson H. Brown, a thirty-two-year-old Douglas County, Oregon farmer who enlisted in the First Oregon Volunteer Infantry, wrote in his diary that he tended cattle at Camp Wright (October 1865) and cut hay at Camp Currey (February 1866).[41]

And when there was nothing else, it was drill time.

Life was ruled by the clock. Some posts had buglers who blew the call to get up, go to bed, eat and drill. Others had drummers who performed the same function. John Buel Dimick wrote from his camp in eastern Oregon: "The cursed whisiling (sic) sticks awaked me again from a pleasant dream."[42]

Drill was conducted by volunteer officers, many of whom knew little more of the procedure than the men they were commanding. It consisted of marching drill based on *Hardee's Manual*, including loading of the clumsy muzzle-loader rifles "by the numbers," a drill more suited to the massed armies of Napoleon than the Indian fighters of the West. Recruits who did not readily learn the drill were assigned to the "Awkward Squad."[43] There is little mention of marksmanship training. Men of the West were presumed to know how to hit what they aimed at.

When in garrison, drill was conducted five days a week. Much of the time drill was done by squad. When there were enough men to do it, the men drilled in platoon and company formations. At some posts, Saturday was the day to prepare for the Sunday morning standing inspection. At Fort Hoskins, no drills were held on Saturday and Sunday. All units were required to stand formation twice a year while the Articles of War were read aloud to them.[44]

The men drew additional duties as guards both at day and night on the perimeters of the fort and at its guardhouse. The army also cleared trails, built roads and built and maintained the buildings and facilities at the installations.

Julie Schablitsky quoted the daily routine at Fort Hoskins. At the start of the war, the schedule allowed only two meals, breakfast and supper. Under Lieutenant James Garden in April 1863 a third meal was added to the schedule:

Reveille 5:30 a.m.
Breakfast 6:15 a.m.

Fatigue call 7:00 a.m.
Guard Mount 8:00 a.m.
Surgeon call 8:00 a.m.
Recall 12:00 noon
Orderly call   12:00-5:00 p.m.
Dinner 12:30 p.m.
Fatigue 1:30 p.m.
Recall 4:45 p.m.
Supper   5:00 p.m.
Tattoo 8:45 p.m.
Taps 9:15 p.m.[45]

Life in the field was more relaxed. William Hilleary preferred it. He wrote in his diary:

> I think this is the best place for here we have no opportunity to spend our money if we had any more to borrow, for everyone is broke. There is no sutler to give us things on tick. No dress parade or drills, no guard house with "grim monsters" in the shape of cells, no chopping wood for officers without pay and many other annoyances (of garrison life).[46]

Sergeant James Shelley of Company A, First Oregon Volunteer Infantry, wintered at Camp Polk 1865-66. He wrote that his commanding officer, Captain Charles LaFollett, held no roll call or guard mount, saying: "Well, boys. We've lost no Indians and if they'll let us alone, we'll let them alone." Shelley said he and the rest of the detachment "spent much of our time hunting mule deer."[47]

Troops also wondered whether they had the stuff should they finally face real combat. Dimick wrote: "They say there is a good chance for us to get a fight out of the redskins up in that country (the headwaters of the John Day River). God knows I hope so. I would like to know whether I am a coward or not."[48]

SPARE TIME ACTIVITIES

On their off-duty time, soldiers made their own entertainment.

In the army's District of Oregon there were no organized army bands. The Fourth U.S. Infantry had a band of sorts at Fort Vancouver before the start of the war, but it went south with the regulars when the troops were withdrawn. The monthly reports of the individual companies show that each company had one or two men listed as musicians. There were drummers and fifers. Some men carried fiddles and mouth harps and made their own music.[49]

There were other more structured spare time activities including spelling bees and ad hoc athletic events. One account tells of soldiers at Fort Hoskins competing with the Indians in a game of "coho"—an Indian version of field hockey played with a wooden ball.[50] Where card-playing was not banned, soldiers played cards for money or matches. They also played checkers, rolled dice, and pitched pennies.

Sometimes, just to show that fun can be found anywhere, the soldier resorted to unusual entertainment. On duty in remote eastern Oregon, John Buel Dimick wrote his girl friend: "Us boys have lots of fun a rooling (sic) rocks down the mountain side. I was out yesterday and passed of a few hours thus very pleasantly."[51]

Many soldiers were interested both in the progress of the war in the East and in current events. At some posts company funds were used to subscribe to newspapers and magazines and there were posts with libraries of sorts. Company F, First Oregon Volunteer Infantry, formed its own literary society.

When a newspaper came in the mail to camp, a good reader with a strong voice would read its contents out loud to the listeners, some of whom themselves were barely literate.

Men put on their own theatrics. Occasional variety acts would come to camp and perform for a fee. Fort Hoskins had a 40 x 60-foot building called a theater. Captain Frederick Seidenstriker, post commander, had it torn down in 1862 and used the salvage to repair other buildings. At Fort Hoskins later in the war, two jugglers put on their act on the bottom floor of the barracks. Admission was 25¢ and collected at the door. Most of the crowd came in through the window.[52]

There were few chaplains on the frontier. In May 1865 General Alvord asked the Secretary of War for an army chaplain for the remote and unchurched Fort Colville, in Washington Territory. He noted that he had only two chaplains in the District of Oregon, one at Fort Steilacoom and the other at Fort Vancouver.[53]

Preachers visited and held services at posts near established communities. At Fort Hoskins, soldiers organized a Bible study group, and one officer organized a Bible study class that met regularly.

Soldiers also womanized, gambled, and drank. Occasionally they went to town and fought with any local secessionists who might call them out. Sometimes the soldiers provoked the fights themselves.[54] It broke the monotony.

In 1864 a money order system was established that allowed soldiers to send part of their minute pay home to the family more safely. In populous areas, the army had special postal units that kept track of the units and forwarded mail to soldiers on the move.[55]

WHISKEY, GAMBLING AND SEX

One constant element in most contemporary accounts of the life of the Civil War soldier involved whiskey, gambling, and sex.

Whiskey, homemade and otherwise, went by a variety of names. Liquor purchased from Mormon traders in the Idaho country was called "Mormon Tan" Or "Valley Tan." Other nicknames included "O, Be Joyful," "How Come You So," "Red Eye," "Tanglefoot," "The Ardent," "Hoochinoo," "Tarantula Juice," "Nockum Stiff," "Take a Horn," and "Oil of Gladness."

Rodney Glisan, a teetotaler army surgeon who served before the Civil War both in Oregon and Texas, blamed liquor for 90 percent of the offenses for which soldiers were charged.[56] In the summer of 1864, bad whiskey played in the death of Private Sam P. Strang, at Jacksonville, Oregon, as was noted in a letter to the Surgeon General from his commanding officer at Fort Klamath:

> ....Deceased Private Sam. P. Strang, Company Clerk of Co. C, 1st Ogn. Cav., left this Post, Capt. Wm. Kelly, for Jacksonville, Oregon,...Soon after arriving at Jacksonville, Strang became drunk. He was to return to the Post on the 12th but was so drunk that he was left behind by Sergt. in charge of the party, where he remained until he died on the 21st, evidently Delirium Tremens which he had been subject to. Ten or fifteen minutes before he died he was running up the streets of Jacksonville after an imaginary person when he dropped in a fit. The day was warm and the man very fat....[57]

Liquor was prohibited on military installations. It was a prohibition that didn't work. Archaeological excavations at Fort Hoskins uncovered numerous bottles from that period--beer, whiskey, brandy, champagne, cognac, wine, schnapps and ale.[58]

Sutlers, the private merchants who sold to the soldiers, were not supposed to sell cards and whiskey. But they did anyway. Permanent installations attracted entrepreneurs who opened drinking establishments off-post. On January 12, 1863 the provost guard from Fort Hoskins rousted a handful of drunken soldiers from a deadfall operated by two men from Corvallis below the fort's main gate. Immediately afterwards the building burst into flames. The clerk in charge accused the soldiers of starting the fire but the post commander, Captain F. Seidenstriker, was so glad to get rid of the place that he asked no questions.[59]

For some, drinking was a destination. Diarist Royal Bensell noted that two colleagues, McCarthy and Howard, "went to Hoskins for a drunk." Some soldiers traded uniform clothing for whiskey to the peddlers who clustered outside the camps.

On a river steamer heading back to winter quarters at Fort Dalles in 1863, Lieutenant Colonel Reuben Maury was insulted by a passenger who his regimental adjutant, William V. Rinehart, described as a "gentleman gambler of Southern birth and prejudice." The gambler sneered at Maury's uniform. But the gambler himself was wearing a brand new cavalry greatcoat.

Maury told the gambler: "Men wearing such clothing usually salute shoulder-straps whether they like me or not." Then Maury turned to Rinehart and ordered him to seize "that coat and every one like it, not in possession of a United States soldier."

Rinehart did as he was told. "When I had finished collecting overcoats I found I had piled up on the deck over 30 coats, and began to see a reason for the general order requiring us to stop the purchase, by citizens, of army clothing." The gambler, under arrest until the boat docked, was released, coatless, after profuse apologies to Maury.[60]

Sometimes too much drink made for marvelous stories. Bensell's diary tells of a holiday dinner to which he and his messmates at Fort Yamhill invited guests—including young ladies—from the area:

> July 4, 1864. Clear. Independence Day. Pvt. Lewee purchased a pig and a mutton. Bowery, Moran and Doc Getzendanner attempted to cook the same. All got gloriously

fuddled. Just before dinner "Bowery" went to the rear and lost the Kitchen Key down the privy hole. He went outside and tried to crawl down where he could see the key, but being a little too Drunk he lost his balance and found himself in a nice fix. Finally he got out, cleaning his clothes with a bunch of grass. He reported for duty as a waiter just as several Ladies got seated. The curiosity that follows defies description. Everybody was seen to examine the soles of their Boots carefully. All to no purpose. "Bowery" was discovered and hustled out in "Double Quick." Of course, much fun followed, and the 4th passed jollily after all. The Dinner was a "lifter," you may depend.[61]

Soldiers in the Pacific Northwest were young, single and bored. In contemporary accounts there is little mention of military involvement with white prostitutes, likely because they charged for their pleasures. Soldiers stationed near Indian reservations frequently consorted with Indian women who did it for much less money and occasionally out of affection.

Men were disciplined for sneaking off from their duty stations at night to be with their Indian girl friends. Officers also got involved. At Fort Hoskins before the war, Lieutenant H. H. Garber had an affair of the heart with an Indian woman from the Siletz reservation. He was suspended from duty in 1858 by his commanding officer, Captain C. C. Augur.[62]

Lieutenant Philip Sheridan, who was later to become chief of staff of the postwar army, reportedly had relations with three Indian women while stationed before the war at Forts Yamhill and Hoskins. He was unmarried at the time. The photo of one, a quite handsome Frances Johnson of the Rogue tribe, is in the Oregon Historical Society archives.

Another, a seventeen-year-old Klickitat young woman named Jennie, reportedly was sold by her aunt to Sheridan, but refused to go through with the deal.[63] Her daughter-in-law, Mrs. Sam Riggs, told an *Oregon Statesman* reporter in 1965 that Jennie arrived at Sheridan's quarters, saw her image for the first time in a mirror, concluded that Sheridan already had a wife and left, refusing to return.[64]

Some Indian women were forced into prostitution by their men. Bensell was a member of a twenty-two-man party sent from Fort Hoskins to the blockhouse at the Indian reservation at Siletz. He wrote twice of the relations between soldiers and the women of the Siletz tribe:

> Feb. 12, 1864....There is all around the Post any amount of Squaws, young & old, some good looking and some not, and to say virtue could be found out of the cradle is to lie, and to deny the existence [of] Soldiers concubines would be equally untrue.[65]
>
> Mar. 9, 1864....[T]hese Indians, all of them, sell their women to any persons wishing to purchase. Prices according "to age and appearance," some $5 and others $50, and the whole tribe or tribes will see that the bargain is sustained. Should the Squaw "vamoose" the tribes will refund the money. Some of the Boys invest in this doubtful traffic.[66]

In March 1862, Captain J. C. Schmidt, then commanding officer, ordered his troops at Fort Hoskins and Siletz to keep the soldiers and the Indians apart. At Siletz Agency, Indians were not permitted within 200 yards of the blockhouse. Further, he ordered: "No non com officers or privates will be allowed squaws in quarters nor will they be allowed to sleep out of quarters."[67]

DISCIPLINE

Military discipline in the Pacific Northwest, as elsewhere, was harsh and unpredictable. In the field, many unit commanders didn't bother. "Just get the job done," was the unwritten rule and one accepted by the non-professional volunteers. But during the winter months, when the men and their officers were stuck in garrison until spring opened up the roads, rules and punishment for their violation took on more importance.

Informal punishment was accomplished through a "black list" of those men who had committed non-court martial offenses. This list was referred to when obnoxious jobs needed filling—digging latrine trenches, policing the camp and burying dead animals.[68]

Over-all, Oregon and Washington Territory troops appear better disciplined than troops in many units in the East, perhaps because troops raised for Pacific Northwest units were mostly frontiersmen and it took a degree of internal discipline to survive on the western frontier.

The 1861-65 General Orders of the District of Oregon showed more serious courts martial for desertion, assault without law, drunkenness on duty, habitual drunkenness, sleeping on his post, selling property belonging to the government of the United States, mutinous subordinate conduct, striking a superior officer, theft, conduct to the prejudice of good order and discipline, and mutiny.

Some prisoners sentenced to confinement were sent to work on the fortifications at Fort Cape Disappointment, where a lack of available civilian laborers delayed completion of construction.

At least two officers, First Lieutenant Peter Fox and Captain Daniel O'Regan[69], both of the Washington Territory Volunteer Infantry, were discharged for misappropriating government property.

A usual punishment for enlisted soldiers was additional drill, often while carrying a weight. John Buel Dimick wrote his sweetheart: "I had a soldier carrying a sack of sand weighing 40 lbs today in front of the Guard house in charge of No 1 sentinel. His offence was getting drunk and missing roll call."[70] Others spent brief tours in the guardhouse or were shackled with a ball and chain, usually until they sobered up.

Punishment was also extended to civilian employees of the army and to the Indians confined to reservations. In his memoirs, William V. Rinehart wrote of a Fort Walla Walla civilian interpreter, Tom Hughes, who got drunk and shot his government-issue horse. His officer put him to work in the broiling summer sun, made him dig a hole, bury the horse's carcass, and then banned him from the fort.[71]

Reservation Indians who got drunk, stole, or fled the reservation without permission were imprisoned in the guard house, flogged with a whip, or beaten with a hoe handle. The worst punishment for an Indian was to have his (or her) head shaved.[72]

DESERTION

Desertion was a continuing problem for the army in all theaters of operation during the Civil War, including the Pacific Northwest. In the District of Oregon, desertions increased in the spring when better-paying civilian jobs beckoned.[73]

Adjutant General Reed's war-end report in 1866 listed 149 men deserted from Oregon Volunteer units during the Civil War. War Department records show 209 deserters from the Washington Territory Volunteer Infantry.[74] Those who were recaptured were either returned to duty or court-martialed. Punishment varied. Some were summarily dismissed from the service. [75]

After the government started paying cash bonuses for enlistments, some men enlisted, collected their bonuses, deserted, enlisted again in different units, collected their bonuses and deserted over and over again. On March 11, 1865, as the war wound down, President Lincoln granted pardons to all deserters who would surrender.

The penalty for desertion in the face of the enemy was death. Only one soldier in the District of Oregon suffered the ultimate penalty. Francis Ely, a twenty-one-year-old Irish-born private in Co. A, First Oregon Volunteer Cavalry, deserted in July 1863 as his company was preparing for an anticipated battle with Chief Pocatello and his band of Snake Indians on the Port Neuf River in eastern Idaho. The battle never materialized because Chief Pocatello had already signed a peace agreement.

The exact circumstances of Ely's desertion are not clear. Historian Glenn Thomas Edwards, Jr. opines that Ely fell under the influence of anti-Union Mormon traders and the bootleg they dispensed, and abandoned his military career for fame and fortune in the recently opened gold mines of Montana.[76]

Ely headed for the frontier town of Beaver Head. He was found by a squad of soldiers in pursuit, asleep by the side of the road with his horse's picket rope tied to his foot. He was taken to Fort Walla Walla and in November 1863 he was court-martialed and sentenced to death.

Ely's company had multiple desertions that summer. Its commanding officer, Captain Thomas S. (Smiley) Harris, resigned his commission at the request of his superiors for, among other things, lax discipline.

In at least nine previous instances, General George Wright, commander of the Department of the Pacific, had reduced the death penalty to imprisonment.

No clemency came for Francis Ely. Wright directed that the court martial verdict of execution be carried out.[77] Captain William V.

Rinehart, Harris' successor as commanding officer of Company A, was responsible for the job.

In 1907, Rinehart wrote his recollection of the event.[78] It was Rinehart's duty to tell Ely that he would be executed on March 11, 1864 and to offer him the benefit of clergy. Ely chose a Methodist minister, Reverend Boswell whose son-in-law was stationed at the fort. When Boswell visited the fort, he would also visit the men and act as volunteer chaplain. As the time for his execution approached, Ely changed his mind and sent for a Catholic priest.

Ely was to be executed on a Friday. For three days prior no passes were issued at Fort Walla Walla, not even to visit the town a mile away. After midnight each night the captain and first sergeant went quietly from bunk to bunk checking off names to see that every man was in his bed.

Hoping that there might be a reprieve, Colonel Maury at Fort Dalles ordered men from Company B there, and Company A at Walla Walla, to take posts every twelve miles along the 175-mile road to serve as couriers to carry forward the hoped for reprieve from General Wright at San Francisco.

No reprieve came. The firing squad took four men from Company A and six from Company E. As 2 p.m. approached, Ely was taken to a cart. He rode backward sitting on the rough board coffin that would be his last resting place. They proceeded to the corral:

> [W]hich was surrounded by a high board fence. The formation there was three sides of a hollow square, with the condemned Ely facing the two firing parties at ten paces in the open fourth side. After Adjt. Kapus had read the order for his execution, the black cap was drawn down over his eyes and one volley sent four balls through his heart. His body was carted away by the fatigue party and buried without the honors of war.[79]

QUARTERS

Although primitive at best, Pacific Northwest housing for the Civil War soldier wasn't much worse than the rude country cabins in which many families then lived. In the field, if a soldier had a tent he slept in it. Otherwise he wrapped himself in a blanket and slept on the ground.

Near Phoenix (then Gasburg), recruits to the new First Oregon Volunteer Cavalry Regiment mustered at the remains of Camp Baker, a deserted Indian war post. There, they built their own barracks and stables and two-man bunks.[80]

At Salem, the recruits of the new First Oregon Volunteer Infantry bunked through winter 1864 in the livestock pavilion at the State Agricultural Society's fairgrounds.

On their three-day march from Salem to their first duty station at Fort Hoskins, Private William Hilleary's Company F of the First Oregon Volunteer Infantry had no tents and slept one night in the barn on the farm of U.S. Senator James W. Nesmith near Dixie (now Rickreall).

At Fort Hoskins, a permanent installation built in the 1850s, the barracks was a two-story wooden building. It was designed to house two companies of about 175 men.

The second floor was the sleeping area for enlisted men. The ground floor held a kitchen, mess room, and wash room.[81] The first floor also was a day room of sorts and was where the soldiers made their rude entertainment.

As noted earlier, Fort Hoskins was unique in that it had running water piped to the barracks and other buildings from a spring above the fort site. The barracks had no stoves. Heat came from two inefficient open fireplaces. Through the winter the troops stayed warm cutting and hauling the two cords of wood these fireplaces consumed each day. The men bunked in double-decker bunks, two men to a bed. Private Hilleary wrote:

> We had no stoves, not even cook-stoves, but open fireplaces in every room....The usual style of bunk was two stories high, arranged for four persons, two above and two below. The end of the bunk was set against the wall with a space of two feet between it and the next one. On the end of the bunk next the aisle a gun rack was fixed up for four guns and the necessary fixtures. There was a row of such bunks on either side of the squad room. The bed sacks were generally made single width, hence there was no grumbling that one or the other had all the straw on their side.[82]

Fort Hoskins also had three small cottages, each fenced with a picket fence. This is where the officers lived. Designed originally for officers and their families, the cottages were shared by two bachelor officers during the war.

At the Siletz Blockhouse, a separate building was built to house the troops.

In eastern Oregon, John Buel Dimick wrote of the three-sided brush wickiup he and his bunkies constructed at Camp Five Mile Creek in August 1863:

> We all have nice bush (sic) houses built. Near the lower end of our camp a large bush house can be seen built under some nice spreading oaks. Three sides of which are closed up by interwoven bushwork. The fourth side or end is left open & there may be seen a humble soldier with pen in hand bending over a rude table (made by driving four crotches in the ground and building there on a rude table out of poles and covered on the tip of the poles by a pan of macheers(?).... In the Back end of the rude house may be seen to beds made of oak leaves.... And on pegs made for that purpose hangs the impliments of War consisting of Guns pistols and sabers.[83]

At the Lapwai conference with the Indian tribes in 1863, the attending army units bivouacked in tents and hauled firewood from fourteen miles away.[84]

Since army policy called for bringing all troops in from the field to permanent winter quarters at established posts, the field camps had little in the way of substantial structures until the winter campaign of 1865-66. Then structures of log chinked with clay provided shelter.

LEADERSHIP

At the start of the war, the army left a handful of regular army officers along with two companies of regular troops in the Pacific Northwest.

The volunteer units were led by volunteer officers. Some had served in volunteer or regular units during the war with Mexico. Others had service of indifferent value with militia units organized during the Indian wars.

The quality of volunteer officers varied.

Some officers performed well. One of the brilliant home-grown leaders of the war in the Pacific Northwest was George B. Currey, who started the series of winter campaigns that finally subdued the renegade Indian bands of the area east of the Cascades.

Others were less competent. Diaries complain of officers who had failed to master the drill or overindulged in drink.

Overall the volunteer officers were a good fit for their volunteer enlisted men. Observers found the Pacific Northwest volunteer army more democratic. There was less distinction between the frontier officers and the frontier enlisted men than between the prewar West Pointers and enlisted troops, many of whom were foreign-born immigrants. The editor of San Francisco's *Alta* newspaper wrote that the egalitarian attitude of the volunteer units would:

> [T]each the officer that in his intercourse with the rank and file, he is dealing with men, some of whom may be one day his equals: or may be, his superiors, and the private soldiers [would learn] that fame and distinction do not belong exclusively to any one class by right of West Point.[85]

Some promising enlisted men became officers. John Buel Dimick was promoted to second lieutenant and transferred to Fort Vancouver in January 1865, where he was able to marry his sweetheart, Almira Eberhard.

At the end of the war, Dimick applied for a commission in the peacetime army and failed.

Few of the volunteers reenlisted in the regular army. Most returned to civilian life. They were veterans of the Civil War. But for most their experience in the Pacific Northwest was far different from the domestic wartime experience they had anticipated when they enlisted.

Chapter 16 notes

1 Wiley, Bell Irvin, *The Life of Billy Yank; The Common Soldier of the Union*, 9.
2 Gould, Benjamin Apthorp, *Investigations in the Military and Anthropological Statistics of American Soldiers*, (New York, Riverside Press, 1869) 30, cited in Schablitsky, Julie M., *Duty and Vice: The Daily Life of a Fort Hoskins Soldier*, 37.
3 Ibid, W.O.R. Series 3, 4:1269.
4 Schablitsky, "Duty and Vice," 37-39, 45-46, 48-50.
5 Barth, Gunter, *All Quiet on the Yamhill*, 13.
6 Field, Virgil F., *History of the Washington National Guard*, 1:215-16.
7 Barth, Gunter, *All Quiet On the Yamhill*, 168.
8 Edwards, "The Department of the Pacific," 296.
9 Hilleary, William M., *A Webfoot Volunteer*, 187.
10 Kittell, Allen (Ed.), "Bear Bravely On, Letters from Sergeant John Buell Dimick , First Oregon Volunteer Cavalry, to Amelia Eberhart," 3. Troiani, Don, *Regiments and Uniforms of the Civil War*, (Mechanicsburg, Pa., Stackpole Books, 2002), 107-8
11 Ward, Arthur, interview, 1968.
12 Schablitsky, Julie M., "Duty and Vice," 94.
13 Kittell, "Bear Bravely On," 2-4.
14 W.O.R., Series 3, 1:399.
15 Wiley, *Life of Billy Yank*, 224.
16 W.O.R., 3, 1:531.
17 Schablitsky, "Duty and Vice," 68.
18 Rinehart, William V., "With the Oregon Cavalry," mss. 471, OHS, 1907, unnumbered.
19 U.S. Army, Fort Hoskins, Oregon, General Order No. 3, March 4, 1859, Post Returns.
20 Wiley, *Life of Billy Yank*, 242.
21 One recorded bit of camp dialogue: SERGEANT – "I was eating a piece of hardtack this morning and I bit on something soft. What do you think it was?" PRIVATE – "A worm?" SERGEANT – "No, by God, it was a ten-penny nail." Wiley, Bell Irvin, *The Life of Billy Yank; The Common Soldier of the Union*, (Garden City, N. Y., Doubleday and Co., 1971), 237.
22 Hilleary, *A Webfoot Volunteer*, 82.
23 Hoop, Oscar Winslow, "History of Fort Hoskins," OHQ, (1929) 30:359.
24 Barth, *All Quiet on the Yamhill*, 8.
25 Hilleary, *A Webfoot Volunteer*, 42-46, 50-53.
26 Schablitsky, "Duty and Vice," 76
27 Hoop, "History of Fort Hoskins," 353-54.
28 Schablitsky, "Duty and Vice," 77.
29 Holburt, Charles, Camp Curry Documents, mss. 1514, OHS.
30 Trussell, Timothy D., "Frontier Military Medicine at Fort Hoskins, 1857-1866: An archaeological and Historical Perspective," (Master's thesis, Oregon State University, 1996) 36.
31 Ibid., 37.
32 Wiley, *Life of Billy Yank*, 126-127.
33 Kittell, "Bear Bravely On," A-18.
34 Trussell, Timothy D., *Frontier Military Medicine*, 23.
35 Ibid., 84.
36 Ibid.
37 Ibid., 62-63.
38 Colmache may have been considered for a state commission, but records show federal service only as an enlisted man.
39 Trussell, Timothy D., *Frontier Military Medicine*, 37.
40 Barth, *All Quiet on the Yamhill*, 10.
41 Brown, A.H., Diary, 1864-1866, mss., Justine Jones collection, n.p.
42 Kittell, Allen (ed.), "Bear Bravely On," C-13.
43 Shelley, James M., Untitled Manuscript Read to Reunion of 1st Oregon Veterans, Newport, Oregon, June 24, 1908, OHS, n.p.
44 Wiley, *Life of Billy Yank*, 25.
45 Schablitsky, "Duty and Vice," 61.
46 Kittell, "Bear Bravely On," X-3.
47 Shelley, James M., Untitled Manuscript, n.p.
48 Kittell, "Bear Bravely On," E-1.
49 Schablitsky, "Duty and Vice," 70.

50 Schablitsky, "Duty and Vice," 73.

51 Kittell, "Bear Bravely On," E-17.

52 Schablitsky, "Duty and Vice," 72.

53 U.S. Army District of Oregon, correspondence file, p. 284, National Archives, Washington, D.C.

54 Hilleary, *A Webfoot Volunteer*, 46.

55 Billings, John D., *Hardtack and Coffee* (Chicago, R.R. Donnelly and Sons Co., 1960) 94, cited in Kittell, Allen (Ed.), App. IV, 2.

56 Edwards, "The Department of the Pacific," 36.

57 U.S. Army, Fort Klamath, Correspondence book, National Archives, Washington, D.C.

58 Bowyer, Gary, *Archaeological Symbols of Status and Authority; Fort Hoskins, Oregon, 1856-1865*, 57-58.

59 Schablistsky, "Duty and Vice," 89-90; Maxwell, Ben, "Worse Duty No Man Could Find," *Frontier Times*, December-January 1968, 36-37.

60 Rinehart, William V., "With the Oregon Cavalry."

61 Barth, Gunter, *All Quiet on the Yamhill*, 164.

62 Maxwell, Ben, "Worse Duty No Man Could Find," 36-37.

63 Charles Crookham, formerly presiding judge of the Multnomah County Circuit Court at Portland and Oregon Attorney General, recounted to me in 1991 an account told him by his uncle, Arthur Crookham, one-time city editor of the *Oregon Journal*. Crookham's uncle said that he was approached sometime in the 1920s by promoters of the annual "Phil Sheridan Days" celebration at Sheridan, accompanied by two elderly Indian women who claimed to be Philip Sheridan's illegitimate daughters.

64 Lockley, Fred, "Reminiscences of Martha E. Gilliam Collins,", *OHQ*, 17(1916):367; Cooper, Grace E., "Benton County Historical Society Meeting," *OHQ*, 57(1956):83, both cited in Schablitsky, Julie M., "Duty and Vice," 81; Wright, Tom, "The Almost Wife of General Phil Sheridan," *Oregon Statesman*, Nov. 28, 1965, cited in *Historically Speaking*, 15(2007), Polk County Historical Society.

65 Barth, *All Quiet on the Yamhill*, 123.

66 Ibid., 131.

67 Schablitsky, "Duty and Vice," 82.

68 Ibid., 92.

69 U.S. Army, Department of the Pacific, General Orders No. 61, January 5, 1864, and December 29, 1864.

70 Kittell, "Bear Bravely On," 15.

71 Rinehart, William V., "With the Oregon Cavalry."

72 Schablitsky, "Duty and Vice," 56.

73 Ibid., 87.

74 Field, *The Official History of the Washington National Guard*, 1:239.

75 A 20 percent desertion rate is astonishingly high, but probably can be attributed to the fact that the majority of the regiment's enlisted men were recruited in California and had few ties with the Pacific Northwest.

76 Edwards, "Oregon Regiments in the Civil War Years," 199-201.

77 *Oregon Statesman*, February 22, 1864.

78 Rinehart, William V., "With the Oregon Cavalry."

79 First Lt. T.W. Kapus, 1st Washington Volunteer Infantry, also was the Judge Advocate, or presiding officer, at Ely's court martial.

80 Taylor, Hobart, unpublished diary, Southern Oregon Historical Society, Medford, Oregon.

81 Maxwell, "Worse Duty No Man Could Find," 36-37.

82 Hilleary, *A Webfoot Volunteer*, 42.

83 Kittell, "Bear Bravely On," 16-17.

84 Kittell, "Bear Bravely On," E-15.

85 *San Francisco Alta*, October 26, 1862, cited in Edwards, *The Department of the Pacific in the Civil War Years*, 293.

Chapter 17

WHEN THE WAR ENDED

N ews of the capture of the Confederate capitol of Richmond, General Robert E. Lee's surrender at Appomattox, and the assassination of President Lincoln trickled to the Pacific Northwest over the single hand-pounder telegraph line that linked the Willamette Valley and Puget Sound cities with Sacramento and the East.[1]

The surrender of Richmond on April 3, 1865 was recognized by most of the Oregon Country as the virtual end of the Confederacy and of the war. Every cannon in the region was fired. Those who had no cannon fired anvil guns by priming the holes in their anvils with gunpowder and touched them off with a rousing crash. Speeches were made, and people listened to them. Fireworks were set off. Some cities celebrated with a "Grand Illumination" and put lamps and candles in all the windows of business houses and homes. Patriotic red, white, and blue transparencies were cast on the sides of buildings.

The first news of the fall of Richmond came to Salem April 4, 1865. The *Oregon Statesman* reported:

> [E]verybody was taken by surprise and many looked incredulous....The telegraph office was besieged all day for a confirmation; and when it did come, Union men threw their hats with a right good will. The cannon was brought in the square and a hundred rounds fired in honor of the event. In the evening, an immense crowd gathered on Commercial Street and Gov. Gibbs made a speech.

An unnamed correspondent in Independence reported that anvils were fired and shouts were uttered on receipt of the news, "but a leading democrat of that place came out on his steps and hurrahed for Jeff. Davis."

In Dallas, the Democrat proprietor of the Eagle Hotel grudgingly gave up her flag and local Unionists ran it up the town flagpole.[2]

Lee surrendered to Grant on April 9 and the news made it to Portland three days later. The patriotic juices flowed again. A parade was organized and passed down the city's main thoroughfare with three bands, marching firemen, and illuminated horse-drawn floats.[3] In Salem, students from Willamette University stacked up a huge bonfire on the site of the old territorial capitol building, destroyed by fire in 1854. They used four timbers left behind after the original fire as a foundation and topped the stack of combustibles with several tar and oil barrels. That evening, they touched it off.[4]

All agreed it was quite a fire. The *Oregon Statesman* commented the bonfire was "equalized in size only by the conflagration of the hotel last summer." Local luminaries and six Willamette students made formal speeches. The crowd made three cheers for four former Willamette University students then in Union military service.[5]

This exultation was followed by the news of President Lincoln's death April 15. Funeral services were held in Washington, D.C., on April 19, and most Portland business houses closed. Governor Gibbs declared April 27 a day of mourning for Oregon.[6]

Some communities were not served by telegraph. There, the news came late. It arrived in The Dalles when the river steamer from Portland docked at the wharf. The steamer's flag was at half mast and its bell was being tolled.

This was not readily noted by celebrating townspeople who had just learned that Washington had decided to locate a new federal mint at The Dalles. Aboard the ship was William H. Newell, the man who was credited with the achievement of this federal effort.

The noisy crowd, accompanied by the town band, met Newell and hauled him to Moody's Hall, which was over a saloon, for speeches. Two volunteers fired their anvils. Then word spread of President Lincoln's death. The anvils were hauled back to the shop, the speechmaking fizzled out and The Dalles joined the nation in its mourning.[7]

Not all Pacific Northwest residents mourned the President's passing.

At Bruceport, in Washington Territory, a noisy rebel exu
Lincoln's death. The *Oregon Statesman* reported that local patr

> [G]rabbed him, slipped a rope around his neck, threw it
> over a beam, and strung him up, as long as it was safe without
> utter strangulation, when he was let down and put through
> the process, until he had signed every oath of allegiance to be
> found in town—with the stars and stripes unfurled over his
> head.[8]

At Eugene City, Patrick Henry Mulkey, a Long Tom River
secessionist, was jailed for drunkenly and loudly applauding Lincoln's
death. This incident almost precipitated the only North-South armed
conflict of the Civil War in the Pacific Northwest. It also spawned
Oregon's first documented free speech lawsuit.

The incident sometimes is referred to as the Long Tom Rebellion.
Patrick Henry Mulkey[9] was a native of Kentucky. He was in his early
thirties, one of nine children of Philip Mulkey, a farmer and preacher
in the rural Long Tom River area who came to Oregon with his family
in 1853.[10]

It was May 6, 1865. The war was over. Eugene City, like the nation,
still mourned the death of Abraham Lincoln. There were more people
than usual on Eugene's dirt streets. It was a Saturday, and market day.

Among those who came to town was Patrick Henry Mulkey. Some
said he was drunk. In any event, he was embittered at the collapse of
the Southern cause. He gave vent to his distress by marching up and
down the principal streets of Eugene City shouting: "Hurrah for Jeff
Davis. Old Lincoln is dead—he should have been shot years ago."[11]

This aggravated Mayor J. B. Underwood. He sought the help of
Captain William V. Rinehart, who was in town to recruit men for the
First Oregon Volunteer Infantry.

Rinehart arrested Mulkey, and had him frog-marched from
Willamette Street to the city jail, which was located in the former
Eugene Hotel building at the corner of Eighth and Pearl Streets. Rinehart
then telegraphed his superior, Lieutenant Colonel T. C. English at Fort
Vancouver, and waited for orders. The army's perceived authority for
arresting Mulkey was General McDowell's order of April 17, 1865,[12]
declaring that those who rejoiced over Lincoln's assassination were
"virtual accessories after the fact and will at once be arrested by any

officer or provost marshal or member of the police having knowledge of the case."[13]

Mulkey's actions and arrest galvanized the community. A lynch crowd gathered and the jail door was kicked down. Mulkey had a small knife that had not been discovered by his captors. He took a slice at one of the crowd, which then retreated.[14]

The Long Tom Secessionists met, and rumors flew through the community. Lieutenant Colonel George B. Currey, the commanding officer at Fort Hoskins, north of Corvallis, was ordered to hold ready his two companies of infantry to come to the relief of Eugene.[15] Rinehart gathered his young recruits, who had signed up but were not yet mustered into federal service, and local Unionists scavenged up firearms in case they were needed to repel a Secessionist attempt to free Mulkey.

Finally on May 17, orders were received to take Mulkey downriver to the hamlet of Lancaster (at that season the head of navigation of the Willamette River) to board a steamboat there and take him to headquarters at Fort Vancouver.

The night before he was to be moved, Mulkey escaped. Allowed out of the jail for exercise, Mulkey knocked down his guard, sixteen-year-old recruit James Burnap, and bolted for the Willamette River. Burnap shouted, a group of off-duty recruits pitching horseshoes nearby set out in pursuit, and Mulkey was found a few minutes later hiding in a garden.[16]

The next day Mulkey and an escort of fifteen soldiers set out by foot for Lancaster. Two hours after they left, two Unionists galloped into town to breathlessly report that a mob of 200 armed secessionists was waiting at Lancaster to free Mulkey. Rinehart sent Lieutenant Ivan (also known as Ivon) Applegate by horse to catch the escort and divert them to meet the steamer at Harrisburg.

Mulkey was confined to the guardhouse at Fort Vancouver. A summary of his case was sent to the Army's Department of the Pacific headquarters at San Francisco for review.[17]

In August 1865 Mulkey was released without trial. He arrived home to a tumultuous welcome from his Long Tom neighbors.[18]

Mulkey brooded over his confinement for nearly a year and a half. Then, in March 1867, he did the American thing. He sued William Rinehart, Ivan D. Applegate, and three enlisted members of the escort that had taken him to Vancouver claiming assault and false imprisonment.[19]

Mulkey asked damages of $10,000, a lot of money for that time. Rinehart, the principal defendant, answered the complaint with six separate defenses:

1. He was an officer of the U.S. Army at the time.

2. A state of rebellion then existed.

3. President Lincoln previously had suspended the right of habeas corpus.

4. Mulkey, by hurrahing for Jeff Davis, was guilty of disloyal practices in aid of the rebellion.

5. Because "the loyal people of the United States were lamenting the death of their late President," Mulkey's conduct threatened a conflict between the "loyal and disloyal people of the United States."

6. Rinehart ordered Mulkey transported to Vancouver because he was ordered to do so by his military superior and Rinehart didn't have anything to do with Mulkey after that.

The case was heard at Eugene by Supreme Court Justice Alonzo A. Skinner, who also rode circuit as its trial judge in Lane County and southern Oregon.

After the usual pleadings and a delay to obtain certified copies of Lincoln's habeas corpus order, the case came on for trial before a twelve-member jury October 7, 1867.

At the close of testimony, Rinehart's lawyers moved for an Order of Dismissal. Skinner allowed the motion.[20]

Mulkey promptly appealed to the Oregon Supreme Court. On September 8, 1868, the Supreme Court reversed Skinner's ruling and sent the case back for a new trial.[21]

It is unclear why the Supreme Court reversed. No opinion was published in the *Oregon Reports*. The remand order indicated the justices ruled from the bench the day of argument. The appellant's brief, which sets forth the arguments in favor of reversal, is missing from the file.

A likely reason for reversing the Circuit Court's decision to dismiss was the failure of Rinehart's lawyers to raise the issue of jurisdiction in the pleadings initially filed in the case. The Circuit Court file is silent as to any further action in the case.

Rinehart reported in his memoirs that the federal government finally paid Mulkey $200 to settle the case. But Rinehart said he got stuck with about $1,200 in attorney fees and other costs for his defense.[22]

Chapter 17 notes

1 Hansen, *Public Response*, 53.

2 *Oregon Statesman,* April 10, 1865.

3 *Daily Oregonian,* April 13, 14, 1865.

4 Gatke, Robert Moulton, *Chronicles of Willamette; The Pioneer University of the West,* (Portland, Or., Binfords and Mort, 1943) 234.

5 *Oregon Statesman,* April 17, 1865.

6 *The Daily Oregonian,* April 19, 1865.

7 Ibid., April 29, 1865.

8 *Astoria Gazette,* quoted in *Oregon Statesman,* May 22, 1865.

9 Previous published articles dealing with this incident identify Patrick Henry Mulkey varyingly as Philip Henry Mulkey and John Thomas Mulkey. Philip Mulkey was Patrick Henry Mulkey's father. Patrick Henry Mulkey was referred to locally as Henry, and so appears in the 1860 Lane County census.

10 Walling, Albert G., *Illustrated History of Lane County, Oregon* (Portland, Or., A. G. Walling Publishing Co., 1884), 498.

11 Richter, William, "War in the Great Northwest," *Washington Historical Quarterly,* 22(1931):84.

12 McDowell's authority for his order was President Lincoln's order of September 24, 1862 which suspended the right of habeas corpus and allowed the arrest of all persons who, among other things, committed any disloyal act. The U.S. Supreme Court later, on December 17, 1866, ruled that martial law can be exercised over civilians only where invasion is threatened and the civilian courts are closed. Ex Parte Milligan, U.S. Supreme Court, December term, 1866.

13 U.S. Army, Department of the Pacific, General Orders No. 27, April 17, 1865, cited in Edwards, "The Department of the Pacific," 287.

14 Williams, James C., "The Long Tom Rebellion," *OHQ,* 67(1966):54-60.

15 Carey, *History of Oregon,* 1:641.

16 Williams, "The Long Tom Rebellion," 493.

17 U.S. Army, District of Oregon, Correspondence Book, 358, National Archives, Washington, D.C.

18 *Oregon State Journal,* Aug. 12, 26, 1865.

19 Pleadings, *Patrick Henry Mulkey v. W.V. Rinehart et al,* Case No. 625, Lane County Circuit Court, Oregon State Archives, Salem, Oregon.

20 By today's ethical rules, Alonzo Skinner probably should have recused himself from hearing the case. He had served during part of the war as a civilian assistant to the Provost Marshal, and as such had directed registration for the draft and had investigated reported secessionist activities in the Eugene area. But getting a new judge in an Oregon court in the 1860s posed a significant logistical challenge. And no one complained.

21 Ibid.

22 Rinehart, William V., "With the Oregon Volunteers, 1862-1866," mss. Oregon Historical Society.

Chapter 18

THE WAR AND THE ECONOMY

P olitically and economically, the Civil War had a cataclysmic effect on the Pacific Northwest and its citizens. During the war years, the flow of immigrants to the Pacific Northwest became a flood. A new life, free land, and economic advantage continued to beckon those in the states to the East.

Some were refugees from the war who came from the Border States, beset with military strife. A number were deserters from the Confederate and Union armies. Many were attracted to the newly-discovered gold deposits in eastern Oregon and Idaho Territory. Others came to the Pacific Northwest and headed north to the Fraser River gold camps in British territory.

The army protected these new immigrants. It also became a social service agency that provided food and clothing to destitute travelers, miners, and occasionally, to the non-reservation Indians who caused the immigrants and miners concern.[1] The conflict between the whites and the non-reservation renegade Indian bands east of the Cascades was beginning to dwindle.

With the dismissal of General Alvord and the death of his successor, General George Wright, Colonel Reuben Maury, a non-career officer, took command of the military in the region. Maury launched a pro-active, all-weather campaign against the Indian bands. His troopers starved the principal band of renegades out of its winter quarters and brought them to the reservation.

Although there were later outbreaks among the Modoc and the elements of the Nez Perce tribes, Maury's military plan, hatched by Oregon volunteer officers who finally had a chance to battle the Indians western-style, put an effective end to the Indian troubles. Maury's plan was continued by his non-regular army successors, Colonel George Currey and Lieutenant Colonel John M. Drake.

The war brought massive government expenditures to the Pacific Northwest. Because of the expense of transportation, the army proved to be a ready market for what could be made, grown, or raised locally.[2] That, together with the opening of the gold fields in eastern Oregon and Idaho, meant a skyrocketing market for the products of the Pacific Northwest, and jobs at a good wage for its workmen.

Life continued apace for the farmers. Before enlisting in the First Oregon Volunteer Infantry, Anderson H. Brown farmed in the Roseburg area. He wrote that he raised sugarcane, row crops, and cattle, ran a syrup press powered with cattle, tended sheep, rendered lard, salted and resalted meat, ran ashes to make lye for his own soap, and carried wheat to Roseburg to have it ground into flour.[3]

Lumber had been a staple export of Washington Territory and Oregon since 1851. Washington sent three shipments annually to the East Coast and to Pacific ports, including Spanish naval stations.

In the early 1860s an extensive codfish fishery was developed in the Straits of Juan de Fuca. In Puget Sound, there was a heavy harvest of dogfish, a species of small shark whose oil was used as a lubricant in saw mills and as a cheap substitute for cod liver oil.[4]

The exploitation of the natural oyster beds in Yaquina Bay on Oregon's Pacific Coast brought oyster harvesters from San Francisco.

Oregon was a significant source of wool for military uniforms.[5] The Willamette Woolen Mills at Salem,[6] the largest of Oregon's woolen mills, shipped 100,000 pounds of raw wool to Boston in February 1863.[7]

After 1860, up to 13,000 tons of coal was exported each year from western Washington. Coal mines in the Issaquah Valley of King County and near Bellingham on Puget Sound were opened to feed the boilers of steam vessels on Puget Sound and in the Northwest waters.

The Pacific Northwest was not the only area to benefit from the war. Demands of the military resulted in significant income in the production of farm products in the Midwest and East. These were shipped not only to the army but to markets in Western Europe, which suffered from crop failures in the early 1860s.

In the 1850s gold was discovered in the Rogue Valley of southern Oregon. But this discovery paled in comparison to the gold deposits found east of the Cascades during the 1860s. The first of the discoveries was in summer 1860 on Orofino Creek forty miles east of the site of Lewiston, Idaho.[8] Another strike was made in September 1861 in the Salmon River area 140 miles southeast of Lewiston. Yet another strike was made in 1862 thirty-five miles northeast of what now is Boise, Idaho.

In eastern Oregon, discoveries were made in 1861 and 1862 on the John Day, Burnt, and Powder Rivers.

There was but one practical way to get men and supplies into the mines and the gold out. That was to travel along the Columbia and Snake Rivers, dominated by the Oregon Steam Navigation Company. This was immensely profitable for the businessmen of Portland, and made Portland the gateway to the interior.[9]

Gold came out. Each dollar mined was spent and spent again. Millions were spent for tools, equipment, food, clothing, and other supplies as well as for the transportation that took it from its source in the remoteness of the interior to the consumer.

The Oregon Steam Navigation Co. reported carrying 213,000 passengers and 60,000 tons of freight between 1861 and 1864.

The war years brought a greater military presence to the Pacific Northwest. Principal army posts were built and manned at Fort Boise, Fort Colville, and Fort Klamath. Other more temporary installations guarded the main roadways of eastern Oregon and Idaho Territory.

Yet Portland was not to remain the uncontested beneficiary of trade with the interior. Other communities considered themselves the proper entry point to this new area of great wealth.

Under the guise of defense and the expeditious movement of troops and the mails, the U.S. Army became involved in the mapping and development of new roads through the Cascade Mountains to the east.

In the summer of 1864, Lieutenant Colonel C. W. Drew of the First Oregon Volunteer Cavalry led an expedition to locate a road from southern Oregon past Fort Klamath and through the Warner Valley and Goose Lake to the Alvord Valley and eastward. The army had earlier opened a road from Jacksonville to Fort Klamath. Folks in the Rogue River Valley asked other southern Oregon communities to join in trying to block government support for a proposed road eastward from Red Bluff and Shasta City in northern California.

In 1864 both Congress and the Oregon Legislature approved a land grant to the Oregon Central Military Road Company. That company proposed to build a wagon road up the middle fork of the Willamette River, over a pass in the Cascades and east to Idaho. The road was never made fully passable and it was infrequently used until the road company sold its holdings in 1873.[10]

The McKenzie Fork Wagon Road Company was formed in 1862. It proposed building a toll road from near the current community of Vida east of Springfield and over what is now known as the McKenzie Pass to the Deschutes River and eventually to the gold mines of Canyon City and Auburn in Baker County. This was followed by a series of successor corporations.

In 1864, the Willamette Valley and Cascade Mountains Wagon Road Company was formed to open a road from Lebanon over what was then called Wiley Pass. This road was actually opened by 1865 and in late summer of 1865, Company A, First Oregon Volunteer Infantry passed over this road en route to its winter quarters at Camp Polk near what now is Sisters, Oregon.

Washington Territory Governor William Pickering championed the construction of wagon roads through the Washington Cascades opening up communication and transport to the eastern part of the territory.

Stimulated by a need to tie the Pacific Coast states to the rest of the Union, telegraph lines were extended to San Francisco and then north to Portland and to the Puget Sound country.[11]

The Pacific Coast states and territories long had agitated for both a transcontinental telegraph and a railroad. Proponents of the Pacific Republic—and Oregon's pre-war Senator Joseph Lane—had opposed it. In July 6, 1862 President Lincoln signed a bill to aid construction of a transcontinental telegraph and railroad.[12]

The transcontinental railroad finally tied California to the East in 1869. Rails were extended to Oregon in 1883.

With their eyes focused on what might occur after the war, the Washington Territory Legislature memorialized Congress to acquire the Russian holdings in Alaska. They thought it contained incredible wealth.

The end of the war also brought an economic change to the Pacific Northwest. In February 1865 Congress submitted the Thirteenth Amendment to the Constitution (which abolished slavery) to the states. Governor Addison C. Gibbs called a special session of the Oregon Legislature which ratified that amendment on December 11, 1865. The federal amendment nullified Article I, Section 35 of the Oregon Constitution that prohibited free Negroes and mulattos within the state.

The volunteer soldiers gradually were mustered out as regular army troops arrived to take their places. Discharged troopers were allowed to take their weapons with them—for a price. A standard-issue revolver or rifle cost $8. A sabre and belt cost $3.[13]

The muster-out was not uniformly smooth. Volunteer officers were sometimes lax in record keeping. One unnamed headquarters captain at Fort Vancouver waspishly complained in a letter to the commanding officer of Camp Watson that Private John R. Scott showed up at Fort Vancouver to be discharged from Company F of the First Oregon Volunteer Cavalry. But by that time Company F didn't exist anymore. The captain threatened to ask that the pay of the company officer responsible for the error be docked for the extra wages paid. Poor Private Scott cooled his heels at Fort Vancouver while waiting for the proper paperwork to allow him to be discharged.[14]

The Democrats, who had managed to elect only five members to the Oregon House of Representatives in 1864, soon seized political control in Oregon.

Part of this was the result of scandals during the administration of Republican Governor George L. Woods (1866-70), whose refusal to appoint successors for those members of the House of Representatives who had resigned at mid-session left Oregon government in limbo for nearly two years.

Much of the credit for revitalizing the Democratic Party was given to Lafayette Grover, a state rights champion who was elected as Oregon's first member of the U.S. House of Representatives. His term of office expired eighteen days after Oregon finally became a state in 1859.

The Democrats seized control of the legislature in 1868 and attempted unsuccessfully to undo the ratification by the previous legislature of the Fourteenth Amendment.[15]

Grover was elected governor in 1870 and served until he resigned to be appointed to the U.S. Senate in 1877. The Republicans did not reclaim the governor's office until 1882.[16]

Joseph Lane stayed on his farm seven miles east of Roseburg. He and his wife were baptized in the Catholic faith in 1867. She died in 1870. Lane moved to Roseburg in 1878 to live near his daughter. He roused himself on three occasions to go to the political stump.

Lane appeared at the less-than-successful Democratic Party convention at Albany in 1864 to champion the successful legislative campaign of his son, Lafayette Lane, a member of the Knights of the Golden Circle. Lane again campaigned when Lafayette Lane ran in 1875 to succeed U.S. Representative George LaDour, who had died in office.

Lane stirred himself from old age to run for the state senate in 1880—and lost handily. He died April 19, 1881 and was buried in the Masonic Cemetery at Roseburg after a service followed by the largest funeral cortege seen to that date in Roseburg.[17]

General Benjamin Alvord, summarily relieved from his wartime position as the army's commanding general of the District of Oregon, reported to Washington, D.C. as ordered and was sent home on leave to Vermont. From Vermont on June 14, 1865, Alvord wrote General W. A. Rawlins, army chief of staff, to urge that troops be stationed at Virginia City, Montana, to protect settlers and miners in Montana from attack by the Indians.[18]

On July 28, 1865, as a part of a wholesale reassignment of general officers, Alvord was ordered to report for occupation duty in the Department of Florida.[19] He resigned his commission as Brigadier General of Volunteers eleven days later.

Alvord served as Chief Paymaster of the Distict of Omaha and Department of the Platte from 1867 to 1871. He was appointed Paymaster General of the Army January 1, 1872, and served until he retired June 8, 1880.[20]

The Democratic press, stifled during the war, blossomed forth in true "Oregon Style." It clamored against the newly-bestowed rights of the Negro and championed the repudiation of the U.S. war debt.[21]

Army volunteers used skills learned during the war to succeed in business and industry. The old Oregon volunteers almost uniformly joined the Grand Army of the Republic and headed patriotic parades through the 1920s.[22]

Oregon's last Civil War veteran was James W. Smith, who served as a private in Nathan Olney's short-lived cavalry detachment in eastern Oregon. Smith, who lived at Waterloo, in Linn County, died March 22, 1951 at the age of 108.[23]

The last Civil War veteran in Washington was Hiram R. Gale, who served in the Wisconsin volunteers. He died March 15, 1951 at the age of 104.[24]

OREGON'S UNPAID CIVIL WAR DEBT

The federal government never paid Oregon for what it spent raising volunteer troops during the Civil War. As early as July 1861 Congress passed an act directing the Secretary of the Treasury to pay for the "costs, charges, and expenses" incurred for "enrolling, subsisting, clothing, supplying, arming, equipping, paying, and transporting its troops."[25]

In 1864 the Oregon Legislature authorized two bond issues. The first was in the amount of $100,000 payable in eleven years. Oregon troops were paid in depreciated paper money, and this amount was to bring the pay of the troops up to a value of $13 a month payable in gold. The second, a $100,000 issue redeemable in twenty years, was to provide a $150 mustering-out bonus for new recruits and those already in the Oregon units who reenlisted. It was an amount intended to equal the bonus given peacetime volunteers in the Pacific Northwest. That bonus was what the army figured it cost to bring a recruit to Oregon from the army's prewar central recruiting depot in New York City.[26]

Oregon's lawmakers acted on the assurances of Secretary of State William H. Seward that issuing the bonds would only require "temporary use of its (Oregon's) means." Similar assurances came from General McDowell and General Alvord.

For years after the war, Oregon chief executives intermittently sought payment from the federal government. No money came. Part of the problem was that Oregon delayed in making a serious press for payment. A collateral factor undoubtedly was the bad odor left behind by Oregon's claim for questionable expenses incurred during the Indian Wars of the 1850s.

Meanwhile, in March 1873 Congress passed an act setting June 30, 1874 as the final date for any state to submit claims for the mustering of recruits during the Civil War. California and Nevada also had not been paid. The California Legislature authorized the hiring of outside attorneys to press California's claim.

Both Oregon and California hired attorney Thomas Mullan, (who, as a regular army captain, had blazed the Mullan Road from Walla Walla to the east) to help move the claim.

In 1882 Congress authorized examining the claims of all three states, but the claims of all states were hung up on an administrative rule issued by Secretary of the Treasury Salmon P. Chase in July 1861. Chase's rule said that the federal government wouldn't have to pay for the cost of mustering volunteer troops unless they were authorized by the President or Secretary of War. Neither Oregon nor California's action was specifically authorized by Lincoln or Secretary Seward.[27]

Finally, in 1906, Oregon hired the Washington, D.C. firm of attorneys representing California to press its claim with Congress.[28] The matter was referred to the U.S. Court of Claims which two years later ruled that the state's bonus pay was not a federal matter, but the state could collect for its bounty money. It ruled that Oregon was entitled to recover the cost of its bond issue and a few side expenses in the total amount of $192,543.02.

The claim was then referred to the Treasury Department for auditing. This took two additional years. Oregon's bookkeeping was imprecise and, among other problems, the state had paid off some counterfeit interest coupons. The Treasury Department estimated the sum due Oregon at $193,929.82.

The state's Washington lawyers, the firm of Ralston Siddons and Richardson, then obtained the introduction of a revenue measure in Congress that failed to pass.

About this time, the settlement of California's claim for expenses of the Modoc War of 1872-73 alerted the state's lawyers to the possibility of more money due Oregon. The federal government had paid Oregon about $38,000 for its costs in the Umatilla Indian War of 1877 and $70,000 for the Modoc Indian War. But the 1910 California settlement gave hope that Oregon might recover a good part of the $73,000 it still claimed due.

The Oregon Legislature authorized Attorney General A. W. Crawford to make yet another try at getting the federal government to pay. The contract with the Washington law firm was a contingent fee case—the lawyers got paid 15 percent of whatever they collected. But Oregon was too late. The federal government already had paid $44,000,000 to twenty-eight other states for Civil War indemnities.[29] By then, Congress was tired of paying for a war more than forty years old.

Oregon's congressional delegation over several sessions of Congress dutifully introduced a bill to pay Oregon its Civil War expenses. Like legislation was introduced for the benefit of California. The bills went nowhere, although California was still trying to collect as late as 1963.[30]

Since 1911, when Oregon made its claim for indemnification, only one other Civil War claim was paid. That was a $595,000 payment made to Nevada in 1929. Nevada's claim, according to Oregon's Washington lawyers, was virtually identical to that of Oregon.

In 1963, Attorney General Robert Y. Thornton made another mild pitch for payment. Oregon's Al Ullman was chairman of the Ways & Means Committee of the House of Representatives, which Thornton thought might be helpful. It wasn't.

All was not lost, however. Some of Oregon's bonds never were turned in for payment, and Oregon got to keep an estimated $4,935.

In 1966, Deputy State Treasurer Kenneth Johnson reported that about forty bonds, issued to pay Civil War bonuses and the cost to the state of the militia in the Modoc and Umatilla Indian Wars, were never presented for payment.[31]

The last Indian bonds were presented and paid in 1925.

The State Treasurer now says that if any bond were to be presented, it would not be honored.[32]

Chapter 18 notes

1 Edwards, "The Department of the Pacific," 304.

2 Ibid., 303-304..

3 Brown, Anderson H., unpublished diary, Justine Jones collection.

4 Richter, "Washington and Idaho Territories, The Civil War in the Western Territories," 33.

5 Hageman, *Lincoln and Oregon,* 58-68.

6 The production of wool was an important part of Oregon's early economy. The Willamette Woolen Mill at Salem started operation in December 1857 and turned out blankets and yard goods for Pacific Coast trade. The mill purchased a total of 199,686 pounds of wool from producers in almost every Oregon county. Other woolen mills were begun at Brownsville, Oregon and Ellendale (Dallas).

7 Lomax, "Woolen Mills in Oregon," *OHQ,* 30(1929):238.

8 Throckmorton, *Oregon Argonauts,* 247.

9 W.O.R., Vol. 50, Pt. 2, 327-28, 666-67.

10 Merriam, L.C., Jr., ed. "The First Oregon Cavalry and the Central Oregon Military Road Survey of 1865," *OHQ,* 60(1959): 89-124.

11 Hageman, *Lincoln and Oregon,* 68.

12 Ibid., 61.

13 Hilleary, *A Webfoot Volunteer.*

14 U.S. Army, Department of the Columbia, Correspondence files, National Archives, Seattle, Wash.

15 LaLande, "'Dixie' of the Pacific Northwest," 69.

16 Oregon Blue Book, Oregon Secretary of State, 2001-2002 Edition.

17 Kelly, *The Career of Joseph Lane, Frontier Politician,* 189-93. Hendrickson, *Joe Lane of Oregon, Machine Politics and the Sectional Crisis, 1949-1861,* 255-58.

18 W.O.R., Series 1, Vol. 50, Pt. 1, 888.

19 Ibid., 680.

20 U.S. War Department, Printed Obituary of Benjamin Alvord, quoted in *OHQ,* 45(1944):328.

21 Scott, "Disunion Journalism in Oregon," *Oregonian,* April 7, 1885.

22 Carey, *General History of Oregon,* 645-46.

23 *Oregon Statesman,* March 23, 1951.

24 *Oregonian,* March 16, 1951.

25 12 U.S. Statues at Large, 276.

26 *State of Oregon v. The United States*, Findings, U.S. Court of Claims, December 31, 1908, Senate Document No. 28, 61st Congress.

27 U.S. Senate, 51st Congress, Executive Document No. 17, Report on War Claims files, State Archives, Salem, Oregon.

28 Ralston & Siddons, letter, September 7, 1906, Oregon Attorney General, war claims files, State Archives, Salem, Oregon.

29 California Attorney General, letter, August 2, 1963.

30 Dyer, Brainard, "California's Civil War Claims," *Southern California Quarterly,* 45(1963):1-18.

31 *Salem Capital Journal,* August 4, 1966.

32 Oregon State Treasurer, letter, February 5, 2002.

Appendix A

Chapter 8

Secret sign of the Knights of the Golden Circle

As the organization of the Knights of the Golden Circle, its successors, and sister organizations became fragmented, so too did the rituals and secret signs of these groups. The Knights thrived on secrecy and arcane rituals designed to set its members apart. The ritual apparently changed frequently, and the published versions vary significantly.

In February 1865, John O. Shelton, a civilian spy employed in Oregon by Adj. Gen. Cyrus Reed, reported on one version that was in use in Oregon and the Pacific Northwest. If the Oregon version of the Knights had more than one degree, then Shelton appears to have penetrated only the first degree.

A summary of the Oregon Ritual follows:

Oath: A member agrees to resist the draft and to assist in subverting the present administration. He would furnish himself with a good rifle, musket or shotgun (the latter preferred), a six-shooter revolver and 40 rounds of ammunition, more if possible.

Hailing sign or means of identification on the street: Both men stand with thumbs extended on the breast of the coat, and begin the following:

Q: Have you read the Old Guard?

A: Which Guard?

Q. The one published by C. Chaney Burr.

A. Ney.

Q. What Ney?

A. The Commander of the Old Guard.

Handshake or grip: Shake hands with right hands. Insert the little finger between the little finger and the next one and extend thumbs across the knuckles of each hand.

Hailing sign or sign of identification useable anywhere: Challenger strokes his mustache twice with the two first fingers of the right hand, closed against the thumb. Responder gently scratches behind his ear with the right hand. This is accompanied by the verbal challenge:

> Q. Were you out last night?
> A. I were.
> Q. Did you see that lone star?
> A. I did.
> Q. Which way did it point?
> A. To the Southwest.
> Q. Right, Brother.
> (Followed by the grip.)

Hailing or identification sign between soldiers in uniform: Challenger raises his hat slightly and flourishes it with his right hand. Responder raises his hat and slowly presses it down with his right hand.

Hailing or identification sign in the field: The ramrod is drawn by each and returned with a flourish over the right shoulder.[1]

Notes
1   Shelton, John O., Report, Knights of the Golden Circle, Mss. 468, Oregon Historical Society.

APPENDIX B
LOCATION OF NORTHWEST TROOPS

The semi-annual manpower reports listed in the *War of the Rebellion* show where all Army Regular and Volunteer troops and artillery on the Pacific Coast and federal troops in the Military District of Oregon during the Civil War were located. The manpower reports also listed a total of officers and men present for duty. But many of the totals reported varied from the number of men and officers separately listed, and have been deleted. This information has been organized by state or territory and alphabetized.

DECEMBER 31, 1860
Present for Duty, Department of the Pacific
Officers 143, Men 2245.
Present for Duty, Department of Oregon
Officers 71, Men 1195.

Oregon
Fort Dalles, Co. H, 1st U.S. Dragoons, and Co. G, 9th U.S. Infantry.
Fort Hoskins, Cos. F and G, 4th U.S. Infantry.
Fort Yamhill, Co. K, 4th U.S. Infantry.

Washington Territory
Camp Chehalis, Co. A, 4th U.S. Infantry.
Camp Pickett, Co. D, 9th U.S. Infantry.
Fort Cascades, Co. H, 4th U.S. Infantry.
Fort Colville, Cos. A, C, I and K, 9th U.S. Infantry.
Fort Steilacoom, Cos. F and H, 9th U.S. Infantry.
Fort Townsend, Co. C, 4th U.S. Infantry.
Fort Vancouver, Cos. A, B, C, D, G, and M, 3rd U.S. Artillery, and Ordnance Detachment.
Fort Walla Walla, Cos. C, E and I, 1st U.S. Dragoons, and Cos. B and E, 9th U.S. Infantry.

JUNE 30, 1861
Present for Duty, Department of Pacific

Officers 114, Men 2064.
Artillery: Heavy 79, Light 33
Present for Duty, District of Oregon
Officers 31, Men 488.
Artillery: Heavy 0, Light 16.

Oregon
Fort Dalles, Co. H, 1st U.S. Dragoons.
Fort Hoskins, Co. G, 4th U.S. Infantry, and Co. B, 9th U.S. Infantry.
Fort Umpqua, Detachment of Co. L, 3rd U.S. Artillery.
Fort Yamhill, Detachment of Co. K, 1st U.S. Dragoons.

Washington Territory
Camp Pickett, Co. D, 9th U.S. Infantry.
Fort Colville, Cos. A, C and K, 9th U.S. Infantry.
Fort Steilacoom, Cos. F and H, 9th U.S. Infantry.
Fort Vancouver, Co. D, 3d U.S. Artillery, and Co. G, 9th U.S. Infantry and detachment of Ordnance.
Fort Walla Walla, Cos. C, E and I, 1st U.S. Dragoons.

December 31, 1861
Present for Duty, Department of the Pacific
Officers 232, Men 4400.
Artillery: Heavy 81, Light 21
Present for Duty, District of Oregon
Officers 36, Men 620.
Artillery: Heavy 0, Light 10.

Oregon
Fort Dalles, one company 2nd California Volunteer Infantry.
Fort Hoskins, Oregon, one company 2nd California Volunteer Infantry.
Fort Yamhill, Oregon, one company 4th California Volunteer Infantry.

Washington Territory
Camp Pickett, Battery D, 3rd U.S. Artillery.
Fort Colville, two companies 2nd California Volunteer Infantry.
Fort Steilacoom, Co. E, 4th California Volunteer Infantry.
Fort Vancouver, One company 2nd California Volunteer Infantry, One company 4th California Volunteer Infantry, Cos. A and C, 9th U.S. Infantry, Ordnance Detachment.

Fort Walla Walla, two companies 4th California Volunteer Infantry.

June 30, 1862

Present for Duty, Department of the Pacific
Officers 258, Men 4,808.
Artillery: Heavy 167, Light 23.

Present for Duty, District of Oregon:
Officers 46, Men 686.
Artillery: Heavy 0, Light 9.

Oregon

Fort Dalles, Co. B, 4th California Volunteer Infantry.
Fort Hoskins, Co. B, 2nd California Volunteer Infantry.
Fort Yamhill, Co. D, 4th California Volunteer Infantry.
Mullan Road Expedition, 9th U.S. Infantry (detachment).

Washington Territory

Camp Pickett, Co. C, 9th U.S. Infantry.
Fort Colville, Cos. C and D, 2nd California Volunteer Infantry.
Fort Steilacoom, Co. E, 4th California Volunteer Infantry.
Fort Vancouver, Co. A, 9th U.S. Infantry, Cos. A and D, 1st Washington
Territory Volunteer Infantry, Co. C, 1st Oregon Volunteer Cavalry,
and detachment of Ordnance.
Fort Walla Walla, Cos. A and C, 4th California Volunteer Infantry, and
Cos. B and E, 1st Oregon Volunteer Cavalry.

December 31, 1862

Present for Duty, Department of the Pacific:
Officers 239, Men 4138.
Artillery: Heavy 167, Light 28.
Present for Duty, Division of Oregon:
Officers 62, Men 1068.
Artillery: Heavy 0, Light 5.

Oregon

Fort Dalles, Co. H, 1st Oregon Cavalry and Co. F, 1st Washington
Territory Volunteer Infantry
Fort Hoskins, Co. D, 1st Washington Territory Volunteer Infantry.
Fort Yamhill, Co. D, 4th California Infantry.

Washington Territory

Camp Lapwai, Washington Territory (later Idaho Territory), Co. E, 1st Washington Territory Volunteer Infantry and Co. F, 1st Oregon Volunteer Cavalry.

Camp Pickett, Co. C, 9th U.S. Infantry.

Fort Colville, Cos. B and C, 1st Washington Territory Infantry.

Fort Steilacoom, Cos. G and K, 1st Washington Territory Infantry.

Fort Vancouver and Vancouver Arsenal, Co. I, 1st Washington Territory Volunteer Infantry

and Co. A, 9th Infantry and detachment of Ordnance.

Fort Walla Walla, Cos. B, D and E, 1st Oregon Cavalry and Cos. A and H, 1st Washington Territory Infantry.

JUNE 30, 1863

Present for Duty, Department of the Pacific

Officers 232, Men 3,637.

Artillery: Heavy 174, Light 22.

Present for Duty, District of Oregon:

Officers 63, Men 893.

Artillery: Heavy 0, Light 6.

Oregon

Fort Dalles, Co. B, 1st Oregon Cavalry and Co. F, 1st Washington Territory Infantry.

Fort Hoskins, detachment of Co. D, 4th California Infantry.

Fort Yamhill, Detachment of Co. D, 4th California Infantry.

En route to new station, Co. B, 1st Oregon Cavalry.

On expedition three companies of 1st Oregon Cavalry and four companies of 1st Washington Territory Infantry.

Washington Territory

Camp Lapwai, Co. F, 1st Oregon Cavalry and Co. E , 1st Washington Territory Infantry.

Camp Pickett, Co. C, 9th U.S. Infantry.

Fort Colville, Cos. B and C, 1st Washington Territory Infantry.

Fort Steilacoom, Co. K, 1st Washington Territory Infantry.

Fort Vancouver, Co. A, 9th U. S. Infantry and Ordnance Detachment.

Fort Walla Walla, Co. A, 1st Washington Territory Infantry.

DECEMBER 31, 1863
>Present for Duty, Department of the Pacific

Officers 259, Men 4032.

Artillery: Heavy 178, Light 41.
>Present for Duty, District of Oregon:

Officers 61, Men 709.

Artillery: Heavy 4, Light 20.

Idaho Territory

Fort Boise, Cos. D and G, 1st Washington Territory Infantry.

Oregon

Fort Dalles, Co. D, 1st Oregon Cavalry and Co. F, 1st Washington Territory Infantry.

Fort Hoskins, (none listed).

Fort Yamhill, (none listed).

Washington Territory

Camp Pickett, Co. C, 9th U.S. Infantry.

Fort Colville, Cos. B and C, 1st Washington Territory Infantry.

Fort Lapwai, Co. F, 1st Oregon Cavalry and Co. E, 1st Washington Territory Infantry.

Fort Steilacoom, Co. K, 1st Washington Territory Infantry.

Fort Vancouver, Cos. B and C, 1st Oregon Cavalry, Co. A, 9th U.S. Infantry, and detachment of Ordnance.

Fort Walla Walla, Cos. A and E, 1st Oregon Cavalry and Cos. A and H, 1st Washington Territory Infantry.

JUNE 30, 1864
>Present for Duty, Department of the Pacific

Officers 216, Men 3933.

Artillery: Heavy 197, Light 49.
>Present for Duty, District of Oregon

Officers 48, Men 584.

Artillery: Heavy 10, Light 27.

Idaho Territory

Fort Boise, three companies Washington Territory Infantry.

Oregon

Fort Dalles, Co. F, 1st Washington Territory Infantry.

Fort Hoskins, Co. D, 4th California Volunteer Infantry.

Fort Yamhill, (none listed).

On expedition, Cos. D and G, 1st Oregon Cavalry.

On expedition, Cos. A and E, 1st Oregon Cavalry.

On Canyon City expedition, Co. B, 1st Oregon Cavalry.

Washington Territory

Camp Lapwai, Co. F, 1st Oregon Cavalry.

Camp Pickett, Co. C, 9th U.S. Infantry.

Cape Disappointment, Co. A, 9th U.S. Infantry

Fort Colville, Co. C, 1st Washington Territory Infantry.

Fort Steilacoom, Co. K, 1st Washington Territory Infantry.

Fort Vancouver, Cos. E and H, 1st Washington Territory Infantry, Co. D, 9th U.S. Infantry, and Ordnance Detachment.

Fort Walla Walla, Cos. A and B, 1st Washington Territory Infantry.

En Route, Fort Walla Walla to Fort Vancouver, Co. H, 1st Washington Territory Infantry.

DECEMBER 31, 1864

Present for Duty, Department of the Pacific

Officers 234, Men 4295.

Artillery: Heavy 230, Light 45.

Present for Duty, District of Oregon:

Officers 52, Men 668.

Artillery: Heavy 18, Light 23.

Idaho Territory

Fort Boise, three companies 1st Washington Territory Infantry.

Oregon

Camp Watson, Oregon, Co. G, 1st Oregon Cavalry.

Fort Dalles, Co. E, 1st Oregon Cavalry, and Co. F, 1st Washington Territory Infantry.

Fort Hoskins, (none listed).

Fort Yamhill, (none listed).

Washington Territiory:

Camp Lapwai, Co. F, 1st Oregon Cavalry.

242

Camp Pickett, Co. C, 9th U.S. Infantry.[1] (2)
Fort Cape Disappointment, Washington Territory, Co. A, 9th U.S. Infantry.
Fort Colville, Co. C, 1st Washington Territory Infantry.
Fort Steilacoom, Co. K, 1st Washington Territory Infantry.
Fort Vancouver, three companies 1st Oregon Cavalry, Cos. E and F, 1st Washington Territory Infantry, Co. D, 9th U.S. Infantry.
Fort Walla Walla, Cos. A and B, 1st Washington Territory Infantry.

June 30, 1865
Present for Duty, Department of the Pacific
Officers 270, Men 5,551.
Artillery: Heavy 267, Light 45.
Present for Duty, District of Oregon:
Officers 56. Men 1019.
Artillery: Heavy 27, Light 26.

Idaho Territory
Fort Boise, Idaho Territory, four companies of 1st Oregon Cavalry (en route from Fort Vancouver and Fort Dalles), and Cos. B and G, 1st Oregon Infantry (en route from Fort Hoskins), and Co. I, 1st Washington Territory Infantry.

Oregon
Camp Watson, Oregon, Co. H, 1st Oregon Infantry and Co. G, 1st Oregon Cavalry.
Fort Dalles, Oregon, Co. K, 1st Oregon Infantry and Co. H, 1st Washington Territory Infantry.
Fort Hoskins, (none listed.)
Fort Klamath, Oregon, Co. C, 1st Oregon Cavalry, and Co. I, 1st Oregon Infantry.
Fort Stevens, Oregon, Co. B, 8th California Infantry.
Fort Yamhill, Oregon, Co. D, 4th California Infantry.

Washington Territory
Cape Disappointment, Co. A, 8th California Infantry and Co. A, 9th U.S. Infantry.
Fort Colville, Co. E, 1st Oregon Infantry.
Fort Steilacoom, Co. C, 1st Oregon Infantry.
Fort Vancouver, Co. A, 1st Oregon Infantry, Co. E, 1st Washington

Territory Infantry, Co. D, 9th U.S. Infantry. Ordnance Detachment.
Fort Walla Walla, Cos. D and F, 1st Oregon Infantry.
Fort Lapwai, Co. F, 1st Oregon Cavalry.
San Juan Island, Washington Territory, Co. C, 9th U.S. Infantry.

(1) The manpower reports also listed a total of officers and men present for duty. But many of the totals reported varied from the number of men and officers separately listed, and have been deleted.

Appendix B notes

1   Camp Pickett in Washington's San Juan Islands, was named after George Pickett, its first commanding officer. Pickett resigned in 1861. On June 3, 1863, Pickett, then a general in the Confederate Army, led the ill-fated charge at Gettysburg. Eighteen months later, on December 31, 1864, the U.S. Army still referred to the installation as Camp Pickett.

Appendix C

DRAFT REGISTRY

(From *Oregon Statesman*, March 28, 1864.)

- - - -

ENROLLMENT OF OREGON
Provost Marshal's Office
Salem, March 23, 1864

Sub-Dist.	County	Enrolling Officer	No. of 1st Class	No. of 2d Class
1	Jackson	Chas W. Savage	737	181
2	Josephine	George Thrusher	336	46
3	Curry	Michael Riley	55	24
4	Douglas	L. L. Williams	617	235
5	Coos	A. J. Moody	143	34
6	Lane	Wm. H. Haley	715	244
7	Linn	John Smith	1076	415
8	Benton	A. R. McConnell	452	156
9	Polk	Wm. Grant	453	145
10	Marion	Wm. Porter	1100	376
11	Clackamas	J. E. Hurford	526	206
12	Yamhill	Henry Warren	509	189
13	Tillamook	C. H. Davidson	29	12
14	Multnomah	J. S. Newell	1420	431
15	Washington	Harvey Scott	458	180
16	Columbia	J. H. Watts	106	12
17	Clatsop	P. W. Gillette	121	43
18	Wasco	Nathan Olney	1580	220
19	Umatilla	Jasper W. Johnson	237	47
20	Baker	Wm. R. Park	752	93
Total			11,422	3,289

The above may be taken as the result of the Enrollment of Oregon as required by the Act for "Enrolling and Calling Out the National Forces," with the exception of the 19th Sub District (Umatilla County), not yet complete.

JULIUS M. KEELER
Captain and Prov. Marshal

BIBLIOGRAPHY

BOOKS AND MONOGRAPHS

Anderson, Martha. *Black Pioneers of the Northwest, 1800-1918.* No publication information, 1980.

Bancroft, Hubert Howe. *History of Oregon.* San Francisco: The History Co., 1886.

_____. *History of the Pacific States.* San Francisco: The History Company, 1886.

_____. *History of Washington, Idaho, and Montana.* San Francisco: The History Co., 1890.

Barth, Gunter. *All Quiet on the Yamhill.* Eugene, Oregon.: University of Oregon Press, 1959.

Bartlett, John. *Familiar Quotations.* 10th ed., New York: Halcyon Press, 1919.

Basler, Roy (ed.). *The Collected Works of Abraham Lincoln.* New Brunswick, New Jersey: Rutgers University Press, 1955.

Bates, Samuel P. *History of the Pennsylvania Volunteers, 1861-1865.* B. Singerly, State Printer, Harrisburg, Pennsylvania., 1869-1871.

Billings, John D. *Hardtack and Coffee.* Chicago: R.R. Donnelly and Sons Co., 1960.

Bowyer, Gary C., "Archaeological Symbols of Status and authority, Fort Hoskins, Oregon." Master's thesis, Oregon State University, 1992.

Boyd, Robert. *The Coming of the Spirit of Pestilence.* Seattle, Washington: University of Washington Press, 1999.

Campbell, Patricia. *With Pride in Heritage; History of Jefferson County.* Port Townsend, Washington: Jefferson County Historical Society, 1966.

Carey, Charles H., *History of Oregon,* Author's Edition, Chicago: The Pioneer Historical Publishing Co., Vol. 3, 1922.

246

_____. *General History of Oregon through Early Statehood,* Portland, Or., Binfords and Mort, 1971).

Colton, Ray C. *The Civil War Years in the Western Territories.* Norman, Oklahoma: University of Oklahoma Press, 1959.

Corning, Howard McKinley, ed. *Dictionary of Oregon History.* Portland, Oregon: Binfords and Mort, 1956.

Crawford, Medorem. *Journal of Medorem Crawford.* Fairfield, Washington: Ye Galleon Press, 1967.

Cross, Osborn. *March of the Regiment of Mounted Riflemen to Oregon in 1849.* Fairfield, Washington: Ye Galleon Press, 1967.

Deady, Matthew P. *The Organic and Other General Laws of the United States, 1845-1864.* Portland, Oregon: State Printer, 1866.

Deady, Matthew P. and Lane, Lafayette, *General Laws of Oregon, 1845 to 1872.* Salem, Oregon: State Printer, 1894.

Edwards, Glenn Thomas, Jr. *Oregon Regiments in the Civil War.* Master's thesis, University of Oregon, 1960.

———.*The Department of the Pacific of the Pacific in the Civil War Years.* PhD diss., University of Oregon, 1963.

Fee, Chester Anders. *Chief Joseph; The Biography of a Great Indian.* New York: Wilson-Erickson, 1936.

Field, Virgil F. *The Official History of the Washington National Guard, Vol. 1.* Tacoma, Washington: Washington Military Department, 1961.

Fowler, Dorothy Canfield. *Unmailable.* Athens, Georgia: University of Georgia Press, 1977.

Gallas, Stanley. *Lord Lyons and the Civil War, 1859-1864, A British Perspective.* PhD diss., University of Illinois, Chicago, 1992.

Gatke, Robert Moulton. *Chronicles of Willamette: The Pioneer University of the West.* Portland, Oregon: Binfords and Mort, 1943.

Geer, T. T. *Fifty Years in Oregon.* New York: The Neale Publishing Co., 1912.

Gilbert, Benjamin Franklin. *Naval Operations in the Pacific, 1861-1866.* PhD diss., University of California, 1951.

Goodell, Phoebe Judson. *A Pioneer's Search for an Ideal Home.* Tacoma, Washington: Washington Historical Society, 1966.

Gould, Benjamin Apthorp. *Investigations in the Military and Anthropological Statistics of American Soldiers.* New York: Riverside Press, 1869.

Hageman, Todd. *Lincoln and Oregon.* Master's thesis, Eastern Illinois University, 1988.

Hanft, Marshall. *Fort Stevens, Oregon's Defender at the River of the West.* Salem, Oregon: Oregon State Parks and Recreation Branch, 1980.

Hansen, David Kimball. *Public Response to the Civil War in Washington Territory and Oregon, 1861-1865.* Master's thesis, University of Washington, 1971.

Hardee, W. H., *Rifle and Light Infantry Tactics for the Exercise and Manoeuvres of Troops When Acting as Light Infantrymen or Riflemen.* Philadelphia: Lippincott, Grambo & Co., 1855.

Heitman, Francis B., *Historical Register and Dictionary of the United States Army, From Its Organization September 29, 1789, to March 2, 1903.* Washington, D.C.: Government Printing Office, 1903.

Hendricks, Robert, *Innnnnnnng Haaaaaaaa!, The War To End The White Race.* Salem, Oregon: n.p., 1937.

_____, *The West Saved America and Democracy, Number Two.* Salem, Or., n.p., 1939.

Hendrickson, James E. *Joe Lane of Oregon; Machine Politics and the Sectional Crisis.* New Haven, Connecticut: Yale University Press, 1967.

Hibbard, Charles Gustin. *Fort Douglas, 1862-1916, Pivotal Link on the Western Frontier.* PhD diss., University of Utah, 1980.

Higgins, David Williams. *The Mystic Spring, and Other Tales of Western Life.* Toronto: W. Briggs, 1908.

Hill, Daniel G., Jr. *The Negro Question in Oregon, A Survey.* Master's thesis, University of Oregon, 1932.

Hilleary, William M. *A Webfoot Volunteer: The Diary of William M. Hilleary, 1864-1866. Edited by Herbert B. Nelson and Preston Onstad in Cooperation with the Oregon Historical Society.* Corvallis, Oregon: Oregon State University Press, 1965.

Historically Speaking, Vol. XV, (Rickreall, Oregon:, Polk County Historical Society, 2007).

Hunt, Aurora. *The Army of the Pacific.* Glendale, California: Arthur H. Clark Co., 1951.

Jackson, John C., *Little War of Destiny,* Fairfield, Washington: Ye Galleon Press, 1996.

Johansen, Dorothy. *Empire of the Columbia.* New York: Harper & Row, 1967.

Johnston, William P. *The Life of General Albert Sidney Johnston.* New York, DaCapo Press, 1997.

Josephy, Alvin H. *The Civil War in the American West.* New York, Alfred A. Knopf, 1991.

Kelly, Sister M. Margaret Jean. *The Career of Joseph Lane, Frontier Politician.* PhD diss., Catholic University of America, 1942.

Kennedy, Elijah R. *The Contest for California; How Colonel E. D. Baker Saved the Pacific States for the Union.* Boston: Houghton Mifflin Co., 1912.

Keyes, Erasmus. *Fifty Years' Observation of Men and Events,* New York: Scribner and Sons, 1884.

Lyman, Horace S. *History of Oregon: The Growth of an American State.* New York: North Pacific Publishing Society, 1903.

McArthur, Lewis, *Oregon Geographic Names,* 4th ed. Portland, Oregon: Oregon Historical Society, 1974.

McPherson, James M., and McPherson, Patricia R. *Lamson of the Gettysburg; The Civil War Letters of Roswell H. Lamson, U.S. Navy.* New York: Oxford University Press, 1997.

McCurdy, James G. *By Juan de Fuca's Strait.* Portland, Oregon: Binfords and Mort, 1937.

Merk, Frederick (ed.). *Fur Trade and Empires, George Simpson's Journal.* Harvard University Press, 1968.

Morgan, Murray C., *Confederate Raider in the North Pacific,* Pullman, Washington: Washington State University Press, 1995.

Morrow, Curtis Hugh. "Politico-Military Secret Societies of the Pacific Northwest, 1860-1865." PhD diss., Clark University, 1929.

Official Records of the Union and Confederate Navies in the War of the Rebellion, (Washington, D.C., U.S. Government Printing Office, 1890-1922), Series 1, Vol. 3.

Oliver, Egbert S. *Obed Dickinson's War Against Sin in Salem, Oregon,* Portland, Oregon: Napi Press, 1987.

Oregon Blue Book, Salem, Oregon: Oregon Secretary of State, 2001-2002 Edition.

249

Oregon Federal Writers' Project. *Oregon Oddities and Items of Interest,* Oregon Federal Writers' Project, 1940.

Oregon Military Department. *Historical Annual,* National Guard of the State of Oregon, 1939.

Patton, Rodney C. "Knights of the Golden Circle; Fact or Fiction", (Master's thesis, Kansas State College of Pittsburg, 1964).

Payne William Kenneth. "How Oregonians Learned About the Civil War." Master's thesis, University of Oregon, 1963.

Peltier, Jerome. *Black Harris.* Fairfield, WA: Ye Galleon Press, 1986.

Phelps, Thomas Stowell, and Harriman, Alice. *Reminiscences of Seattle, Washington Territory and the U. S. Sloop of War Decatur During the Indian Wars of 1855-56.* Seattle, Washington: The Alice Harriman Co., 1908.

Roberts, Allen E. *House Undivided; The Story of Freemasonry and the Civil War.* Macoy Publishing and Masonic Supply Co. Inc., 1990.

Robinson, William Morrison Jr. *The Confederate Privateers.* New Haven, Connecticut: Yale University Press, 1928.

Ross, Alexander, *Adventures of the First White Settlers on the Oregon or Columbia River,* (London, Elder and Co., 1849).

Sager, Elizabeth, and Wilson, Mrs. E. M. *The Last Day at Wailatpu,* Walla Walla, Washington: Whitman College, 1897.

Schablitsky, Julie M. "Duty and Vice: The Daily Life of a Fort Hoskins Soldier." Master's thesis, Oregon State University, 1966.

Schneider, Franz M. "The 'Black Laws' of Oregon." Master's thesis, University of Santa Clara, 1970.

Schweninger, Joseph Michael. "'A Lingering War Must Be Prevented;' The Defense of the Northern Frontier, 1812-1871." PhD diss., Ohio State University, 1999.

Scott, Harvey W. (Leslie M. Scott, ed.) *History of the Oregon Country.* Cambridge, Massachusetts: Riverside Press, 1924.

Sheridan, Philip H. *Indian Fighting in the Fifties in Oregon and Washington Territories.* Fairfield, Washington: Ye Galleon Press Reprint, 1987.

Snowden, Clinton A., *History of Washington,* (New York, The Century History Co., 1909).

Steeves, Sarah Hunt. *Book of Remembrances of Marion County, Oregon, Pioneers, 1840-1860.* Portland, Oregon: The Berncliffe Press, 1927.

Stone, Buena Cobb. *Fort Klamath; Frontier Post in Oregon.* Dallas, Texas: Royal Publishing Co., 1964.

Throckmorton, Arthur L. *Oregon Argonauts, Merchant Adventurers on the Western Frontier.* Portland, Oregon: Oregon Historical Society, 1961.

Tobie, Harvey Elmer. *No Man Like Joe.* Portland, Oregon: Binfords and Mort, 1949.

Troiani, Don, *Regiments and Uniforms of the Civil War.* Mechanicsburg, Pa., Stackpole Books, 2002.

Trussell, Timothy D. *Frontier Military Medicine at Fort Hoskins, 1857-1866: An archaeological and Historical Perspective.* Master's thesis, Oregon State University, 1996.

University of Oregon Bureau of Population Research and Service, *Population of Oregon Cities, Counties and Metropolitan Areas, 1850 to 1957,* Information Bulletin No. 106, April, 1958.

Van Winkle, Roger A. "A Crisis in Obscurity; A study of Pro-Southern Activities in Oregon, 1854-1865." Master's thesis, Western Oregon State College, 1968.

Victor, Frances Fuller. *The Early Indian Wars in Oregon.* Salem, Oregon: State Printer, 1894.

Walling, Albert G., *Illustrated History of Lane County, Oregon,* Portland, Oregon: A. G. Walling Publishing Co., 1884.

War of the Rebellion; A compilation of the Official Records of the Union and Confederate Armies. Washington, D.C., U.S. Government Printing Office, 1880-1901.

Waters, Gary L. *The Western Territories in the Civil War.* Manhattan, Kansas: Sunflower University Press, 1971.

Wiley, Bell Irin. *The Life of Billy Yank, The Common Soldier of the Union.* Garden City, N.Y.: Doubleday and Co., 1971.

Winkenwerder, Kathleen O., "Treated as Enemies; The Suppression of Oregon's Copperhead Press." Master's thesis, University of Oregon, 1985.

Winks, Robin W. *The Civil War Years, Canada and the United States,* 4th ed. Montreal: McGill University Press, 1998.

Winther, Oscar Osburn. *The Great Northwest.* New York: Alfred A. Knopf, 1952.

Wright, E. R. *Lewis and Dryden's Marine History of the Pacific Northwest.* Portland, Oregon: Lewis and Dryden Printing Co., 1895.

PERIODICALS

____, "Lincoln-Time Letters," *Washington Historical Quarterly,* 16 (1925).

____, "The Years Without Laws." *Idaho Yesterdays, The Journal of the Idaho Historical Society,* 25(1981).

____, *Missouri Historical Review* January, 1931, cited in *Oregon Historical Quarterly, (OHQ* hereafter*)* 32(1931):83-84.

Athearn, Robert G. "West of Appomatox, Civil War Beyond the Great River." *Magazine of Western History* 12(April 1982).

Bovey, Wilfrid. "Confederate Agents in Canada During the American Civil War." *The Canadian Historical Review, New Series II (1921).*

Case, Victoria, "It Began With McMinnville Ladies Sanitary Aid Society," *Sunday Oregonian,* February 19, 1961.

Clark, Robert Carlton. "Military History of Oregon, 1849-1959." *OHQ* 36(1935).

Cook, S. F. "The Epidemic of 1830-1833 in California and Oregon." *University of California Publications in American Archaeology and Ethnology* 43(1955).

Cooper, Grace E. "Benton County Historical Society Meeting." *OHQ* 57(1956).

Davenport, T. W. "Slavery Question in Oregon." *OHQ* 31(1930).

Dennis, Elsie Frances. "Indian Slavery in the Pacific Northwest." *OHQ* 31(1930).

Dorpat, Paul, "Now & Then: Snowbound", *Seattle Times,* January 28, 2001, Magazine section, 22.

Drake, John M. "The Oregon Cavalry in the Indian Country, 1864." Priscilla Knuth, Ed., *OHQ* 65(1964).

Dustin, Charles Mail. "The Knights of the Golden Circle." *Pacific Monthly Magazine* November 1911.

Dyer, Brainard. "California's Civil War Claims," *Southern California Quarterly,* 45,1(1963).

Ellison, Joseph. "Designs for a Pacific Republic, 1845-1862." *OHQ* 9(1908): 254-73

Ekland, Roy E. "The Indian Problem; Pacific Northwest" *OHQ* 70(1969).

Fendall, Lon W. "Medorem Crawford and the Protective Corps." *OHQ* 72(1971): 54-77.

Hanft, Marshall. "The Cape Forts, Guardians of the Columbia," *OHQ* 74(1973).

Hart, Newell. "Rescue of a Frontier Boy," *Utah Historical Society Quarterly,* (Fall, 1963).

Historically Speaking, 15(2007): (Rickreall, Oregon, Polk County Historical Society).

Hoblitt, Flora F., "When Silverton was Young," *Silverton Appeal-Tribune*, June 25, 1954.

Hoop, Oscar Winslow. "History of Fort Hoskins." *OHQ,* 30(1929).

Huebner, Michael. "The Regulars." *Civil War Times*, 33(2000).

Hull, Dorothy. "The Movement in Oregon for the Establishment of a Pacific Coast Republic." *OHQ,* 17(1916).

Hunt, Aurora. "The Far West Volunteers." *Montana, The Magazine of Western History.* 12(April 1962).

Johannsen, Robert W. "Spectators of Disunion, The Pacific Northwest and the Civil War." *Pacific Northwest Quarterly,* 54(June, 1953).

Kenney, Judith Keyes. "The Founding of Camp Watson." *OHQ* 58(1957).

Kittredge, Frank A. "Washington Territory in the Civil War." *Washington Historical Society Quarterly* 2(1907).

Klooster, Karl, "Portland's Part in the Civil War," *Oregonian*, Nov. 21, 1990.

Knuth, Priscilla, Ed. "John M. Drake: Private Journal." *OHQ* 65(1964).

LaLande, Jeff. "'Dixie' of the Pacific Northwest: Southern Oregon's Civil War." *OHQ* 100(1999): 32-70.

Lockley, Fred. "Some Documentary Records of Slavery in Oregon." *OHQ* 17(1916).

Lockley, Fred. "Reminiscences of Martha E. Gilliam Collins." *OHQ* 17(1916).

_____, "Impressions and Observations of the Journal Man," *Oregon Journal*, Portland, Oregon., March 24, 1934.

Lomax, Alfred L. *"Brother Jonathan*; Pioneer Steamship of the Pacific Coast." *OHQ* 60(1959).

_____, "Woolen Mills in Oregon," *OHQ* 30(1929).

Maxwell, Ben. "Free Negroes Unwanted in State as First News Came in 1861," Salem *Capital Journal*, Jan. 2, 1961, 1.

_____."Oregon Proved Apathetic to Arms Raising Efforts During Civil War," *Salem Capital Journal,* January 3, 1961.

___. "War's End Gets Short News Space in Oregon." *Salem Capital Journal.* January 6, 1961.

_____. "Worse Duty No Man Could Find." *Frontier Times* January, 1968.

Merriam, L. C., Jr. (Ed.) "The First Oregon Cavalry and the Central Oregon Military Road Survey of 1865," *OHQ* 60(1959).

Meyer, J. A. "River of Slaves or River of the West." *Washington Historical Quarterly* 13(1922).

Minto, John. "Reminiscences." *OHQ* 2(1901).

Onstad, Preston. "The Fort on the Luckiamute, a Resurvey of Fort Hoskins." *OHQ,* 65(1964).

Platt, Robert Trent. "Oregon in the Civil War." *OHQ* 4(1903).

Pollard, Lancaster. "Golden Circle Knights Opposed Union Banner," *Oregonian,* December 31, 1961.

Prosch, Thomas W., "The Military Roads of Washington Territory," *Washington Historical Quarterly,* II:2(118-126).

Richter, Sara Jane. "Washington and Oregon Territories, The Civil War in the Western Territories." *Journal of the West,* 16(1977).

Richter, William V. "War in the Great Northwest." *Washington Historical Quarterly,* 22(1931).

Robertson, James O. "Origin of Pacific University." *OHQ* 6(1905).

Scott, Cameron. "Catalina, The Real Far West," *Golden West Magazine,*[volume # or month] 1966.

Scott, Harvey, "Disunion Journalism in Oregon," *Oregonian,* April 7, 1885.

Scott, Leslie M. "The Oregon Boundary Treaty of 1846." OHQ 29(1928).

_____."The Yaquina Railroad." *OHQ* 16(1915).

Seaman, N. G. "The Amateur Archaeologist's 50 Years in Oregon." *OHQ,* 52(1951).

Shippee, Lester Burrell. "The Federal Relations of Oregon, *OHQ,* 20(1919).

Spaid, Stanley. "Life of General Joel Palmer," *OHQ,* 55(1951).

Swing, William, "Civil War Falls Upon Nation; Rains Invade Portland Sector," *Oregonian,* April 9, 1961, 24.

Thomison, Joel D. "Old U. S. Mint at The Dalles is Monument to Argonaut Era." *OHQ* 41(1940).

Victor, Frances Fuller. "The First Oregon Cavalry" *OHQ* 3(1902).

Wang, Peter Haywood. "The Mythical Confederate Plot in Southern California," *San Bernardino County Museum Association Quarterly.* 16(1969).

West, Oswald. "First White Settlers on French Prairie." *OHQ* 43(1942).

Williams, George H., "The Free State Letter," *Oregon Statesman*, July 28, 1857, 1, 2, reprinted in *OHQ*, 9(1908):254-273.

Williams, James C. "The Long Tom Rebellion," *OHQ* 67(1966).

Woodward, W. C. "Political Parties in Oregon," *OHQ* 13(1912)..

Young, F. G. "Financial History of Oregon." *OHQ* 9(1910).

NEWSPAPERS

Albany Inquirer, September 17, 1862.

Eugene Democratic Register, August 23, 1862.

Idaho Sunday Statesman, July 17, 28, August 21, 1924.

Jacksonville Sentinel, January 11, 1862.

Oregon Journal, January 8, 1920; March 24, 1934.

Oregon Sentinel, June 15, 1861.

Oregon Statesman, June 6, September 16, 1851; June 27, 1854; June 6, 1856; April 14, June 28, July 28, 1857; July 3, 17, 1860; May 6, 1861; June 30, July 14, 1862; June 19, July 20, 27, August 3, December 21, 1863; February 22, March 3, 12, 14, August 8, 15, 29, November 14, December 11, 1864; January 7, 16, April 10, May 25, December 25, 1865; August 13, 1866; March 23, 1951; November 28, 1965.

Oregonian (Weekly), October 20, 1855; April 10, 1858; March 19, 1859; December 15, 1860; May 30, 1862.

Oregonian, April 30, May 9, 1861; November 11, 1864; April 13, 14, 29, 1865; October 15, 1870; April 7, 1885; March 16, 1951; August 15, 1956; February 19, April 9, November 20, 1961; November 21, 1990.

Polk County Observer, March 13, 1905. Applegate, Jesse, "First Settlement of Polk County," *Polk County Observer*, March 13, 1903.

Puget Sound Herald, June 20, 1864.

Sacramento Bee, September 21, 1880.

Salem Capital Journal, January 2, 3, 6, 1961.

San Francisco Alta, October 26, 1862; August 6, September 28, 1864.

San Francisco Bulletin, February 25, 1863.

Seattle Times, January 28, 2001.
Silverton Appeal-Tribune, June 25, 1954.
State Journal, July 8, 1864.
Washington Standard, October 28, 1871.
Weekly Union, October 25, 1862.

PERSONAL CONTACTS
California Attorney General, letter, August 8, 1963.
Oregon State Treasurer, letter, February 5, 2002.
Ward, Arthur, interview, 1968.

OREGON HISTORICAL SOCIETY RESEARCH LIBRARY
Bowlby, Wilson., and others to A. C. Gibbs, letter, Addison C. (Crandall) Gibbs Papers, Mss 685, Box 1, file 11.
Dimick, John Buell, papers.
Holburt, Charles, "Camp Currey Documents," mss. 1514.
Jones, D. H., mss. 898.
Rinehart, William V., "With the Oregon Volunteers, 1862-6," mss. 471.
Shelley, James M., mss. 391.
Shelley, James H., Untitled Manuscript Read to Reunion of 1st Oregon Volunteers, Newport, Or., June 24, 1908.
Shelton, John O., "Statements in Regard to Secret Political Organization in Oregon," July 10, 1865, mss. 465.
Wells, W.W. letter to Governor A. C. Gibbs, Gibbs Collection.

OREGON STATE ARCHIVES
Curry, George L., Governor, Proclamation Declaring the Results of the Election For and Against the Constitution.
Mulkey, Patrick Henry v. Rinehart, W.V., et al, Pleadings, Case No. 625, Lane County Circuit Court.
Oregon Adjutant General, Correspondence File, 1862-1863, 1864.
Oregon Adjutant General, "Report for the Year 1863," House of Representatives Journal, Oregon Legislature, 1864 Session.
Oregon Adjutant General, "Report for the Year 1865-1866."
Oregon Governor's Office, Executive Order of November 19, 1878.
Oregon Legislature, Act of October 20, 1870.
Oregon Legislature, "Journal of the House of Representatives," 1859 Session,

Oregon Legislature, "Report of the Committee of Military Affairs," Territorial Council, 1858-1859 Session.

Oregon Legislature, Journal of the House of Representatives, 1864 Session.

Oregon Legislature, Session Laws of the First Regular Session Begun September 10, 1860.

Ralston & Siddons, letter, September 7, 1906, Oregon Attorney General War Claims.

State v. Samuel E. May, Marion County Circuit Court records, Oregon States Archives.

Territory of Oregon ex rel Robin Holmes v. Nathaniel Ford, Pleadings, Polk County District Court.

U.S. Senate, 51st Congress, Executive Document No. 17, Report on War Claims of Oregon, December 16, 1889.

Vincent v. Umatilla County, 14 Oregon Reports 375, 12 Pacific Reports 732 (1887).

Whitaker et al v. Haley, 2 Oregon Reports 128 (1865).

NATIONAL ARCHIVES, WASHINGTON, D.C.

Congressional Globe. 2nd Session, 36th Congress, Part 1.

U.S. Army, Department of the Pacific, General Orders No. 53, November 23, 1864.

___.U.S. Army, Department of the Pacific, General Orders No. 2, January 5, 1865; General Orders No. 61, December 29, 1865.

U.S. Army, District of Oregon, Correspondence Book.

U.S. Army, First Oregon Cavalry, Fort Klamath, Oregon, Correspondence Files.

U.S. Army, Fort Hoskins, Oregon, General Orders No. 3, March 4, 1859.

U.S. House of Representatives, 2nd Session, 36th Congress, Executive Document No. 29, Dent, Captain F. T., Report of November 8, 1860, "Indian Depredations in Oregon."

U.S. Senate, 2nd Session, 35th Congress, Senate Document No. 24, Slacum, William A., "Memorial."

U.S. Senate, 61st Congress, Senate Document No. 28, Findings, U. S. Court of Claims, December 31, 1908, "State of Oregon vs. The United States."

U.S. War Department, Printed Obituary of Benjamin Alvord.

NATIONAL ARCHIVES, SEATTLE, WASHINGTON BRANCH

Consulate of the United States, Victoria, Vancouver Island, Correspondence Files.

U.S. Army, Department of the Columbia, Commissary of Musters, Letters Sent files.

U.S. Army, District of Oregon, Correspondence Files, Letter Book, 1865.

U.S. Army, District of Oregon, Office of the Acting Assistant Provost Marshal General, Correspondence Book.

U.S. Army, District of Oregon, Office of the Provost Marshal General, Letter Book, Records Group 100.

U.S. Army, District of Oregon, Recruiting Rendezvous, Correspondence File.

MISCELLANEOUS

Bancroft, Hubert Howe, Manuscripts, Inyo Marble Co. and Julius M. Keeler, Bancroft Library, University of California, Berkeley, California.

Brown, Anderson H., unpublished diary, 1864-1866, Justine Jones Collection, Salem, Oregon.

Burch, Pauline, Mss. 107, Oregon State Library.

Butler, Ira F. M., Letter, December 29, 1861, Butler Family Letters, Oregon State Library, Salem, Oregon.

Constitution, Bylaws and Minutes of the Multnomah Council of the Union League of the State of Oregon, December 28, 1863-May 3, 1864, Multnomah County Library, Portland, Oregon.

Douglas to Newcastle, December 28, 1861, Vancouver Dispatches, Provincial Archives, Victoria, B. C.

Grand Lodge of Ancient, Free and Accepted Masons of Oregon, Annual Proceedings, 1861, Grand Lodge of AF&AM Library, Forest Grove, Oregon.

Hubbard, Cora, "Early Settlement of Independence, Oregon.," mss., Independence Public Library, Independence, Oregon.

Kittell, Allan (Ed.), "Bear Bravely On; Letters from Sergeant John Buell Dimick, First Oregon Volunteer Cavalry, to Almira Eberhard, 1862-1865." Mss.: Lewis and Clark College Archives, Portland, Oregon.

McLarney, Donald F., "The American Civil War in Victoria, Vancouver, Island Colony," mss., Highline Community College, Des Moines, Washington.

Oregon Federal Writers Project, "Oregon Oddities," 1940.

Taylor, Hobart, unpublished diary, Southern Oregon Historical Society, Medford, Oregon.

Territory of Idaho v. Williams, Idaho Supreme Court Reports, 85 (1864).

U.S. Army, Department of the Pacific, General Orders No. 20, September 3, 1861; General Orders No. 34, September 17, 1862; General Orders No. 60, December 28, 1864, University of Oregon Library, Eugene, Oregon.

U.S. Army, Fort Hoskins Post Returns, University of Oregon Library, Eugene, Oregon.

U.S. Sanitary Commission, Oregon Branch, Circular, "To the Friends of the Sanitary Commission," March 9, 1865, University of Oregon Library, Eugene, Oregon.

Washington State Military Department Records, Record Group 82, Historical Record Notes, Washington State Archives, Olympia, Washington,

State of Oregon v. The United States, Findings, U.S. Court of Claims, December 31, 1908, Senate Document No. 28, 61st Congress.

Scott McArthur

Scott McArthur, Monmouth, Oregon writer and retired lawyer, is the author of five books dealing with the history of the Pacific Northwest. He holds degrees from the University of Puget Sound, University of Oregon and Northwestern School of Law of Lewis and Clark College.

Scott is a Civil War reenactor and a student of military music of the Civil War and Mexican-American War. He has worked as a writer for daily newspapers and for the Associated Press and United Press International and has taught in both the public schools and at the college level.

INDEX

For a free catalog of Caxton titles write to:

CAXTON PRESS
312 Main Street
Caldwell, Idaho 83605-3299

or

Visit our Internet web site:

www.caxtonpress.com

Caxton Press is a division of THE CAXTON PRINTERS, Ltd.